Contents at a Glance

Table of Contents

Introduction

You've decided to take the General Education Development (GED) test to earn the equivalent of a high school diploma. Congratulations! You're about to clear a major hurdle standing between you and your educational and professional goals. But now you realize that you need extra guidance in reading, writing, and reasoning to tackle the GED Science test. Perhaps you took the test once or even twice and didn't do so well. Perhaps you've done an honest self-assessment and now realize that science was never your favorite or best subject. Whatever the reason, you need to quickly review the essentials and practice answering questions like those you'll encounter on the test. You want to know what to expect, so you're not blindsided on test day.

Welcome to *GED Science Test For Dummies* — your key to excelling on the GED Science test. Here, you find everything you need to do well on the test, from guidance on how to improve reading speed and comprehension to whirlwind tours of biology, physics, chemistry, ecology, earth science, and astronomy that get you up to speed on the basics. You also find out how to write top-notch short response essays. Along the way, you find plenty of practice questions to reinforce your newly acquired knowledge and skills.

About This Book

As we were writing *GED Test For Dummies,* 3rd edition (Wiley), we didn't have the space to cover all four sections of the GED test in great detail. In that book, we provided a general overview of the GED test and two full-length practice tests that covered all four sections — Reasoning Through Language Arts (RLA), Mathematical Reasoning, Science, and Social Studies.

Knowing that each section of the GED test can be taken separately and that test-takers probably need more guidance in some subject areas than in others, we decided to develop a separate book for each section — four books, each with a balance of instruction and practice. In this book, *GED Science Test For Dummies,* we focus exclusively on the GED Science test. Our goal is twofold: to prepare you to answer correctly any science question you're likely to encounter on the test, so that you'll receive a high score, and to help you do well on the short response questions.

We begin by giving you a sneak peek at the test format and an overview of what's on the GED Science test. We then provide a diagnostic test that presents you with science questions that challenge your reading and reasoning knowledge and skills and identify your unique strengths and weaknesses. The diagnostic test and answer explanations following the test guide you to specific skills and knowledge areas where you may need to focus your test-prep activities. When you feel ready, you can then tackle the full-length practice test in Chapter 11 and turn to Chapter 12 for answers and explanations. Check the answers even for questions you answered correctly because the answers provide additional insight.

We wrap up with two Part of Tens chapters — one that presents ten performance-enhancing tips and another that highlights ten science facts and concepts you're likely to bump into on the test.

Foolish Assumptions

When we wrote this book, we made a few assumptions about you, dear reader. Here's who we think you are:

- ✔ You're serious about earning your GED as soon as possible.

- ✔ You're looking for additional instruction and guidance, specifically to improve your score on the GED Science test, not the Reasoning Through Language Arts (RLA), Mathematical Reasoning, or Social Studies tests. We have a separate book for each of those tests when you're ready to tackle them.

- ✔ You've made earning your GED a priority in your life because you want to advance in the workplace or pursue higher learning that requires a GED or high school diploma.

- ✔ You're willing to give up some activities so you have the time to prepare, always keeping in mind your other responsibilities.

- ✔ You meet your state's requirements regarding age, residency, and the length of time since leaving school that make you eligible to take the GED test. (See Chapter 1 for details.)

- ✔ You have sufficient English language skills to handle the test.

- ✔ You want a fun and friendly guide that helps you achieve your goal.

If any of these descriptions sounds like you, welcome aboard. You're about to embark on a journey that takes you from point A (where you are right now) to point B (passing the GED Science test with flying colors).

Icons Used in This Book

Icons — little pictures you see in the margins of this book — highlight bits of text that you want to pay special attention to. Here's what each one means:

Whenever we want to tell you a special trick or technique that can help you succeed on the GED Science test, we mark it with this icon. Keep an eye out for this guy.

This icon points out information you want to burn into your brain. Think of the text with this icon as the sort of stuff you'd tear out and put on a bulletin board or your refrigerator.

Take this icon seriously! Although the world won't end if you don't heed the advice next to this icon, the warnings are important to your success in preparing to take the Science test.

We use this icon to flag example questions that are much like what you can expect on the actual GED Science test. So if you just want to get familiar with the types of questions on the test, this icon is your guide.

Beyond the Book

In addition to the book content, you can find valuable free material online. We provide you with a Cheat Sheet that addresses things you need to know and consider when getting ready for the GED Science test. You can access this material at www.dummies.com/cheatsheet/gedsciencetest.

We also include additional articles at www.dummies.com/extras/gedsciencetest that provide even more helpful tips and advice to help you score your best on the GED Science test.

Where to Go from Here

Some people like to read books from beginning to end. Others prefer to read only the specific information they need to know now. Here we provide a road map so you can find your way around.

Chapter 1 starts off with an overview of the GED test and how to register for the exam. Chapter 2 brings you up to speed on what the Science test covers. Chapter 3 is a must-read — a diagnostic test followed by answers and explanations that point you to the chapters where you can find out more about answering each question type. Based on the questions you struggled with, the answers and explanations send you to the specific chapters in Part II you need most:

- Chapter 5 for guidance in improving reading speed and comprehension and writing short answer responses on the test.
- Chapter 6, where you find out about the scientific method of answering questions and solving problems and discover how to evaluate evidence.
- Chapter 7 for more about reasoning through science questions that involve math.
- Chapter 8 to find out more about life sciences, which cover everything from cell theory and human anatomy to ecosystems and evolution.
- Chapter 9, where you find out more about the physical sciences — physics and chemistry.
- Chapter 10, which brings you up to speed on earth science and astronomy.

When you're ready to dive into a full-length practice test that mimics the real GED Science test, check out Part III. After the test, you can check your answers with the detailed answer explanations we provide. (But be sure to wait until *after* you take the practice test to look at the answers!).

If you need a break, turn to the chapters in Part IV, where you'll find ten tips for boosting your score and ten key science facts and concepts that will help you answer science questions faster and more accurately.

Part I
Getting Started with the GED Science Test

getting started
with the

GED science
test

In this part . . .

- ✔ Get oriented to the test format, question types, test scheduling, and scoring, and find out what steps to take if English isn't your first language.

- ✔ Find out what's on the GED Science test and the knowledge and skills you'll be required to demonstrate on the test.

- ✔ Take a diagnostic test to identify your strengths and weaknesses and highlight the areas where you may need additional practice.

- ✔ Prepare for the actual test day and find out what you should or shouldn't do on the day(s) before and the day of the test and during the exam.

Chapter 1

Taking a Quick Glance at the GED Science Test

. . . .

In This Chapter

▶ Warming up to the GED test format

▶ Glancing at what's covered on the GED Science test

▶ Registering for the exam

▶ Completing the GED test when English is your second language

▶ Understanding what your scores mean and how they're determined

. . . .

The GED test offers high-school dropouts, people who leave school early, and people who were educated outside the United States an opportunity to earn the equivalent of a U.S. high-school diploma without the need for full-time attendance in either day or night school. The GED certificate is a recognized standard that makes securing a job or college placement easier.

The GED test complies with current 12th grade standards in the United States and meets the College and Career Readiness Standards for Adult Education. The GED test also covers the Common Core Standards, used in most states in the country. These standards are based on the actual expectations stated by employers and postsecondary institutions.

The GED test measures whether you understand and can use what high-school seniors across the country have studied before they graduate. Employers want better-educated employees. In addition, some colleges may be uncertain of the quality of foreign credentials. The GED certificate provides those assurances. When you pass the GED test, you earn a high-school equivalency diploma. That can open many doors for you — perhaps doors that you don't even know exist at this point.

The new GED test is now given on a computer and has taken advantage of many different formats that the computer can create. Most of them are variations of multiple choice. You can see examples of all these formats and how they would appear on the computer screen by looking at any of the new editions of the *GED Test For Dummies* books (published by Wiley).

For the purposes of this book, we use mainly the multiple-choice option because it's one of the universally accepted formats for testing of this type, and if you can acquire the skills to answer a multiple-choice question, you can easily manage any of its variations.

Ready to get started? This chapter gives you the basics of the GED Science test: how the test is administered and what it looks like, how to schedule the test, including whether you're eligible, and how your score is calculated (so you know what you need to focus on to pass).

Note: The diagnostic test in Chapter 3 helps you discover your weaknesses and strengths so that with additional practice, you can convert your weaknesses into strengths.

Knowing What to Expect: The GED Test Format

A computer administers the GED test. That means that all the questions appear on a computer screen, and you enter all your answers into a computer. You read, evaluate, analyze, and write everything on the computer. Even when drafting an essay, you don't use paper. Instead, the test center provides you with an erasable tablet. If you know how to use a computer and are comfortable with a keyboard and a mouse, you're ahead of the game. If not, practice your keyboarding. Also, practice reading from a computer screen because reading from a screen is very different from reading printed materials. At the very least, you need to get more comfortable with computers, even if that means taking a short course at a local learning center. In the case of the GED test, the more familiar you are with computers, the more comfortable you'll feel taking the computerized test.

Under certain circumstances, as a special accommodation, the sections are available in booklet format. Check with the GED Testing Service to see what exceptions are acceptable.

The computer-based GED test allows for speedy, detailed feedback on your performance. When you pass (yes, we said *when* and not *if,* because we believe in you), the GED Testing Service provides both a diploma and a transcript of your scores, similar to what high-school graduates receive. They're available online at www.gedtestingservice.com within a day of completing the test. You can then send your transcript and diploma to an employer or college. Doing so allows employers and colleges access to a detailed outline of your scores, achievement, and demonstrated skills and abilities. This outline is also a useful tool for you to review your progress. It highlights areas where you did well and areas where you need further work. If you want to (or have to) retake the test, these results provide a guide to what you should work on to improve your scores. Requests for additional copies of transcripts are handled online and also are available within a day.

Getting a Glimpse of What's on the Science Test

The GED Science test is 90 minutes long. The test includes two short-answer questions, but these questions are not timed separately. Students are expected to manage their time and spend about 10 minutes on each of the short-answer questions. To prepare for the Science test, read as much science material as you can get your hands on. Whenever you don't understand a word or concept, look it up in a dictionary or online. The items on the Science test assume a high-school level of science vocabulary.

You don't have to be a nuclear physicist to answer the questions, but you should be familiar with the vocabulary normally understood by someone completing high school. If you work at improving your scientific vocabulary, you should have little trouble with the Science test. (***Note:*** That same advice applies to all the GED test's sections. Improve your vocabulary in each subject and you'll perform better.)

The Science test concentrates on two main themes:

✔ Human health and living systems
✔ Energy and related systems

In addition, the content of the problems focus on one of the following areas:

- **Physical science:** About 40 percent of the test focuses on physics and chemistry, including topics such as conservation, transformation, and energy flow; work, motion, and forces; and chemical properties and reactions related to living systems.

- **Life science:** Another 40 percent of the Science test deals with life science, including biology and, more specifically, the human body and health, the relationship between life functions and energy intake, ecosystems, the structure and function of life, and heredity and evolution.

- **Earth and space science:** This area makes up the remaining 20 percent of this test and includes astronomy — interactions between Earth's systems and living things, Earth and its system components and interactions, and the structure and organization of the cosmos.

Go ahead and type one of the three content areas into your favorite search engine to find material to read. You'll find links to articles and material from all different levels. Filter your choices by the level you want and need — for example, use keywords such as "scientific theories," "scientific discoveries," "scientific method," "human health," "living systems," "energy," "the universe," "organisms," and "geochemical systems" — and don't get discouraged if you can't understand technical material that one scientist wrote that only about three other scientists in the world can understand.

Items in the Science test are in multiple-choice, fill-in-the-blank, hot-spot, and drop-down format. In addition, the Science test includes two short answer items that are basically short essays to be completed in about ten minutes each, based on a stimulus and a response to a prompt. For additional details about what's covered on the Science test, check out Chapter 2.

It's a Date: Scheduling the Test

To take the GED test, you schedule it based on available testing dates. Each state or local testing center sets its own schedule for the GED test, which means that your state decides how and when you can take each section of the test. It also determines how often you can retake a failed section and how much such a retake will cost. Because a computer administers the test, many testing centers allow you to schedule an individual appointment. Your test starts when you start and ends when your allotted time is completed. The test centers are small computer labs, often containing no more than 15 seats, and actual testing facilities are located in many communities in your state.

You book your appointment through the GED Testing Service (www.gedtestingservice.com). Your local GED test administrator can give you all the information you need about scheduling the test. In addition, local school districts and community colleges can provide information about local test centers in your area.

Sending a specific question or request to www.gedtestingservice.com may come with a charge for the service. To save money, you're better off asking a person at your local testing center. That way, you don't have to pay for the privilege of asking a question, and your answer will be based on rules and conditions specific to your area.

The following sections answer some questions you may have before you schedule your test date, including whether you're even eligible to take the test, when you can take the test, and how to sign up for the test.

Determining whether you're eligible

Before you schedule your test, make sure you meet the requirements to take it. You're eligible to apply to take the GED test only if

- ✔ **You're not currently enrolled in a high school.** If you're currently enrolled in a high school, you're expected to complete your diploma there. The purpose of the GED test is to give people who aren't in high school a chance to get an equivalent high-school diploma.

- ✔ **You're not a high-school graduate.** If you're a high-school graduate, you should have a diploma, which means you don't need to take the GED test. However, you can use the GED to upgrade or update your skills and to prove that you're ready for further education and training.

- ✔ **You meet state requirements regarding age, residency, and the length of time since leaving high school.** Check with your local GED test administrator to determine your state's requirements concerning these criteria. Residency requirements are an issue because you may have to take the test in a different jurisdiction, depending on how long you've lived at your present address.

Knowing when you can take the test

If you're eligible, you can take the GED test whenever you're prepared. You can apply to take the GED test as soon as you want. Just contact your local testing center or `www.gedtestingservice.com` for a test schedule. Pick a day that works for you.

You can take all four sections of the GED test together. That takes about seven hours. However, the test is designed so that you can take each section separately, whenever you're ready. In most areas, you can take the test sections one at a time, in the evening or on weekends, depending on the individual testing center. If you pass one test section, that section of the GED test is considered done, no matter how you do on the other sections. If you fail one section, you can retake it at any time. The scheduling and administration of the test varies from state to state, so check with `www.gedtestingservice.com` or your local high-school guidance office.

Because the test starts when you're ready and finishes when you've used up the allocated time, you should be able to take it alone and not depend on other people. You may be able to find locations that offer the testing on evenings or weekends as well as during regular business hours. Even better, because you don't have to take the test with a group, you may be able to set an individual starting time that suits you.

If circumstances dictate that you must take the paper version of the test, you'll probably have to forgo the flexibility afforded by the computer. Check well in advance to see what the rules are for you.

You can also apply to take the test if you're not prepared, but if you do that, you don't stand a very good chance of passing. If you do need to retake any section of the test, use your time before your next test date to get ready. The rules vary by state, but generally, you can retake the test three times in a year without waiting, but after the third failed attempt you must wait 60 days. In most jurisdictions, taking the test costs money (check with your local testing center to find out specifics for your area). The GED Testing Service does offer a discounted retake up to twice a year, but these promotions change. Some states include free retakes in the price of the test. Check with the GED Testing Service or your state to find out what special discounts may be available. To save time and money, prepare well before you schedule the test. Refer to the later section "Retaking the test(s) if you score poorly" for details.

Are special accommodations available?

If you need to complete the test on paper or have a disability that makes it impossible for you to use the computer, your needs can be accommodated. However, other specifics apply: Your choice of times and testing locations may be much more restricted, but times to complete a test may be extended. Remember also that if accommodation is required, the GED testing centers will ask for documentation of the nature of the accommodation required.

The GED testing centers make every effort to ensure that all qualified people have access to the tests. If you have a disability, you may not be able to register for the tests and take them the same week, but, with some advanced planning, you can probably take the tests when you're ready. Here's what you need to do:

✔ Check with your local testing center or check out www.gedtestingservice.com/testers/accommodations-for-disability.

✔ Contact the GED Testing Service or your local GED test center and explain your disability.

✔ Request any forms that you have to fill out for your special circumstances.

✔ Ensure that you have a recent diagnosis by a physician or other qualified professional.

✔ Complete all the proper forms and submit them with a medical or professional diagnosis.

✔ Start planning early so that you're able to take the tests when you're ready.

Note that, regardless of your disability, you still have to be able to handle the mental and emotional demands of the test.

The GED Testing Service in Washington, D.C., defines specific disabilities, such as the following, for which it may make special accommodations, provided the disability severely limits your ability to perform essential skills required to pass the GED test:

✔ Medical disabilities, such as cerebral palsy, epilepsy, or blindness

✔ Psychological disabilities, such as schizophrenia, major depression, attention deficit disorder, or Tourette's syndrome

✔ Specific learning disabilities, including perceptual handicaps, brain injury, minimal brain dysfunction, dyslexia, and developmental aphasia

Signing up

When you're ready to sign up for the test, follow these steps:

1. **Contact your local GED test administrator or go to** www.gedtestingservice.com **to make sure you're eligible.**

   Refer to the earlier section "Determining whether you're eligible" for some help.

2. **Ask the office for an application (if needed) or an appointment.**

3. **Complete the application (if needed).**

4. **Return the application to the proper office, with payment, if necessary.**

   Testing fees vary by state, so contact your local administrator or testing site to find out the fee amount. In some states, low-income individuals may be eligible for financial assistance.

Note: You can do all this online, including submitting the payment, with your computer, tablet, or smartphone. Go to www.gedtestingservice.com to start the process.

Never send cash by mail to pay for the GED test. Most local administrators have payment rules and don't accept cash.

Working with unusual circumstances

If you feel that you may have a special circumstance that prevents you from taking the GED test on a given day, contact the GED test administrator in your area. If, for example, the test is going to be held on your Sabbath, the testing center may make special arrangements for you.

When applying for special circumstances, keep the following guidelines in mind:

- ✔ Document everything in your appeal for special consideration.

- ✔ Contact the GED test administrator in your area as early as you can.

- ✔ Be patient. Special arrangements can't be made overnight. The administrator often has to wait for a group with similar issues to gather so arrangements can be made for the entire group.

- ✔ Ask questions. Accommodations can be made if you ask. For example, allowances include extended time for various special needs, large print and Braille for visual impairments, and age (for individuals older than 60 who feel they may have a learning disability).

Taking the GED Test When English Isn't Your First Language

English doesn't have to be your first language for you to take the GED test, because it's offered in English, Spanish, and French. If you want to take the test in Spanish or French, contact your local GED test administrator to apply. However, individuals who speak another language as their first language must take the test in English.

If English, Spanish, or French isn't your first language, you must decide whether you can read and write English as well as or better than 40 percent of high-school graduates because you may be required to pass an English as a Second Language (ESL) placement test. If you write and read English well, prepare for and take the test in English. If you don't read or write English well, take additional classes to improve your language skills until you think you're ready. An English Language Proficiency Test (ELPT) is also available for people who completed their education in other countries. If you're not sure of your English language skills, consider taking an ELPT to assess your language skills before taking the GED test.

For more information about the language component of the GED test, check out www.gedtestingservice.com/testers/special-test-editions-spanish and www.gedtestingservice.com/testers/special-test-editions-french.

In many ways, the GED test is like the Test of English as a Foreign Language (TOEFL) comprehension test. If you've completed the TOEFL test with good grades, you're likely ready to take the GED test. If you haven't taken the TOEFL test, enroll in a GED test-preparation course to see whether you have difficulty understanding the subjects and skills assessed on the test. GED test courses provide you with some insight into your comprehension ability with a teacher to discuss your skills and struggles.

Websites that can help you plan to take the GED test

The Internet is a helpful and sometimes scary place. Some websites are there to help you in your GED test preparation, while others just want to sell you something. You have to know how to separate the good from the bad. Here are a couple of essential websites (most are accessible through www.gedtestingservice.com):

✔ adulted.about.com/od/getting yourged/a/stateged.htm links to the GED test eligibility requirements and testing locations in your state.

✔ usaeducation.info/Tests/GED/ International-students.aspx explains GED test eligibility for foreign students.

If you're curious and want to see what's out there, type "GED test" into any search engine and relax while you try to read about 3 to 4 million results, ranging from the helpful to the misleading. We suggest leaving this last activity until after you've passed the tests. As useful as the Internet can be, it still provides the opportunity to waste vast amounts of time. And right now, you need to spend your time preparing for the test — and leave the rest until after you get your diploma.

Taking Aim at Your Target Score

To pass the GED test, you need to score a minimum of 150 on a scale of 100 to 200, and you must pass all other subjects of the test to earn your GED diploma. If you achieve a passing score, congratulate yourself: You've scored better than at least 40 percent of today's high-school graduates, and you're now a graduate of the largest virtual school in the country. And if your marks are in the honors range (score of 170 or more), you're ready for college or career training.

Be aware that some colleges require scores higher than the minimum passing score. If you plan to apply to postsecondary schools or some other form of continuing education, check with their admissions office for the minimum admission score requirements.

The following sections address a few more points you may want to know about how the GED test is scored and what you can do if you score poorly on one or more of the test sections.

Identifying how scores are determined

Correct answers may be worth one, two, or more points, depending on the item and the level of difficulty.

Because you don't lose points for incorrect answers, make sure you answer all the items on each test. After all, a guessed answer can get you a point. Leaving an answer blank, on the other hand, guarantees you a zero. The information and practice in this book provides you with the knowledge and skills you need to answer most questions on the Science section with confidence and to narrow your choices when you're not quite sure which answer choice is correct.

Retaking the test(s) if you score poorly

If you discover that your score is less than 150 on any test section, start planning to retake the test(s) and make sure you leave plenty of time for additional study and preparation. Retake the diagnostic test in Chapter 3 and carefully review the answers and explanations to determine your weaknesses and strengths. Concentrate on understanding your weaknesses and try several more GED sample tests to make sure. If none of this helps, enroll in a preparation course or a study group. Remember that you're trying to complete several years of high school in a concentrated time. Don't get discouraged.

As soon as possible after obtaining your results, contact your local GED test administrator to find out the rules for retaking the failed section of the test. Some states may require that you wait a certain amount of time and/or limit the number of attempts each year. Some may ask that you attend a preparation course and show that you've completed it before you can retake the GED. Some may charge you an additional fee. However, you need to retake only those sections of the test that you failed. Any sections you pass are completed and count toward your diploma. Furthermore, the detailed evaluation of your results will help you discover areas of weakness that need more work before repeating any section of the test.

One advantage of taking the GED test on a computer is that you can receive, within a day, detailed feedback on how you did, which includes some specific recommendations of what you need to do to improve your scores.

No matter what score you receive on your first round of the section, don't be afraid to retake any section that you didn't pass. After you've taken it once, you know what you need to work on, and you know exactly what to expect on test day.

Chapter 2

From Aardvarks to Atoms: Confronting the GED Science Test

. . . .

In This Chapter

▶ Discovering what skills you need to succeed on the Science test

▶ Checking out the format and content of the Science test

▶ Reading text passages and interpreting visual materials

▶ Mastering effective preparation strategies

. . . .

The GED Science test assesses your ability to ferret out information presented in passages or visual materials and does so using some vocabulary specific to the sciences. You're not expected to be able to name the planets in the solar system, explain the 12 systems of the human body, or define *cell theory*. However, you should have at least a passing knowledge of scientific vocabulary and concepts, so you can understand a passage written about a scientific topic.

One of the best ways to improve your scientific vocabulary is to read scientific material, science magazines, websites, and even old textbooks. Look up any words you don't know. Rest easy that you aren't expected to know the difference between *fission* and *fusion* — but just being familiar with them can help you on the test.

The Science test covers material from life science, physical science (chemistry and physics), and earth and space science. Don't panic — you don't need to memorize material from those subjects. You just need to be able to read and understand the material and correctly answer questions based on it. In this chapter, we help you get a feel for the Science test, the skills it requires, and some techniques you can use to prepare.

Looking at the Skills the Science Test Covers

If you're totally unfamiliar with science and its vocabulary, you'll likely have trouble with the questions on the Science test. You're expected to have some basic knowledge about how the physical world works, how plants and animals live, and how the universe operates. This material tests you on ideas that you observe and develop throughout your life, both in and out of school. You probably know a little about traction, for example, from driving and walking in slippery weather. On the other hand, you may not know a lot about equilibrium aside from what you read in school.

As you prepare to take the Science test, you're expected to understand that science is all about inquiry. In fact, inquiry forms the basis of the *scientific method* — the process every good scientist follows when faced with an unknown. The steps of the scientific method are as follows:

1. **Ask questions.**
2. **Gather information.**
3. **Do experiments.**
4. **Think objectively about what you find.**
5. **Look at other possible explanations.**
6. **Draw one or more possible conclusions.**
7. **Test the conclusion(s).**
8. **Tell others what you found.**

Look at your studying for the Science test as a scientific problem. The question you're trying to answer is, "How can I increase my scientific knowledge?" Follow the scientific method to come up with a procedure to fix the problem. Your solution should include reading, reading, and more reading! In addition to this book, one or more high-school science books or even a course that teaches the basics of high-school science can go a long way in deepening your understanding of the physical universe. (Go to your local library to get your hands on a copy of one of these books, and check with your local school board or community college to find basic science courses in your area.) If you know people who are preparing for the GED tests at the same time as you are, forming a study group may be helpful.

Understanding the Test Format and Topics Covered

The Science test contains about 50 questions of different formats, and you have 90 minutes to answer them. Within this time limit are two short answer items that the GED Testing Service estimates should take you about 10 minutes each to complete. This leaves you about 70 minutes for the other 48 items (slightly less than one and a half minutes per question). The short answer items aren't timed separately. As with the other test sections, the information and questions on the Science test are straightforward — no one is trying to trick you. To answer the questions, you have to read and interpret the passages or visual materials provided with the questions (and you need a basic understanding of science and the words scientists use when they communicate). The speed at which you read makes a difference. The two skills you should work on for reading are speed and comprehension. Being able to read a passage in less than ten seconds is of no use if you don't understand it.

In terms of organization, some of the items are grouped in sets. Some items are stand-alone questions based on one issue or topic. Some questions follow a given passage, chart, diagram, graph, map, or table. Your job is to read or review the material and decide on the best answer for each question based on the given material.

In terms of subject matter, the questions on the Science test check your knowledge in the following areas:

✔ **Physical science:** About 40 percent of the test is about *physical science,* which is the study of atoms, chemical reactions, forces, and what happens when energy and matter get together. As a basic review, keep the following in mind:

- Everything is composed of atoms. (The paper this book is printed on — or the computer you're reading it on, if you have the e-book version — is composed of atoms, for example.)

- When chemicals get together, they have a reaction — unless they're *inert* (which means they don't react with other chemicals; inert chemicals are sort of like antisocial chemicals).

- You're surrounded by forces and their effects. (If the floor didn't exert a force upon you when you stepped down, you would go through the floor.)

For more information about physical science (which includes basic chemistry and basic physics), read and review a basic science textbook. You can borrow one from your local library. Amazon may rent the book you want for a low price. Check out all possibilities including material on the Internet. You can also find material on the Internet. When reading this material, you may need definitions for some of the words or terms to make understanding the concepts easier. Use a good dictionary or the Internet to find these definitions. (If you use the Internet, type any of the topics into a search engine and add "definition" after it. Become amazed at the number of hits produced, but don't spend time reading them all.) As you gather a larger and larger science vocabulary, keep track of the words and definitions in a book so that you can refer to them as needed.

✔ **Life science:** Another 40 percent of the test covers *life science* — the study of cells, heredity, evolution, and other processes that occur in living systems. All life is composed of *cells,* which you can see under a microscope. If you don't have access to a microscope and a set of slides with cells on them, most life science–related books and the Internet have photographs of cells that you can study. When someone tells you that you look like your parents or that you remind them of another relative, they're talking about *heredity.* Reading a bit about heredity in biology-related books can help you practice answering some of the questions on the Science test.

Use a biology textbook to help you review for this portion of the test. (Get your hands on a copy of one at your local library or use your favorite search engine to look for information on the Web.)

✔ **Earth and space science:** The remaining 20 percent of the test covers *earth and space science.* This area of science looks at the earth and the universe, specifically weather, astronomy, geology, rocks, erosion, and water.

When you look down at the ground as you walk, you're interacting with earth science. When you look up at the stars on a clear night and wonder what's really up there, you're thinking about space science. When you complain about the weather, you're complaining about earth science. In a nutshell, you're surrounded by earth and space science, so you shouldn't have a problem finding materials to read on this subject.

You don't have to memorize everything you read about science before you take the test. All the answers to the test questions are based on information provided in the passages or on the basic knowledge you've acquired over the years about science. However, any science reading you do prior to the test not only helps you increase your basic knowledge but also improves your vocabulary. An improved science vocabulary increases your chances of being able to read the passages and answer the related questions on the test quickly.

As the basis for its questions, the Science test uses the National Science Education Standards (NSES) content standards, which are based on content developed by science educators from across the country.

Tackling the Science Test Questions

The Science test has two main question types — questions about textual passages and questions about visual materials. Having a basic understanding of the item formats can help you avoid any surprises when you sit down to take the test.

You want to make sure you read every word and symbol that appears in the Science test questions, including every chart, diagram, graph, map, table, passage, and question. Information — both relevant and irrelevant — is everywhere, and you never know where you'll find what you need to answer the questions quickly and correctly, especially when dealing with visuals, graphs, tables, and diagrams. Don't skip something because it doesn't immediately look important.

Questions about text passages

The text passages on this test — and the questions that accompany them — are very similar to a reading-comprehension test: You're given textual material, and you have to answer questions about it. The passages present everything you need to answer the questions, but you usually have to understand all the words used in those passages to figure out what they're telling you (which is why we recommend that you read as much science information as you can prior to the test).

The difference between the text passages on the Science test and other reading-comprehension tests is that the terminology and examples are all about science. Thus, the more you read about science, the more science words you'll know, understand, and be comfortable seeing on the test — which, as you may imagine, can greatly improve your chances of success.

Keep the following tips and tricks in mind when answering questions about text passages:

- **Read each passage and question carefully.** Some of the questions on the Science test assume that you know a little bit from past experience. For example, you may be expected to know that a rocket is propelled forward by an engine firing backward. (On the other hand, you won't have to know the definition of *epigenetics* — thank goodness!)

  Regardless of whether an item assumes some basic science knowledge or asks for an answer that appears directly in the passage, you need to read each passage and corresponding question carefully. As you read, do the following:

  - Try to understand the passage and consider what you already know about the subject.

  - If a passage has only one question, read that question extra carefully.

  - If the passage or question contains words you don't understand, try to figure out what those words mean from the rest of the sentence or the entire passage.

- **Read each answer choice carefully.** Doing so helps you get a clearer picture of your options. If you select an answer without reading all the choices, you may end up picking the wrong one because, although that answer choice may seem right at first, another answer choice may be more correct based on the material presented. As you read the answer choices, do the following:

  - If one answer is right from your reading and experience, note it.

  - If you aren't sure which answer is right, exclude the answers you know are wrong and then exclude answers that may be wrong.

  - If you can exclude all but one answer, it's probably correct, so choose it.

Questions about visual materials

Visual materials are pictures that contain information you may need to answer the corresponding questions. They can be in the form of tables, graphs, diagrams, or maps. Understanding information presented in visual materials takes more practice than comprehending textual passages because you likely aren't as familiar with getting information from pictures as you are with getting information from text. This section (and the diagnostic and practice tests) can help you get the practice you need.

Any visual object is like a short paragraph. It has a topic and makes comments or states facts about that topic. When you come across a question based on visual material, the first thing to do is to figure out the content of the material. Usually, visual objects have titles that help you understand their meanings. After you figure out the main idea behind the visual object, ask yourself what information you're being given; rereading the question can be helpful. After you know these two pieces of information, you're well on your way to answering the question.

The following sections take a more detailed look at the different visual materials that you may find on the Science test.

Tables

A *table* is a graphical way of organizing information. This type of visual material allows for easy comparison between two or more sets of data. Some tables use symbols to represent information; others use words.

Most tables have titles that tell you what they're about. Always read the titles first so you know right away what information the tables include. If a table gives you an explanation (or *key*) of the symbols, read the explanation carefully, too; doing so helps you understand how to read the table.

Graphs

A *graph* is a picture that shows how different sets of numbers are related. On the Science test, you can find the following three main types of graphs:

- **Bar or column graphs:** Bars (horizontal) or columns (vertical) present and often compare information.

- **Line graphs:** One or more lines connect points drawn on a grid to show the relationships between data, including changes in data over time.

- **Pie graphs (also called pie charts or circle graphs):** Arcs of circles (pieces of a pie) show how data relates to a whole.

All three types of graphs usually share the following common characteristics:

- **Title:** The title tells you what the graph is about, so always read the title before reviewing the graph.

- **Horizontal axis and vertical axis:** Bar, column, and line graphs have a horizontal axis that runs from left to right and a vertical axis that runs up and down. (Pie graphs don't.) Each axis is labeled to give you additional information.

- **Label:** The label on the axis of a graph usually contains units, such as feet or dollars. Read all axis labels carefully; they can either help you with the answer or lead you astray (depending on whether you read them correctly).

- **Legend:** Graphs usually have a *legend,* or printed material that tells you what each section of the graph is about. They may also contain labels on the individual parts of the graph or explanatory notes about the data used to create the graph, so read carefully.

Graphs and tables are both often called *charts,* which can be rather confusing. To help you prepare for problems with graphs, make sure you look at and problem-solve plenty of graphs before the test. Remember that many graphs show relationships. If the numbers represented on the horizontal axis are in millions of dollars and you think they're in dollars, your interpretation of the graph will be more than a little incorrect.

Diagrams

A *diagram* is a drawing that helps you understand how something works.

Diagrams on the Science test often have the following two components:

- **Title:** Tells you what the diagram is trying to show you
- **Labels:** Indicate the names of the parts of the diagram

When you come to a question based on a diagram, read the title of the diagram first to get an idea of what the diagram is about. Then carefully read all the labels to find out the diagram's main components. These two pieces of information can help you understand the diagram well enough to answer questions about it.

Maps

A *map* is a drawing of some section — large or small — of the earth or another planet, depending on how much space exploration has been done. Because the entire world is too large to show you on one piece of paper, a section of it is drawn to scale and presented to you on the test.

Most maps give you the following information:

- **Title:** Tells you what area of the world the map focuses on and what it shows
- **Legend:** Gives you general information about the colors, symbols, compass directions, or other graphics used on the map
- **Labels:** Indicate what the various points on the map represent
- **Scale:** Tells you what the distance on the map represents in real life (for example, a map with a scale of 1 inch = 100 miles shows a distance of 500 miles on the real earth as a distance of 5 inches on the map)

Although maps are seldom used in science passages, they're used occasionally, so you want to at least be familiar with them. The best way to get familiar with maps is to spend some time looking at road maps and world atlases, which you can find in your local library or bookstore.

The exact meaning of any visual materials may not be obvious or may even be misleading if not examined carefully. You must understand what the legends, scale, labels, and color coding are telling you. Numbers on a table also may be misleading or even meaningless unless you read the legend and labels carefully. Colors on a map aren't just for decoration; each color has a meaning. Each piece of a visual material represents meaning from which you can put together the information you need to determine the correct answers.

Examining Preparation Strategies That Work

To get better results from the time and effort you put into preparing for the Science test, we suggest you try the following strategies:

✔ **Take practice tests.** Take as many practice tests as you can. Start with the diagnostic test in Chapter 3. Chapter 11 provides a full-length practice test. Be cautious about time restrictions and check the answers and explanations when you're finished. If you still don't understand why some answers are correct or incorrect, ask a tutor, take a preparation class, or look up the information in a book or on the Internet. Be sure you know why every one of your answers is right or wrong.

✔ **Create your own dictionary.** Get a notebook and keep track of all the new words (and their definitions) that you discover as you prepare for the Science test. Make sure you understand all the science terminology you see or hear. Of course, this chore isn't one you can do in one night.

✔ **Read as many passages as you can.** We may sound like a broken record, but reading is the most important way to prepare for the Science test. After you read a paragraph from any source (textbook, magazine, article on the Web, and so on), ask yourself some questions about what you read. You can also have friends and family members ask you questions about what you read.

For some general test-taking strategies to help you prepare for all the sections of the GED test, along with additional practice tests, check out *GED Test For Dummies* (Wiley).

Finding science on the Internet

The Internet can increase your scientific knowledge or simply introduce you to a new area of interest. If you don't have an Internet connection at home, try your local library or community center.

To save yourself time as you begin your online search for additional practice in reading science material, we suggest you check out the following sites:

✔ `www.els.net`: Contains tons of information about life sciences

✔ `www.earth.nasa.gov`: Contains lots of intriguing earth- and space-related info

✔ `www.sciencenews.org`: Contains excellent up-to-the-minute science news intended to inform, educate, and inspire

✔ `www.chemistry.about.com`: Contains interesting info related to chemistry (note that this is a commercial site, which means you'll see pesky banners and commercial links amidst the interesting and helpful information)

✔ `www.colorado.edu/physics/2000/index.pl`: Contains some interesting physics lessons that are presented in an entertaining and informative manner

You can also find a great deal of information, general and specific, regarding the Science test on the GED Testing Service's site: `www.gedtestingservice.com`.

To explore on your own, go to your favorite search engine and type the science keywords you're most interested in (*biology, earth science,* and *chemistry,* just to name a few examples). You can also use the same keywords for a YouTube search and find many excellent videos explaining these topics.

Chapter 3

Uncovering Your Strengths and Weaknesses with a Diagnostic Test

*B*efore committing to any serious training regimen for the GED Science test, take the diagnostic test in this chapter and check the answers and explanations to identify the skills you need to work on most. This approach enables you to focus your efforts on your weakest areas, so you don't waste a lot of time on what you already know.

Focus on improving your reading rate and comprehension. The average reading rate with around 60 percent comprehension is about 200 to 250 words per minute. To gauge your rate, time how long it takes to read a passage and then count the number of words in one line, multiply that number by the number of lines in the passage, and divide by the number of minutes it took you to read the passage. If you have no trouble with comprehension, work on picking up speed. Reading this book is one great way to pick up speed because the more familiar you become with science concepts and terminology, the faster you read and the greater your comprehension. (For additional tips on improving your reading speed and comprehension, check out a free article at www.dummies.com/extras/gedrlatest. Even though this article is focused on the GED RLA test, the information is also helpful for reading and comprehending passages in the GED Science test.)

Taking the Diagnostic Test

The GED Science test is comprised of approximately 50 questions intended to measure general science aptitude. The questions are based on short readings that may include a graph, chart, or figure. You have 90 minutes to complete it. This diagnostic test has only 40 questions, but it will still give you a good idea of your strengths and weaknesses.

Simply follow the instructions to mark your answer choices. When you're done, check your answers and read the answer explanations that immediately follow the test. Although you can simply look at the answer key to check which questions you answered correctly and which ones you missed, we encourage you to read the answer explanations for all questions to make sure you understand how to approach similar questions. A few extra minutes on the answers and explanations can make all the difference on the actual test.

Formulas you may need are given on the page before the first test question. Only some of the questions require you to use a formula, and you may not need all the formulas provided. *Note:* If you can memorize the formulas and understand how to use them before beginning the test, you'll save a bit of time on the test; you then can use that time saved for review or for more challenging questions.

Unless you require accommodations, you'll be taking the actual GED test on a computer instead of marking your answers on a separate answer sheet, as you do for the diagnostic and practice tests in this book. We formatted the questions and answer choices in this book to make them appear as similar as possible to the real GED test, but we had to retain A, B, C, and D choices for marking your answers, and we provide a separate answer sheet for you to do so. Because this is a diagnostic test, wrong answers are actually more valuable than correct answers because your mistakes shed light on areas where you need the most preparation.

You can get a good idea of what the tests look like on a computer by going to www.gedtestingservice.com/educators/freepracticetest. While you're there, check out the FAQ. In the wonderful world of GED testing on the computer, changes can and have been made, so go to the source to get the most recent information.

Answer Sheet

1. Ⓐ Ⓑ Ⓒ Ⓓ	21. Ⓐ Ⓑ Ⓒ Ⓓ
2. Ⓐ Ⓑ Ⓒ Ⓓ	22. Ⓐ Ⓑ Ⓒ Ⓓ
3. Ⓐ Ⓑ Ⓒ Ⓓ	23. Ⓐ Ⓑ Ⓒ Ⓓ
4. Ⓐ Ⓑ Ⓒ Ⓓ	24. Ⓐ Ⓑ Ⓒ Ⓓ
5. Ⓐ Ⓑ Ⓒ Ⓓ	25. Ⓐ Ⓑ Ⓒ Ⓓ
6. Ⓐ Ⓑ Ⓒ Ⓓ	26. Ⓐ Ⓑ Ⓒ Ⓓ
7. Ⓐ Ⓑ Ⓒ Ⓓ	27. ▭
8. Ⓐ Ⓑ Ⓒ Ⓓ	28. Ⓐ Ⓑ Ⓒ Ⓓ
9. ▭	29. Ⓐ Ⓑ Ⓒ Ⓓ
10. Ⓐ Ⓑ Ⓒ Ⓓ	30. Ⓐ Ⓑ Ⓒ Ⓓ
11. Ⓐ Ⓑ Ⓒ Ⓓ	31. Ⓐ Ⓑ Ⓒ Ⓓ
12. Ⓐ Ⓑ Ⓒ Ⓓ	32. ▭
13. Ⓐ Ⓑ Ⓒ Ⓓ	33. Ⓐ Ⓑ Ⓒ Ⓓ
14. Ⓐ Ⓑ Ⓒ Ⓓ	34. Ⓐ Ⓑ Ⓒ Ⓓ
15. Ⓐ Ⓑ Ⓒ Ⓓ	35. ▭
16. Ⓐ Ⓑ Ⓒ Ⓓ	36. Ⓐ Ⓑ Ⓒ Ⓓ
17. ▭	37. Ⓐ Ⓑ Ⓒ Ⓓ
18. Ⓐ Ⓑ Ⓒ Ⓓ	38. Ⓐ Ⓑ Ⓒ Ⓓ
19. Ⓐ Ⓑ Ⓒ Ⓓ	39. Ⓐ Ⓑ Ⓒ Ⓓ
20. Ⓐ Ⓑ Ⓒ Ⓓ	40. ▭

Formula Sheet

Area	
Square	$A = s^2$
Rectangle	$A = lw$
Parallelogram	$A = bh$
Triangle	$A = \frac{1}{2}bh$
Trapezoid	$A = \frac{(b_1 + b_2)}{2}h$
Circle	$A = \pi r^2$

Perimeter	
Square	$P = 4s$
Rectangle	$P = 2l + 2w$
Triangle	$P = s_1 + s_2 + s_3$
Circumference	$C = 2\pi r$ or $C = \pi d$, $\pi = 3.14$

Surface area and volume	Surface area	Volume
Rectangular prism	$SA = 2lw + 2lh + 2wh$	$V = lwh$
Right prism	$SA = ph + 2B$	$V = Bh$
Cylinder	$SA = 2\pi rh + 2\pi r^2$	$V = \pi r^2 h$
Pyramid	$SA = \frac{1}{2}ps + B$	$V = \frac{1}{3}Bh$
Cone	$SA = \pi rs + \pi r^2$	$V = \frac{1}{3}\pi r^2 h$
Sphere	$SA = 4\pi r^2$	$V = \frac{4}{3}\pi r^3$

(p = perimeter of base with area B; $\pi = 3.14$)

Data	
Mean	Mean is the average.
Median	Median is the middle value in an odd number of ordered values of a data set or the average of the two middle values in an even number of ordered values in a data set.

Algebra	
Slope of a line	$m = \frac{y_2 - y_1}{x_2 - x_1}$
Slope-intercept form of the equation of a line	$y = mx + b$
Point-slope form of the equation of a line	$y - y_1 = m(x - x_1)$
Standard form of a quadratic equation	$y = ax^2 + bx + c$
Quadratic formula	$x = \frac{-b \pm \sqrt{b^2 - 4ac}}{2a}$
Pythagorean theorem	$a^2 + b^2 = c^2$
Simple interest	$I = Prt$ (I = interest, P = principal, r = rate, t = time)
Distance	$D = rt$ (D = distance, r = rate, t = time)
Total cost	total cost = (number of units) × (price per unit)

GED Science Diagnostic Test

Time: 90 minutes

Directions: Choose the best answer for each question. Mark your answers on the answer sheet provided by filling in the corresponding oval or writing your answer in the box.

1. All living things, from single-cell organisms, such as bacteria, to multi-cell organisms, have one thing in common — cells, the smallest unit of life. Scientists use cell theory to describe the properties of cells. Which of the following is not a principle of cell theory?

   (A) All known living things are comprised of cells.

   (B) All cells come from other cells through cell division.

   (C) Cells contain the hereditary information that's passed from one cell to another when the cell divides.

   (D) All cells are part of larger living organisms.

2. The walrus has a layer of blubber that can be up to 6 inches thick and that helps the walrus retain heat. This adaptation enables the walrus to live in the waters of which of the following biomes?

   (A) tundra

   (B) estuary

   (C) ocean

   (D) the South Pole

Questions 3–4 are based on the following excerpt from "Higgs Boson: Mysterious Particle Could Help Unlock Secrets of the Universe" (www.nsf.gov/news/special_reports/ science_nation/higgsboson.jsp).

The search for a mysterious subatomic particle can certainly involve some enormous tools, not to mention a multitude of scientists. The effort to find the elusive "Higgs boson" includes over 5,800 scientists from 56 countries! It's a subatomic particle that gives other particles, such as quarks and electrons, their mass.

How Do Protons Create a Higgs Boson?

In the Large Hadron Collider (LHC), protons, which are the positive particles in an atom's nucleus, smash together to create new particles. We can again thank Einstein for the idea behind how this is possible: Energy and mass are intimately related. His famous equation $E = mc^2$ says that mass m and energy E are two forms of the same thing and can be converted into each other, related by the speed of light c. This also says that it takes a lot of energy to make a little matter, since the speed of light is such a large number.

As Particle Fever documents, the experiments at the LHC found that the Higgs boson has 125 times more mass than a proton. How can two small protons colliding together make something bigger? One has to boost the protons, giving them a lot more energy to add into the mix. This goes along with David Kaplan's explanation of why the LHC has to be so big — the bigger the contraption, the more energy that can be added! The very strong magnets and huge circular structure of the LHC can accelerate the protons to extremely high speeds, giving each one an energy of about 7,000 times the mass of an ordinary proton.

Go on to next page

When two protons collide at such high speeds and energies, they don't just bounce off each other. Protons actually are made up of particles called quarks, which are held together by gluons. In these collisions, it's the quarks and gluons that hit. This is where the extra energy is key — the whole process takes the quarks, gluons, and energy, smashes them all together, and spits out new particles. When that happens, some of that energy can be converted into mass, making particles such as the Higgs that are bigger than the original particles. The colliding proton beams make a bunch of new particles — bigger and smaller — and it is up to scientists to interpret what the detectors record.

3. Why does the LHC have to be so big?

(A) Scientists need large equipment to see small particles.

(B) Scientists like to build larger and larger equipment.

(C) Einstein did the original research on Higgs boson particles.

(D) Its size enables it to be built with components that provide the extra energy required.

4. According to Einstein's equation that shows the relationship among mass, energy, and the speed of light, you could conclude which of the following?

(A) A stationary object has no energy.

(B) The faster an object moves, the more energy it has.

(C) Lighter objects have just as much energy as heavier objects.

(D) Energy varies according to the mass of the object.

Questions 5–6 refer to the following diagram and excerpt from NASA's Glenn Research Center website for Space Flight Systems (exploration.grc.nasa.gov).

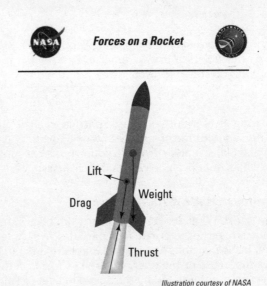

Illustration courtesy of NASA

Many differences exist between the forces acting on a rocket and those acting on an airplane.

1. On an airplane, the *lift force* (the aerodynamic force perpendicular to the flight direction) is used to overcome the *weight*. On a rocket, *thrust* is used in opposition to weight. On many rockets, lift is used to stabilize and control the direction of flight.

Go on to next page

2. On an airplane, most of the aerodynamic forces are generated by the wings and the tail surfaces. For a rocket, the aerodynamic forces are generated by the fins, nose cone, and body tube. For both airplane and rocket, the aerodynamic forces act through the center of pressure (the dot with the black center on the figure) while the weight acts through the center of gravity (the solid dot on the figure).

3. While most airplanes have a high lift to drag ratio, the drag of a rocket is usually much greater than the lift.

4. While the magnitude and direction of the forces remain fairly constant for an airplane, the magnitude and direction of the forces acting on a rocket change dramatically during a typical flight.

5. In the diagram, which force must be the greatest for the rocket to leave the earth?

    (A) drag

    (B) lift

    (C) thrust

    (D) weight

6. Given the fact that gravity between two objects is directly proportional to the mass of the two objects and inversely proportional to the distance between the two objects, the rocket will require

    (A) more thrust to launch than to exit the Earth's atmosphere

    (B) more thrust to exit the Earth's atmosphere than to launch

    (C) an equal amount of thrust to launch and to exit the Earth's atmosphere

    (D) more thrust to land on the moon than to launch from Earth

Question 7 refers to the following passage.

The Jellyfish

One of the creatures living in all the world's oceans is the jellyfish. Although it lives in the ocean, it is not a fish. The jellyfish is an invertebrate — that is, an animal lacking a backbone. Not only does it lack a backbone, but the jellyfish also has no heart, blood, brain, or gills and is more than 95 percent water.

Around the bell-like structure of the body, the jellyfish has *tentacles* — long tendrils that contain stinging cells — which are used to capture prey. The movement of the prey triggers the sensory hair in the stinging cell, and the prey is then in trouble.

Unfortunately, people are also in trouble if they get too close to the tentacles of a jellyfish. The stings generally are not fatal to humans but can cause a great deal of discomfort.

7. Why is a jellyfish classified as an invertebrate?

    (A) It has tentacles.

    (B) It has a small brain.

    (C) It has a primitive circulatory system.

    (D) It has no backbone.

8. In a science experiment, the control group

    (A) isolates the effects of the dependent variable

    (B) isolates the effects of the independent variable

    (C) ensures that only one variable is subject to change

    (D) makes sure the participants do what they are told

Go on to next page

Question 9 refers to the following diagram from NASA's Glenn Research Center website (`www.grc.nasa.gov`).

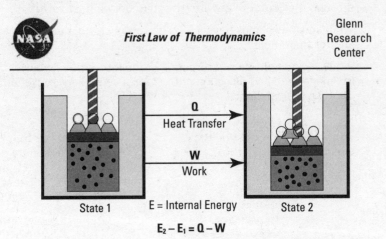

First Law of Thermodynamics

Glenn Research Center

Q
Heat Transfer

W
Work

State 1

E = Internal Energy

State 2

$$E_2 - E_1 = Q - W$$

Any thermodynamic system in an equilibrium state possesses a state variable called the internal energy (E). Between any two equilibrium states, the change in internal energy is equal to the difference of the heat transfer <u>into</u> the system and work done <u>by</u> the system.

9. Which vessel has the lower temperature, State 1 or State 2? ☐

Questions 10–11 are based on the following excerpt from "Predicting Climate Change," by John B. Drake (`web.ornl.gov/info/ornlreview/rev28_2/text/cli.htm`).

Mathematical Models of the Climate

To enable better understanding of the complex climate system, computer programs have been developed to model interactions of climate components. These general circulation models (GCMs) have been used extensively to understand climatic shifts observed in the past and to try to identify possible future responses of the climate system to changing conditions. Can the shifts occur over a short time, such as a decade or century? Will a shift be heralded by phenomena such as an increase in the frequency of El Niños and their surge of warm, western Pacific Ocean water toward South America? What are the different mechanisms of poleward heat transport that might provide the backbone of other climate states? These questions, and many others, indicate the complexity of current climate studies. Simple cause-and-effect arguments are usually not effective explanations in this arena. Complex computer models are practically the only tools available, so they are typically used to justify statements about climate and global dynamics.

For 20 years, climate-modeling researchers have been using some version of the Community Climate Model (CCM1) of the National Center for Atmospheric Research (NCAR). CCM1, which was produced in 1987, was operated on large serial supercomputers. Now, many of these researchers are using CCM2 — a step forward that has been characterized as moving

Go on to next page

from some other planet to the Earth. This step roughly corresponds with the advent of large, shared-memory, parallel, vector computers such as the Cray YMP. Parallel computers allow a more detailed modeling of climate. The detailed examination of the balance of physical processes in the models moves closer to the observed state as modeling of details increases, building confidence that the physics is being captured.

Current atmospheric climate models capture very well the qualitative structure of the global circulation. The transport of energy from the warm equatorial regions to the cold poles and the split of the associated winds into cells are reproduced in simulations both qualitatively and quantitatively. The tropical Hadley cell and the mid-latitude Ferrel cells and jet streams are in good agreement with observations. These are the basic structures of the atmospheric circulation felt on the Earth's surface as the doldrums, trade winds, mid-latitude westerlies, and polar highs.

10. Complex climate conditions are now better understood because of

(A) more repeated climate studies

(B) more cause-and-effect arguments being put forward

(C) modern computer programs that model interactions of climatic components

(D) smaller, more compact, powerful computers

11. CCM2 can now be used on

(A) large, shared-memory, parallel, vector computers

(B) new operating systems

(C) a touch-screen laptop

(D) agreement between atmospheric cells

12. In a food chain, plants are considered "primary producers." Through the process of photosynthesis, they use energy from the sun to convert carbon dioxide and water into carbohydrates and other organic compounds that store energy in a chemical form.

All energy in a food chain can be traced back to which of the following?

(A) plants

(B) carbon dioxide

(C) the sun

(D) oxygen

Question 13 refers to the following passage.

In 1896, Henri Becquerel was using naturally fluorescent minerals to study the properties of X-rays. He exposed potassium uranyl sulfate (uranium) to sunlight and then placed it on photographic plates wrapped in black paper, believing that it absorbed the sun's energy and then emitted it as X-rays. His experiment failed when the clouds moved in and blocked the sunlight required for the uranium to produce an image on the photographic plates. He stuck the uranium and photographic plates in a drawer.

Several days later, Becquerel had the photographic plates developed. He was expecting to see faint images of the uranium crystals. Instead, the images were strong and clear. Becquerel concluded "that the phosphorescent substance in question emits radiation which penetrates paper opaque to light." Becquerel had discovered radioactivity, the spontaneous emission of radiation by a material.

Becquerel used a special apparatus to show that the radiation he discovered was different from X-rays, which had been discovered earlier by Wilhelm Röntgen. X-rays are neutral and do not bend in response to a magnetic field. The radiation Becquerel discovered did bend.

Go on to next page

When he subjected different radioactive substances to the magnetic field, they deflected in different directions or not at all, showing that there were three classes of radioactivity: negative, positive, and electrically neutral.

13. The scientific method involves observation, hypothesis, test, result, and conclusion. Which of the following was the key first step in leading Becquerel to the discovery of radioactivity?

(A) observation

(B) test

(C) result

(D) conclusion

> *Question 14 refers to the following excerpt from NASA's Jet Propulsion Laboratory website* (`www.jpl.nasa.gov`).

We live on a restless planet. Earth is continually influenced by the sun, gravitational forces, processes emanating from deep within the core, and complex interactions with oceans and atmospheres. At very short time scales we seem to be standing on terra firma, yet many processes sculpt the surface with changes that can be quite dramatic (earthquakes, volcanic eruptions, landslides), sometimes slow (subsidence due to aquifer depletion), seemingly unpredictable, and often leading to loss of life and property damage.

Accurate diagnosis of our restless planet requires an observational capability for precise measurement of surface change, or deformation. Measurement of both the slow and fast deformations of Earth are essential for improving the scientific understanding of the physical processes, for optimizing responses to natural hazards, and for identifying potential risk areas.

14. Although people often talk about standing on solid ground, the truth is that

(A) the Earth is capable of supporting huge buildings anywhere on its surface

(B) the ground is solid and stable

(C) the ground is capable of sudden dramatic movement

(D) people should not live near an active volcano

> *Questions 15–17 are based on the following excerpt from "All about Wavelength"* (`science-edu.larc.nasa.gov/EDDOCS/wavelength.html`).

The speed of light is closely related to how rapidly the electric and magnetic fields in a light ray change. How rapidly the fields change is also closely related to how far apart the strong parts of the electric fields are in the wave. The speed of light is the velocity of electromagnetic wave in vacuum, which is 300,000 km/sec. Light travels slower in other media, and different wavelengths travel at different speeds in the same media. When light passes from one medium to another, it changes speed, which causes a deflection of light called *refraction*.

Determining Wavelength

If you study waves, you will find that wavelength and frequency are related by an equation:

$$\text{Speed of Wave} = \text{Frequency} \times \text{Wavelength}$$

Go on to next page

For radio waves or light waves, the speed of the wave is the speed of light. In the United States, we often think of that as 186,000 miles per second. That's as fast as anything can go — according to Einstein's theory of relativity — which is based on Maxwell's equations for electricity and magnetism. In other countries (or when scientists use this equation), they think of the speed of light as 299,792,458 meters per second. The speed of light is the same whether we use miles per second or meters per second — only the number is different.

We use the equation to find the wavelength — we just rearrange it so that the wavelength is on the left:

Wavelength = Speed of wave ÷ Frequency

15. When does light arriving on Earth change its speed?

(A) when it gets dark

(B) depends on the source of the light

(C) passing from one medium to another

(D) depends on the season

16. Why is there no way to make light travel faster?

(A) According to Maxwell's work, it would require more electricity.

(B) According to Einstein's theory, this is as fast as anything can go.

(C) If light did travel faster, we wouldn't notice it.

(D) It is faster in other countries using the metric system.

17. A certain microwave has a wavelength of 0.040 meters. If the speed of light is 3.0×10^8 m/s, what is the frequency of the wave? ☐

18. When identical twins grow up, one is shorter than the other. What is the most likely explanation for the difference?

(A) An organism's genotype is not the only factor that determines its phenotype.

(B) An organism's phenotype is not the only factor that determines its genotype.

(C) One of the parents is shorter.

(D) A genetic mutation caused one of the twins to be shorter.

Questions 19–20 are based on the following excerpt from "Floods: Recurrence Intervals and 100-Year Floods (USGS)" (water.usgs.gov/edu/100yearflood.html)

What is a Recurrence Interval?

"100-year floods can happen 2 years in a row."

Statistical techniques, through a process called *frequency analysis,* are used to estimate the probability of the occurrence of a given precipitation event. The recurrence interval is based on the probability that the given event will be equaled or exceeded in any given year. For example, assume there is a 1 in 50 chance that 6.60 inches of rain will fall in a certain area in a 24-hour period during any given year. Thus, a rainfall total of 6.60 inches in a consecutive 24-hour period is said to have a 50-year recurrence interval. Likewise, using a frequency analysis (Interagency Advisory Committee on Water Data, 1982), there is a 1 in

Go on to next page ➡

100 chance that a streamflow of 15,000 cubic feet per second (ft³/s) will occur during any year at a certain streamflow-measurement site. Thus, a peak flow of 15,000 ft³/s at the site is said to have a 100-year recurrence interval. Rainfall recurrence intervals are based on both the magnitude and the duration of a rainfall event, whereas streamflow recurrence intervals are based solely on the magnitude of the annual peak flow.

Ten or more years of data are required to perform a frequency analysis for the determination of recurrence intervals. Of course, the more years of historical data the better — a hydrologist will have more confidence on an analysis of a river with 30 years of record than one based on 10 years of record.

Recurrence intervals for the annual peak streamflow at a given location change if there are significant changes in the flow patterns at that location, possibly caused by an impoundment or diversion of flow. The effects of development (conversion of land from forested or agricultural uses to commercial, residential, or industrial uses) on peak flows is generally much greater for low-recurrence interval floods than for high-recurrence interval floods, such as 25-, 50-, or 100-year floods. During these larger floods, the soil is saturated and does not have the capacity to absorb additional rainfall. Under these conditions, essentially all of the rain that falls, whether on paved surfaces or on saturated soil, runs off and becomes streamflow.

The weather office keeps statistical data on major events such as floods. In order to attract and keep the public's attention, often events are given catchy names but are based on sound data.

19. Why is it not accurate to call a flood event a "100-year flood"?

(A) They can occur more often than every 100 years.

(B) They have occurred as often as bi-annually.

(C) They are based on data criteria, not on the interval between them.

(D) They have occurred as often as once a year.

20. At least how many years' statistics are needed to determine whether a flood event is a 100-year flood?

(A) 10

(B) 20

(C) 30

(D) any of the above

Questions 21–22 are based on the following excerpt from "Biotechnology Frequently Asked Questions (FAQs)" (www.usda.gov/wps/portal/usda/usdahome?navid= AGRICULTURE&contentid=BiotechnologyFAQs.xml).

Agricultural biotechnology is a range of tools, including traditional breeding techniques, that alter living organisms, or parts of organisms, to make or modify products; improve plants or animals; or develop microorganisms for specific agricultural uses. Modern biotechnology today includes the tools of genetic engineering.

How Is Agricultural Biotechnology Being Used?

Biotechnology provides farmers with tools that can make production cheaper and more manageable. For example, some biotechnology crops can be engineered to tolerate specific herbicides, which make weed control simpler and more efficient. Other crops have been engineered to be resistant to specific plant diseases and insect pests, which can make pest control more reliable and effective, and/or can decrease the use of synthetic pesticides. These crop production options can help countries keep pace with demands for food while

Go on to next page

reducing production costs. A number of biotechnology-derived crops that have been deregulated by the USDA and reviewed for food safety by the Food and Drug Administration (FDA) and/or the Environmental Protection Agency (EPA) have been adopted by growers.

Genetically engineered plants are also being developed for a purpose known as *phytoremediation,* in which the plants detoxify pollutants in the soil or absorb and accumulate polluting substances out of the soil so that the plants may be harvested and disposed of safely. In either case the result is improved soil quality at a polluted site. Biotechnology may also be used to conserve natural resources, enable animals to more effectively use nutrients present in feed, decrease nutrient runoff into rivers and bays, and help meet the increasing world food and land demands. Researchers are at work to produce hardier crops that will flourish in even the harshest environments and that will require less fuel, labor, fertilizer, and water, helping to decrease the pressures on land and wildlife habitats.

The application of biotechnology in agriculture has resulted in benefits to farmers, producers, and consumers. Biotechnology has helped to make both insect pest control and weed management safer and easier while safeguarding crops against disease.

USDA's Economic Research Service (ERS) conducts research on the economic aspects of the use of genetically engineered organisms, including the rate of and reasons for adoption of biotechnology by farmers. ERS also addresses economic issues related to the marketing, labeling, and trading of biotechnology-derived products.

21. USDA researchers conduct major research to

   (A) make crops more palatable

   (B) introduce new crops and animal traits in a safe way

   (C) create super animals

   (D) make agricultural work easier

22. Thanks to genetic engineering

   (A) animals are now bigger

   (B) scientists can modify microorganisms for use in agriculture

   (C) plants mature faster

   (D) farmers have less work to do

---

*Question 23 is based on the following excerpt from "All About The Human Genome Project (HGP)" (*www.genome.gov/10001772*).*

The Human Genome Project (HGP) was one of the great feats of exploration in history — an inward voyage of discovery rather than an outward exploration of the planet or the cosmos; an international research effort to sequence and map all of the genes — together known as the *genome* — of members of our species, Homo sapiens. Completed in April 2003, the HGP gave us the ability, for the first time, to read nature's complete genetic blueprint for building a human being.

23. How can you tell that the HGP was a massive project?

   (A) There are a lot of genomes.

   (B) It involved scientists from all over the world.

   (C) It was completed by 2003.

   (D) Scientists wanted to build a human being.

Go on to next page

Question 24 refers to the following diagram from NASA's Glenn Research Center website (www.grc.nasa.gov).

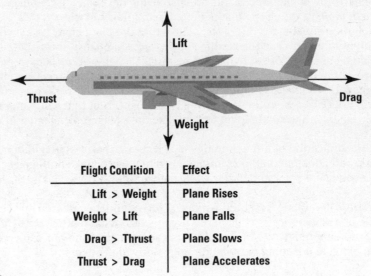

Flight Condition	Effect
Lift > Weight	Plane Rises
Weight > Lift	Plane Falls
Drag > Thrust	Plane Slows
Thrust > Drag	Plane Accelerates

Illustration courtesy of NASA

24. What would cause a plane to descend?

(A) increased drag, increased thrust, or increased weight

(B) increased weight, decreased lift, or increased thrust

(C) decreased drag, decreased lift, or decreased thrust

(D) decreased thrust, increased weight, or increased drag

Question 25 refers to the following excerpt from NASA's website (www.nasa.gov).

On the space shuttle, fuel cells combine hydrogen and oxygen to produce electricity. A fuel cell uses a chemical reaction to provide an external voltage, as does a battery, but differs from a battery in that the fuel is continually supplied in the form of hydrogen and oxygen gas. A byproduct of this reaction ($2H_2 + O_2 \rightarrow 2H_2O$ + electricity) is water, which can be used in a future oxygen generator system to produce oxygen for breathing. Fuel cells can produce electrical energy more safely and efficiently than just burning the hydrogen, to produce heat to drive a generator. The water supply is the limiting factor on the ISS when the space shuttle cannot routinely provide water from its fuel cells. With only two crew members, it is manageable to "truck" water tanks in the Russian Progress resupply ship.

25. Why is $2H_2 + O_2 \rightarrow 2H_2O$ considered to be a balanced chemical equation?

(A) The volume of matter before and after the reaction is the same.

(B) The weight of the matter before and after the reaction is the same.

(C) There are two H's and two O's on either side of the arrow.

(D) Four hydrogen atoms and two oxygen atoms are on either side of the arrow.

Go on to next page

Question 26 refers to the following figure.

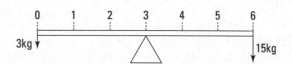

26. Assuming the bar has no weight, where does the fulcrum (the top point of the triangle) need to be positioned for the two sides to be balanced?

   The formula for work is Work = Force × Distance.

   (A) 2

   (B) 3

   (C) 4

   (D) 5

Question 27 refers to the following excerpt from NASA's Science website (`science.nasa.gov`).

New remote sensing technologies are empowering scientists to measure and understand subtle changes in the Earth's surface and interior that reflect the response of the Earth to both the internal forces that lead to volcanic eruptions, earthquakes, landslides and sea-level change and the climatic forces that sculpt the Earth's surface. For instance, InSAR (interferometric synthetic aperture radar) and LiDAR (light detection and ranging) measurements from satellite and airborne sensors are used to provide images of millimeter scale surface changes that indicate an awakening of volcanic activity long before seismic tremors are felt. Ground based geodetic GPS instruments provide time continuous measurements of this activity, though they are often lost during intense volcanic activity. Thermal infrared remote sensing data from NASA satellites signal impending activity by measuring ground temperatures and variations in the composition of lava flows as well as the sulfur dioxide in volcanic plumes. The combination of instruments provides accurate information that can be used for both long-term and short-hazard assessment. These same LiDAR, InSAR, and thermal instruments also provide accurate information on the velocity of ice steams, sub-glacial lake activity, glacial rebound of the Earth's crust, and the retreat and advance of mountain glaciers that are related to climatic changes.

27. New remote sensing technologies provide [_____] that may lead to long- and short-term hazard assessment.

Question 28 refers to the following excerpt from NASA's Earth Observatory website (`www.earthobservatory.nasa.gov`).

Within a single frame of reference, the laws of classical physics, including Newton's laws, hold true. But Newton's laws can't explain the differences in motion, mass, distance, and time that result when objects are observed from two very different frames of reference. To describe motion in these situations, scientists must rely on Einstein's theory of relativity.

Go on to next page

At slow speeds and at large scales, however, the differences in time, length, and mass predicted by relativity are small enough that they appear to be constant, and Newton's laws still work. In general, few things are moving at speeds fast enough for us to notice relativity. For large, slow-moving satellites, Newton's laws still define orbits. We can still use them to launch Earth-observing satellites and predict their motion. We can use them to reach the moon, Mars, and other places beyond Earth. For this reason, many scientists see Einstein's laws of general and special relativity not as a replacement of Newton's laws of motion and universal gravitation, but as the full culmination of his idea.

28. Einstein's theory provides a frame of reference for an explanation of differences in time, length, and mass from

   (A) two very different speeds

   (B) two very different scales

   (C) observations from two very different frames of reference

   (D) two very different perspectives

29. A benefit of aerobic exercise is that it improves your body's ability to produce adenosine triphosphate (ATP), an energy-rich molecule produced by each cell's mitochondria through the process of respiration. What is the primary purpose of mitochondria in a cell?

   (A) It enables the cell to breathe.

   (B) It produces energy for the cell.

   (C) It breaks down waste products.

   (D) It controls reproduction.

> *Questions 30–31 refer to the following excerpt from "About Antimicrobial Resistance" from the Centers for Disease Control (`www.cdc.gov/drugresistance/about.html`).*

Antibiotic/antimicrobial resistance is the ability of microbes to resist the effects of drugs — that is, the germs are not killed, and their growth is not stopped. Although some people are at greater risk than others, no one can completely avoid the risk of antibiotic-resistant infections. Infections with resistant organisms are difficult to treat, requiring costly and sometimes toxic alternatives.

Bacteria will inevitably find ways of resisting the antibiotics developed by humans, which is why aggressive action is needed now to keep new resistance from developing and to prevent the resistance that already exists from spreading.

How Resistance Happens and Spreads

The use of antibiotics is the single most important factor leading to antibiotic resistance around the world. Simply using antibiotics creates resistance. These drugs should only be used to manage infections.

Trends in Drug Resistance

- Antibiotics are among the most commonly prescribed drugs used in human medicine and can be lifesaving drugs. However, up to 50% of the time antibiotics are not optimally prescribed, often done so when not needed, incorrect dosing or duration.

- The germs that contaminate food can become resistant because of the use of antibiotics in people and in food animals. For some germs, like the bacteria *Salmonella* and

Go on to next page ➡

Campylobacter, it is primarily the use of antibiotics in food animals that increases resistance. Because of the link between antibiotic use in food-producing animals and the occurrence of antibiotic-resistant infections in humans, antibiotics that are medically important to treating infections in humans should be used in food-producing animals only under veterinary oversight and only to manage and treat infectious disease, not to promote growth.

• The other major factor in the growth of antibiotic resistance is spread of the resistant strains of bacteria from person to person, or from the non-human sources in the environment.

30. Which of the following precautions should be taken to prevent bacteria from developing resistance to antibiotics?

(A) Stop using antibiotics to treat bacterial infections in humans.

(B) Use antibiotics to treat only bacterial infections in humans and farm animals.

(C) Develop stronger antibiotics.

(D) Remove bacteria from the food supply.

31. How can bacteria adapt so quickly to antibiotics?

(A) Bacteria reproduce quickly, so the chances for a genetic mutation that makes them immune to antibiotics is statistically more likely than in other creatures.

(B) Through epigenetics, bacteria can adapt to a wide variety of environments that would normally be toxic to them.

(C) Bacteria can quickly spread to others who are not taking antibiotics to protect against infection.

(D) If a patient stops taking the antibiotic before it kills off all of the bacteria causing the infection, a few survivors are left behind to multiply.

Questions 32–33 refer to the following passage.

Isotopes

Isotopes are chemical cousins. They are related to each other, but each isotope has slightly different — but related — atoms. Each of the related atoms has the same number of protons but a different number of neutrons. Because the number of electrons or protons determines the atomic number, isotopes have the same atomic number.

The number of neutrons determines the mass number. Because the number of neutrons in each isotope is different, the mass number is also different. These cousins all have different mass numbers but the same atomic number. Their chemical properties are similar but not the same. Like most cousins, they have family resemblances, but each has a unique personality.

32. Different elements would have different numbers of ☐ .

33. Isotopes of a chemical have the same

(A) number of neutrons

(B) mass number

(C) atomic number

(D) chemical properties

Go on to next page

Questions 34–35 refer to the following diagram, which is excerpted from "The Sciences: An Integrated Approach," 3rd Edition, by James Trefil and Robert M. Hazen (Wiley).

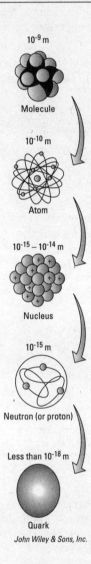

10^{-9} m

Molecule

10^{-10} m

Atom

$10^{-15} - 10^{-14}$ m

Nucleus

10^{-15} m

Neutron (or proton)

Less than 10^{-18} m

Quark

John Wiley & Sons, Inc.

34. According to this diagram, what is the building block upon which the other particles are made?

    (A) atom

    (B) molecule

    (C) neutron

    (D) quark

35. The seat you are sitting on seems solid, but in reality, it is composed of atoms. Each of the atoms is composed of a nucleus, which is composed of neutrons and protons, but much of the space occupied by an atom is just empty space. This means that the chair you are sitting on is mostly empty space. It follows that when you stand on the floor of a building, you are ultimately being supported by ☐ .

Go on to next page

> *Question 36 refers to the following excerpt from "Cryptanalysis and Racketeering Records"*
> *(www.fbi.gov/about-us/lab/scientific-analysis/crypt).*

Mission

The Cryptanalysis and Racketeering Records Unit (CRRU) examines both manually encrypted documents and records of illegal enterprises, as well as provides expert testimony and other forensic assistance to further identify terrorism, foreign intelligence, and criminal activities in support of federal, state, local, and international law enforcement investigations and prosecutions.

The Work

- *Cryptanalysis:* Decrypt manual codes and ciphers found in letters, diaries, ledgers, and other types of written communications, records, and e-mails. Common users of codes ciphers include national and international terrorists, foreign intelligence agents, members, prison inmates, and violent criminals.

- *Racketeering Examinations:* Examine and decode records from illicit businesses, such as loansharking, prostitution, sports bookmaking, and Internet gambling. Such violations are predicate offenses for RICO charges. Examinations may reveal the type of operation, dates of activity, wagering or loan amounts, types of wagers or loans, number and roles of participants, and accounting methods.

- *Drug Records Examinations:* Examine and decode records pertaining to the type of operation, type of drug, quantity of drugs sold or purchased, unit prices, method of payment, transaction dates, roles of participants, gross and net profits, and operating expenses.

The unit members also testify in legal proceedings.

36. If you wanted to develop an encryption hypothesis that triple letter substitution would develop a near impossible encryption protocol, what would be your first step?

(A) Perform experiments to test out your ideas.

(B) Do background research on encryption.

(C) Ask questions to find out more about the subject.

(D) Draw conclusions about the best methods to use.

> *Questions 37–38 refer to the following diagram, which is excerpted from "The Sciences:*
> *An Integrated Approach," 3rd Edition, by James Trefil and Robert M. Hazen (Wiley).*

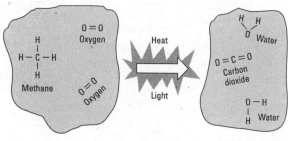

John Wiley & Sons, Inc.

Go on to next page

37. When methane burns, it produces light, heat, carbon dioxide, and water. Why would natural gas be a good choice for keeping your house warm in winter?

    (A) The chemical reaction produces carbon dioxide.

    (B) The chemical reaction produces light.

    (C) The chemical reaction produces water.

    (D) The chemical reaction produces heat.

38. If firefighters were faced with a methane fire, what would they want to eliminate to put out the fire?

    (A) light

    (B) water

    (C) carbon dioxide

    (D) oxygen

Question 39 refers to the following diagram.

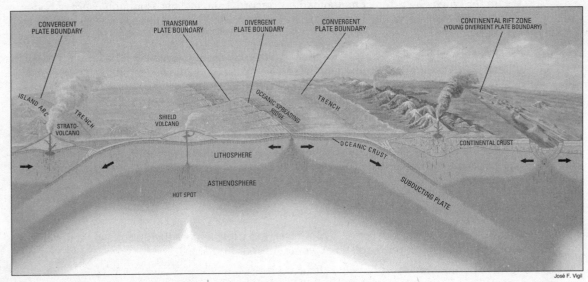

José F. Vigil

Photo created by Jose Vigil and made available courtesy of U.S. Geological Survey.

39. Ocean trenches form along

    (A) convergent plate boundaries

    (B) transform plate boundaries

    (C) divergent plate boundaries

    (D) continental rift zones

Question 40 refers to the following figure.

Go on to next page

40. When the sun, moon, and Earth are in alignment, gravity from both the sun and moon pull on Earth's gravity creating *spring tides* — very low tides and very high tides. When the moon and sun are at right angles to one another, gravity from the sun partially cancels the effect of moon's gravity on the Earth resulting in neap tides — *moderate tides*. During a solar eclipse, you would expect [   ] tides.

Read the following excerpt from "Radiation: Facts, Risks, and Realities," published by the Environmental Protection Agency (www.epa.gov/radiation/docs/402-k-10-008. pdf), and write a brief response to the prompt that follows it.

Stimulus

What Is Radiation?

Radiation is energy. It can come from unstable atoms or it can be produced by machines. Radiation travels from its source in the form of energy waves or energized particles. There are actually two kinds of radiation, and one is more energetic than the other. It has so much energy it can knock electrons out of atoms, a process known as ionization. This ionizing radiation can affect the atoms in living things, so it poses a health risk by damaging tissue and DNA in genes. While there are other, less energetic, types of nonionizing radiation (including radio waves, microwaves — and visible light), this booklet is about ionizing radiation. In the late 1800s, Marie and Pierre Curie were among the first to study certain elements that gave off radiation. They described these elements as "radio-actif," the property that is now called "radioactivity." As scientists studied radioactivity more closely, they discovered that radioactive atoms are naturally unstable. In order to become stable, radioactive atoms emit particles and/or energy waves. This process came to be known as radioactive decay. The major types of ionizing radiation emitted during radioactive decay are alpha particles, beta particles and gamma rays. Other types, such as X-rays, can occur naturally or be machine-produced. Scientists have also learned that radiation sources are naturally all around us. Radiation can come from as far away as outer space and from as near as the ground that you are standing on. Because it is naturally all around us, we cannot eliminate radiation from our environment. We can, however, reduce our health risks by controlling our exposure to it.

Understanding Radiation Risks

Radiation can damage living tissue by changing cell structure and damaging DNA. The amount of damage depends upon the type of radiation, its energy and the total amount of radiation absorbed. Also, some cells are more sensitive to radiation. Because damage is at the cellular level, the effect from small or even moderate exposure may not be noticeable. Most cellular damage is repaired. Some cells, however, may not recover as well as others and could become cancerous. Radiation also can kill cells. The most important risk from exposure to radiation is cancer. Much of our knowledge about the risks from radiation is based on studies of more than 100,000 survivors of the atomic bombs at Hiroshima and Nagasaki, Japan, at the end of World War II. Other studies of radiation industry workers and studies of people receiving large doses of medical radiation also have been an important source of knowledge. Scientists learned many things from these studies. The most important are: The higher the radiation dose, the greater the chance of developing cancer. The chance of developing cancer, not the seriousness of the cancer, increases as the radiation dose increases. Cancers caused by radiation do not appear until years after the radiation exposure. Some people are more likely to develop cancer from radiation exposure than others. Radiation can damage health in ways other than cancer. It is less likely, but damage to genetic material in reproductive cells can cause genetic mutations, which could be passed on to future generations. Exposing a developing embryo or fetus to radiation can

Go on to next page ➔

increase the risk of birth defects. Although such levels of exposure rarely happen, a person who is exposed to a large amount of radiation all at one time could become sick or even die within hours or days. This level of exposure would be rare and can happen only in extreme situations, such as a serious nuclear accident or a nuclear attack.

Determining Radiation Limits

Current science suggests there is some risk from any exposure to radiation. However, it is very hard to tell whether a particular cancer was caused by very low doses of radiation or by something else. While experts disagree over the exact definition and effects of "low dose," U.S. radiation protection standards are based on the premise that any radiation exposure carries some risk.

Prompt

Radiation can both cause and control cancer. In our modern world we are exposed to radiation from many sources, yet we all don't get cancer. Are the beneficial results of radiation worth the possibility of developing the negative side-effects?

This item should take you no more than 10 minutes to complete.

Go on to next page

Go on to next page

STOP DO NOT TURN THE PAGE UNTIL TOLD TO DO SO.
DO NOT RETURN TO A PREVIOUS TEST.

Reviewing Answers and Explanations

This section provides you with answers and explanations for the Science diagnostic test you just completed. The answers tell you whether you answered the questions correctly, but the explanations are even more important. They explain why your answers were right or wrong and give you some hints about the areas tested. Reading the explanations and checking the areas where your answers weren't the best will help you identify where you should spend more time preparing for the test. Some of the explanations refer to other sections and other chapters in other books. It is worth the time to check those out if you got any of the answers wrong.

1. **(D) All cells are part of larger living organisms.** The question mentions the existence of single-cell organisms, such as bacteria, so not all cells are part of larger living organisms. See Chapter 5 to improve reading comprehension and Chapter 8 for more about biology.

2. **(A) tundra.** The tundra biome is very cold and would require a layer of insulation to stay warm enough to live there. If you chose South Pole, you should know that no mammals live at the South Pole. See Chapter 8 for more about biomes and adaptations.

3. **(D) Its size enables it to be built with components that provide the extra energy required.** Choice (D) is stated directly in the passage. Choice (C) mentions Einstein, as does the passage, but this is not the best answer to the question. If you don't read both the passage and the question carefully, you can jump to the wrong conclusion. Choices (A) and (B) may be correct but don't answer the question. See Chapter 5 to improve reading comprehension and Chapter 9 for more about physical science.

   This scientific presentation uses word and phrases which you should understand in order to answer the questions about it. If you have trouble reading because of the vocabulary and can't understand the words in context, you may need to do more reading in the area of science.

4. **(D) Energy varies according to the mass of the object.** Energy equals mass times the speed of light squared. Choice (A) is wrong, because a stationary object has energy stored in the atoms that comprise it. Choice (C) is wrong, because heavier objects would have more energy than lighter objects, according to the equation and common sense, and Choice (D) is correct. See Chapter 7 for more about reasoning through science problems and Chapter 9 for more about physical science.

5. **(C) thrust.** The thrust of the rocket engines must provide more energy than the weight of the rocket for it to leave the Earth. The other forces have an effect, but the thrust lifts it off the ground.

6. **(A) more thrust to launch than to exit the Earth's atmosphere.** If gravity is inversely proportional to the distance between objects, the farther the rocket is from Earth's surface, the less gravitational force will be holding the rocket down, so less force would be necessary to escape the atmosphere than to launch. See Chapter 9 for more about gravity.

7. **(D) It has no backbone.** According to the passage (second sentence in the first paragraph), invertebrates have no backbones. The other choices may be correct, but they don't answer the question. Here, and in all questions on this test, you're looking for the best answer that answers the question posed. Don't get sidetracked by other choices that are correct based on your knowledge or even based on the passage. The answer to the question posed is always the best response on a multiple-choice test. See Chapter 8 to find out more about classification systems.

8. **(B) isolates the effects of the independent variable.** The independent variable is the condition that the researcher changes to determine what effects (dependent variables) are produced. The control group provides data that enables the researcher to observe what happens when the independent variable is unchanged, so any effects produced by changing the independent variable can be attributed to that change and not something else. For more about Experimental Design, check out Chapter 6.

9. **State 1.** According to the diagram, the heat transfer, Q, would be from State 1 to State 2, indicated by the arrow labeled Q. For more about energy transfer, see Chapter 9.

10. **(C) modern computer programs that model interactions of climatic components**, which is mentioned in the passage. Choice (D) talks about the physical size and capabilities of computers but is not the best answer. Choices (A) and (B) are not reflected in any part of the passage. See Chapter 5 for suggestions on how to improve reading comprehension.

11. **(A) large, shared-memory, parallel, vector computers.** This answer is directly stated in the passage. Choice (B) is irrelevant, as is Choice (C), and Choice (D) doesn't make sense in the context of the passage. These questions and the passage are concerned with making predictions based on evidence, and this skill is very important in scientific circles, and it applies here. The question requires you to use information in the passage to make a prediction. If you had problems reading this passage, you have to consider whether it was the length or the vocabulary. If it was the length (363 words), try to improve your reading speed. If the vocabulary tripped you up, continue to read challenging scientific material.

12. **(C) the sun.** Although plants, Choice (A), are primary producers and use carbon dioxide, Choice (B), and oxygen, Choice (D), to create carbohydrates and other organic compounds, the energy is from the sun. See Chapter 8 for more about photosynthesis.

13. **(A) observation.** Had Becquerel not looked at the developed plates and seen that they had been exposed to some form of light energy, he would never have realized that the uranium was emitting wave energy without energy input from the sun. For more about the scientific method, see Chapter 6.

14. **(C) the ground is capable of sudden dramatic movement.** Some of the examples given to support this choice are volcanic eruptions, earthquakes, and landslides. The other choices aren't supported by any content in the passage, although Choice (D) is probably a good idea. See Chapter 10 for more about earth science, including mitigating natural hazards.

15. **(C) passing from one medium to another.** The change of speed when passing from one medium to another is called *refraction*. According to the equation Speed of wave = Frequency × Wavelength, if the speed changes, either the frequency or the wavelength must change. See Chapter 9 for more about waves.

16. **(B) According to Einstein's theory, this is as fast as anything can go.** Careful reading would produce Choice (B) but skimming might lead you to consider Choice (A). Choices (C) and (D) are incorrect. If you're unsure of an answer to a question, read both the passage and the question and answer carefully, but don't spend a great deal of time on this. If time remains at the end, you can check your answer. See Chapter 5 for more about reading passages and answering questions.

17. 7.5×10^9. You're given the equation and the speed of light, so plug in the numbers and do the math:

$$3.0 \times 10^8 \, ^m/_s = 0.04\text{m} \times v$$
$$v = 3.0 \times 10^8 \, ^m/_s \div 0.04\text{m}$$
$$v = 7.5 \times 10^9$$

For more about applying math to science, see Chapter 7. Chapter 9 provides additional details about wavelength and frequency.

18. **(A) An organism's genotype is not the only factor that determines its phenotype.** Although the twins have nearly the same genotype, they may lead different lifestyles that would lead one to be shorter than the other. For example, the taller twin may have eaten a healthier diet and avoided using nicotine, while the other wasn't so health conscious. For more about the difference between genotype and phenotype, see Chapter 8.

19. **(C) They are based on data criteria, not on the interval between them.** As the passage states, the term "100-year flood" is based on a set of criteria but is so named because it is more likely to catch the public's attention and a flood of this magnitude can be extremely dangerous. The other answers are not backed up by information in the passage. See Chapter 7 for more about applying math to science.

20. **(A) 10.** The passage states, "Ten or more years of data are required to perform a frequency analysis for the determination of recurrence intervals." Since this is a statistical determination based on preset criteria, the more data that can be gathered the better, but there is a minimum. Data collection for less than 10 years would not be as accurate as data collected over longer periods of time. This passage and the questions consider your skill of determining the probability of events and give you some insight into how determinations are made using collected data. This is a pure reading comprehension question. If you had trouble with it, turn to Chapter 5 for guidance on reading passages and answering questions.

21. **(B) introduce new crops and animal traits in a safe way.** The passage explains that the USDA conducts major research to ensure food safety. If you had trouble with this question, turn to Chapter 5 for advice.

22. **(B) scientists can modify microorganisms for use in agriculture.** This is stated in the first paragraph, although the rest of the passage provides no detail describing applications for genetically modified microorganisms. If you missed this question, try reading more carefully, as explained in Chapter 5.

23. **(B) It involved scientists from all over the world.** Choice (A) is wrong, because the passage mentions only one genome — the human genome. Choice (C) is wrong, because just mentioning a completion date does not answer the question. Nor did the passage indicate that the people involved were trying to build a human being. Turn to Chapter 9 to read more about the life sciences.

24. **(D) decreased thrust, increased weight, or increased drag.** Decreasing thrust provides the plane with less forward force, increased weight tends to pull it down, and increased drag pulls the plane backward, any of which could cause it to descend, all other factors being equal. See Chapter 5 for suggestions on how to extract details from images and Chapter 9 for more about force and motion.

25. **(D) Four hydrogen atoms and two oxygen atoms are on either side of the arrow.** See Chapter 9 for more about reading chemical equations and for an explanation of balanced chemical equations.

26. **(D) 5.** The formula for work is Work = Force × Distance. To stay balanced, the same amount of work must be applied to both sides, so if you place the fulcrum at 5, you have Work = 3 × 5 = 15 to the left and Work = 1 × 15 = 15 on the right.

27. **information.** According to the passage, all the technologies mentioned provide information that may help scientists in assessing the potential for impending hazards. If you missed this one, check out Chapter 5 for guidance on how to improve reading comprehension.

28. **(C) observations from two very different frames of reference.** As the passage states, Einstein's theory is relevant under these circumstances. The other choices are either incomplete or incorrect. This is another pure reading comprehension question. Check out Chapter 5 for additional insight into answering such questions.

29. **(B) It produces energy for the cell.** ATP is described as an energy-rich molecule that each cell's mitochondria produces, so mitochondria produces energy. If you picked Choice (A), you probably confused "respiration" with breathing. See Chapter 8 for more about how cells function.

30. **(B) Use antibiotics to treat only bacterial infections in humans and farm animals.** The passage states, "These drugs should only be used to manage infections." None of the other choices make much sense. See Chapter 5 for more about reading comprehension and Chapter 8 for more about life sciences.

31. **(A) Bacteria reproduce quickly, so the chances for a genetic mutation that makes them immune to antibiotics is statistically more likely than in other creatures.** Choice (B) would be a good second guess, but the theory of evolution is the best choice — with higher rates of reproduction, the chances for a genetic mutation are greater. See Chapter 9 for more about the forces that drive evolution.

32. **protons.** According to the first sentence of the passage, the atomic number is determined by the number of protons. Skimming the paragraph after reading the question for key words in the question makes choosing the correct answer faster and easier. See Chapter 5 for more about reading comprehension and Chapter 9 for more about atoms and the Periodic Table of Elements.

33. **(C) atomic number.** The last sentence of the first paragraph of the passage states that isotopes have the same atomic number. See Chapter 5 for more about reading comprehension and Chapter 9 for more about atoms and the Periodic Table of Elements.

34. **(D) quark.** The diagram (going from bottom to top) indicates the process of building up a molecule. The quark is the smallest particle, and the molecule is the largest. Sometimes you have to read a diagram in an unfamiliar way to answer the question. See Chapter 5 for suggestions on how to extract information from images.

35. **atoms.** The passage states that everything is composed of atoms. As a result, the floor must be composed of atoms. For more about atoms, turn to Chapter 9.

36. **(B) Do background research on encryption.** In any scientific endeavor, first do your homework. It is important to know what other research has been done on the topic, not so much to copy it but to learn from it. Choice (A) is an important part of the scientific method but not at the very beginning. Questions are important, but answers from the research are more important. Drawing conclusions first may be time-efficient but will never produce good results. This question is really about scientific research and the scientific method. If you had trouble with the question, check out the material about the scientific method in Chapter 6.

37. **(D) The chemical reaction produces heat.** In cold weather, you need a source of heat to warm your house, and methane produces heat in the chemical reaction. The other answers are incorrect. See Chapter 5 for guidance on how to interpret images and Chapter 9 for more about chemical reactions.

38. **(D) oxygen.** Methane requires oxygen to produce light and heat. If there's no oxygen, the methane can't burn. See Chapter 9 for more about chemistry.

39. **(A) convergent plate boundaries.** This is where tectonic plates move toward one another. One plate is a subducting plate, meaning it slides below the other. For more about plate tectonics, check out Chapter 10.

40. **spring.** During a solar eclipse, the moon is between the sun and the Earth, so the three bodies would be aligned, causing a spring tide.

Sample Short-Answer Response

The following sample short answer would receive a reasonable mark. It isn't perfect, but it meets the criteria for an acceptable response. It clearly states a thesis (position) and links directly back to the source material. It uses quotes from the source material and interprets the data. It (mostly) uses correct spelling and grammar and has topic sentences. It also shows that the writer had existing knowledge of the topic. (**Remember:** Your time is restricted. You're not expected to write a fabulous research paper in 10 minutes, only a good, draft-quality one.)

Compare the following sample to the response you wrote.

> Weighing the benefits and drawbacks of radiation is not a question of whether but of the type and amount of radiation people are exposed to, so eliminating potentially beneficial uses of radiation is neither prudent nor necessary. Limiting exposure to all potentially harmful sources of radiation is a more prudent approach.
>
> As the passage points out, the risks very according to the type and amount of radiation. Ionizing radiation, for example, "can affect the atoms in living things, so it poses a health risk by damaging tissue and DNA in genes," but other types of radiation, such as radio waves and visible light are less harmful. Therefore, limiting exposure to some types of radiation makes sense.
>
> The passage points out that X-rays are a form of ionizing radiation that poses a health risk, so people are wise to limit their exposure to X-rays. Radiologists and X-ray technicians receive special training to use the minimum amount of radiation to obtain the results needed. However, doctors should not totally avoid using X-rays, because they are a valuable diagnostic tool, enabling them to see inside a patient's body without using more invasive procedures, such as surgery. Radiation is also beneficial in other diagnostic procedures and in treating certain types of tumors. Until other safer and more effective methods are developed, treatment providers must continue to use these technologies.
>
> Because "radiation sources are naturally all around us," as stated in the passage, we cannot avoid exposure to radiation, but we can limit our exposure even to environmental radiation that can cause harm. For example, limiting exposure to sunlight and using sunscreen can help reduce exposure to ultraviolet (UV) radiation, which can cause skin cancer. Also, in certain areas of the country, exposure to radon gas that builds up in homes increases the risk of lung cancer. Homeowners are wise to test their homes for concentrations of radon gas. If levels are high, a special type of exhaust system may be installed to reduce levels.
>
> It is likely that the cumulative effects of all sources of potentially harmful radiation raise health risks, so becoming more aware of all sources of potentially harmful radiation and limiting exposure to those sources, is the most prudent approach. Totally eliminating sources of radiation, if such a thing were possible, would require eliminating many technologies that improve health.

A more important skill is evaluating your own short answer. If you know how to mark one, you'll know what to watch for when writing one.

The Science short answer is scored between 0 and 3 points. A 3-point answer contains a clear explanation to the question, and supporting evidence from the passage. You need to ensure you actually do answer the question, and use facts and data from the passage to support your answer. The answer can be one, or several, paragraph(s) long, ranging from 50 to 300 words. The answer must be clear and to the point, and your statements must be justified by the stimulus content and your interpretation of that content. Remember, you should take no longer than about 10 minutes on this question. It is not timed separately, so manage your time carefully.

Use this checklist to evaluate your response:

✔ **Content:**

❑ Do you clearly answer the question posed by the stimulus prompt?

❑ Do you give clear evidence using multiple points from the passage to support your answer?

❑ Do you explain how you arrived at your conclusion? (You don't have to agree with the position.)

❑ Have you used evidence from the passage and your own knowledge?

✔ **Style and organization:** Although grammar, spelling, and writing style are not specifically marked as part of the short-answer items, good writing helps produce a clear answer. You can use this part of the checklist to see just how well you did on this aspect of the answer.

❏ Do you start with a clear statement of your position?

❏ Is your evidence presented in a logical order to build your case?

❏ Does your conclusion contain an appropriate summary of the evidence?

❏ Does your answer stay on point?

❏ Do you use proper linking and transition words and phrases between paragraphs?

❏ Do you use varied and clear sentences and sentence structure?

✔ **Writing mechanics:**

❏ Is your answer written in a clear, concise manner?

❏ Do you use grammar and spelling correctly?

❏ Do you use vocabulary appropriately?

When you finish evaluating your response, ask a friend, neighbor, or relative to read it and give you some feedback. Also, check out http://www.gedtestingservice.com/uploads/files/89097368525e28544f77607f31391c4f.pdf to see how the GED Testing Service marks them.

Chapter 4

Succeeding on the GED Science Test

*Y*ou may never have taken a standardized test before. Or if you have, you may wake up sweating in the middle of the night from nightmares about your past experiences. Whether you've experienced the joys or sorrows of standardized tests, to succeed on the GED Science test, you must know how to perform well on this type of test, which consists mostly of multiple-choice questions.

The good news is that you've come to the right spot to find out more about this type of test. This chapter explains some important pointers on how to prepare on the days and nights before the test, what to do on the morning of the test, and what to do during the test to be successful. You also discover some important test-taking strategies to build your confidence.

Gearing Up for Test Time

Doing well on the GED Science test involves more than walking into the test site and answering the questions. You need to be prepared for the challenges on the test. To ensure that you're ready to tackle the test head-on, do the following leading up to the test:

✔ **Get enough sleep.** We're sorry if we sound like your parents, but it's true — you shouldn't take tests when you're approaching exhaustion. Plan your time so you can get a good night's sleep for several days before the test and avoid excess caffeine. If you prepare ahead of time, you'll be ready, and sleep will come easier.

✔ **Eat a good breakfast.** A healthy breakfast fuels your mind and body. You have to spend several hours taking the test, and you definitely don't want to falter during that time. Eat some protein, such as eggs, bacon, or sausage with toast for breakfast. Avoid sugars (donuts, jelly, and so on) because they can cause you to tire easily. You don't want your empty stomach fighting with your full brain.

✔ **Take some deep breaths.** During your trip to the testing site, prepare yourself mentally for the test. Clear your head of all distractions, practice deep breathing, and imagine yourself acing the test. Don't panic.

✔ **Start at the beginning, not the end.** Remember that the day of the test is the end of a long journey of preparation and not the beginning. It takes time to build mental muscles.

✔ **Be on time.** Make sure you know what time the test begins and the exact location of your test site. Arrive early. If necessary, take a practice run to make sure you have enough time to get from your home or workplace to the testing center. You don't need the added pressure of worrying about whether you can make it to the test on time. In fact, this added pressure can create industrial-strength panic in the calmest of people.

Traffic congestion happens. No one can plan for it, but you can leave extra time to make sure it doesn't ruin your day. Plan your route and practice it. Then leave extra time in case a meteor crashes into the street and the crowd that gathers around it stalls your progress. Even though the GED test is now administered on a computer and not everyone has to start at the same time, test centers are open only for certain hours, and if they close before you finish, you won't get any sympathy. Check the times the test center is open. Examiners won't show you a lot of consideration if you show up too late to complete the test because you didn't check the times. They have even less sympathy if you show up on the wrong date.

Using the Diagnostic and Practice Tests to Your Advantage

Taking diagnostic and practice GED Science tests is important for a few reasons, including the following:

✔ **They help you prepare for the test.** Practice tests, the diagnostic test in particular, sheds light on the knowledge and skills you need to focus on leading up to the actual test.

✔ **They give you an indication of how well you know the material.** One or two tests won't give you an accurate indication of how you'll do on the actual test, because you need to do four or five tests to cover all possible topics, but they do give you an indication of where you stand.

✔ **They confirm whether you know how to use the computer to answer the questions.** You don't get this by taking the practice tests in the book, but you can go online at www.gedtestingservice.com/educators/freepracticetest to take a computer-based practice test.

✔ **They familiarize you with the test format.** You can read about test questions, but you can't actually understand them until you've worked through several.

✔ **They can ease your stress.** A successful run-through on a practice test allows you to feel more comfortable and confident in your own abilities to take the GED test successfully and alleviate your overall anxiety.

Turn to Chapter 3 to take the diagnostic test or to Chapter 11 to take the practice test. These tests are an important part of any preparation program. They're the feedback mechanism that you may normally get from a private tutor. To get the most out of any practice test, be sure to check your answers after each test and read the answer explanations.

Packing for Test Day

The GED test may be the most important exam you ever take. Treat it seriously and come prepared. Make sure you bring the following items with you on test day:

✔ **You:** The most important thing to bring to the GED test is obviously you. If you enroll to take the test, you have to show up; otherwise, you'll receive a big fat zero and lose your testing fee. If something unfortunate happens after you enroll, contact the test center and explain your situation to the test administrators. They may reschedule the test with no additional charge.

✔ **Correct identification:** Before test officials let you into the room to take the test, they want to make sure you're you. Bring the approved photo ID — your state GED office can tell you what's an approved form of photo ID. Have your ID in a place where you can reach it easily. And when asked to identify yourself, don't pull out a mirror and say, "Yep, that's me."

✔ **Registration receipt and any fees you still owe:** The same people don't run all test centers. With some, you may have to pay in advance, when booking the test. If so, bring your receipt to avoid any misunderstandings. Others may allow you to pay at the door. If so, find out whether you can use cash, check, debit card, or credit card. The amount of the GED test registration fee also varies from state to state. (Check with your local administrator to confirm when and where the fee has to be paid and how to pay it.) If you don't pay, you can't play.

If needed, you may be able to get financial assistance to help with the testing fees. Further, if you do the test one section at a time, which we recommend, you can probably pay for each test section separately. Check with your state or local education authorities.

✔ **Registration confirmation:** The registration confirmation is your proof that you did register. If you're taking the test in an area where everybody knows you and everything you do, you may not need the confirmation, but we suggest you take it anyway. It's light and doesn't take up much room in your pocket.

✔ **Other miscellaneous items:** In the instructions you receive after you register for the test, you get a list of what you need to bring with you. Besides yourself and the items we list previously, other items you want to bring or wear include the following:

- **Comfortable clothes and shoes:** When you're taking the test, you want to be as relaxed as possible. Uncomfortable clothes and shoes may distract you from doing your best. You're taking the GED test, not modeling the most recent fashions. Consider dressing in layers; you don't want to be too hot or too cold.

- **Reading glasses:** If you need glasses to read a computer monitor, don't forget to bring them to the test. Bring a spare pair, if you have one. You can't do the test if you can't read the screen.

The rules about what enters the testing room are strict. Don't take any chances. If something isn't on the list of acceptable items and isn't normal clothing, leave it at home. Laptops, cellphones, and other electronic devices will most likely be banned from the testing area. Leave them at home or locked in your car. The last place on earth to discuss whether you can bring something into the test site is at the door on test day. If you have questions, contact the test center in advance. Check out www.gedtestingservice.com to start the registration process and find a list of sites close to your home with their addresses and phone numbers. You can also call 877-392-6433 to have real people answer your questions.

Whatever you do, be sure *not* to bring the following with you to the GED testing center:

✔ Books

✔ Notes or scratch paper

✔ MP3 players or tablets

✔ Cellphone (leave it at home or in your car)

✔ Anything valuable, like a laptop computer that you don't feel comfortable leaving outside the room while you take the test

You're provided with an on-screen calculator. You can bring your own hand-held calculator, but it must be a specific make and model. Visit www.gedtestingservice.com/testers/calculator to find out more about the on-screen calculator and which hand-held make and model you're allowed to bring.

Getting Comfortable Before the Test Begins

You usually take the GED Science test in an examination room with at least one official (sometimes called a *proctor* or *examiner*) who serves as a monitor. Some locations have smaller test centers that have space for no more than 15 test-takers at a time. In either case, the test is the same.

As soon as you sit down to take the GED Science test, spend a few moments before the test actually starts to relax and get comfortable. You're going to be in the chair for quite some time, so settle in. Keep these few tips in mind before you begin:

- ✓ **Make sure that the screen is at a comfortable height and adjust your chair to a height that suits you.** Unlike a pencil-and-paper test, you'll be working with a monitor and keyboard. Although you can shift the keyboard around and maybe adjust the angle of the monitor, generally you're stuck in that position for the duration of the test. If you need to make any adjustments, make them before you start. You want to feel as physically comfortable as possible.

- ✓ **Go to the bathroom before you start.** This may sound like a silly suggestion, but it all contributes to being comfortable. You don't need distractions. Even if bathroom breaks are permitted during the test, you don't want to take away time from the test.

The proctor reads the test instructions to you and lets you log in to the computer to start the test. Listen carefully to these instructions so you know how much time you have to take the test as well as any other important information.

Brushing Up on Test-Taking Strategies

You can increase your score by mastering a few smart test-taking strategies. To help you do so, we give you some tips in these sections on how to

- ✓ Plan your time.
- ✓ Determine the question type.
- ✓ Figure out how to answer the different types of questions.
- ✓ Guess intelligently.
- ✓ Review your work.

Watching the clock: Using your time wisely

When you start the computerized version of the GED Science test, you may feel pressed for time and have the urge to rush through the questions. We strongly advise that you don't. You have sufficient time to do the test at a reasonable pace. You have only a certain amount of time for each section on the GED exam, so time management is an important part of succeeding on the test. You need to plan ahead and use your time wisely. Don't spend a great deal of time on a question you don't understand. Leave it until the end and try it again. Never sacrifice an easy question for a difficult one.

During the test, the computer keeps you constantly aware of the time with a clock in the upper right-hand corner. Pay attention to the clock. When the test begins, check that time and record it on your scratchpad, and be sure to monitor how much time you have left as you work your way through the test. The GED Science test is 90 minutes long and consists of approximately 50 questions: 48 standard questions (multiple-choice, fill-in-the-blank, and so forth) and two short answer (essay questions).

Budget your time carefully so you don't run out of time before you have a chance to answer all the questions. You have about 10 minutes to write each short answer response, leaving 70 minutes to answer the other 48 questions — slightly less than 90 seconds per question. As you progress, repeat the calculation, dividing the remaining time by the remaining number of questions, to see how you're doing. Remember, too, that you can do questions in any order. Do the easiest questions first. If you get stuck on a question, leave it and come back to it later, if you have time. Keeping to that schedule and answering as many questions as possible are essential.

If you don't monitor the time for each question, you won't have time to answer all the questions on the test. Keep in mind the following general time-management tips to help you complete the exam on time:

- ✔ **Tackle questions in groups.** For example, calculate how much time you have for each item on the test. Divide the time allowed for the test by the number of questions. Multiply the answer by 5 to give you a time slot for any five test items. Then try to answer each group of five items within the time you calculated. Doing so helps you complete all the questions and leaves you several minutes for review.

- ✔ **Keep calm and don't panic.** The time you spend panicking could be better spent answering questions.

- ✔ **Practice using the sample tests in this book.** The more you practice timed sample test questions, the easier managing a timed test becomes. You can get used to doing something in a limited amount of time if you practice. Refer to the earlier section "Using the Diagnostic and Practice Tests to Your Advantage" for more information.

When time is up, immediately stop and breathe a sigh of relief. When the test ends, the examiner will give you a log-off procedure. Listen for instructions on what to do or where to go next.

Evaluating the different questions

Although you don't have to know much about how the test questions, or items, were developed to answer them correctly, you do need some understanding of how they're constructed. Knowing the types of items you're dealing with can make answering them easier — and you'll face fewer surprises.

To evaluate the types of questions that you have to answer, keep these tips in mind:

- ✔ **As soon as the computer signals that the test is running, start by skimming the questions.** Don't spend a lot of time doing so — just enough to spot the questions you absolutely know and the ones you know you'll need more time to answer.

- ✔ **Rely on the Previous and Next buttons on the bottom of the screen to scroll through the questions.** After you finish skimming, answer all the questions you know first; that way, you leave yourself much more time for the difficult questions. Check out the next section "Addressing and answering questions" for tips on how to answer questions.

✔ **Answer the easiest questions first.** You don't have to answer questions in order. Nobody except you will ever know, or care, in which order you answer the questions, so do the easiest questions first. You'll be able to answer them fastest, leaving more time for the other, harder questions. Just don't forget to go back and do the skipped questions before you finish.

Addressing and answering questions

When you start the test, you want to have a game plan in place for how to answer the questions. Keep the following tips in mind to help you address each question:

✔ **Whenever you read a question, ask yourself, "What am I being asked?"** Doing so helps you stay focused on what you need to find out to answer the question. You may even want to decide quickly what skills are required to answer the question (see the preceding section for more on these skills). Then try to answer it.

✔ **Try to eliminate some answers.** Even if you don't really know the answer, guessing can help. When you're offered four answer choices, some will be obviously wrong. Eliminate those choices and you've already improved your odds of guessing a correct answer.

✔ **Don't overthink.** Because all the questions are straightforward, don't look for hidden or sneaky questions. The questions ask for an answer based on the information given. If you don't have enough information to answer the question, one of the answer choices will say so.

✔ **Find the answer choice you think is best and quickly verify that it answers the question.** If it does, click on that choice and move on. If it doesn't, leave it and come back to it after you answer all the other questions, if you have time. *Remember:* You need to pick the *most* correct answer, not the perfect answer from the choices offered.

Guess for success: Using intelligent guessing

The multiple-choice questions, regardless of the on-screen format, provide you with four possible answers. You get between 1 and 3 points for every correct answer. Nothing is subtracted for incorrect answers. That means you can guess on the items you don't know for sure without fear that you'll lose points if your guess is incorrect. Make educated guesses by eliminating as many obviously wrong choices as possible and choosing from just one or two remaining choices.

When the question gives you four possible answers and you randomly choose one, you have a 25 percent chance of guessing the correct answer without even reading the question. Of course, we don't recommend using this method during the test but thought we would sneak in a bit of probability theory.

If you know that one of the answers is definitely wrong, you now have just three answers to choose from and have a 33 percent chance (1 in 3) of choosing the correct answer. If you know that two of the answers are wrong, you leave yourself only two possible answers to choose from, giving you a 50 percent (1 in 2) chance of guessing right — much better than 25 percent! Removing two or three choices you know are wrong makes choosing the correct answer much easier.

If you don't know the answer to a particular question, try to spot the wrong choices by following these tips:

- ✔ **Make sure your answer really answers the question.** Wrong choices usually don't answer the question — that is, they may sound good, but they answer a different question than the one the test asks.

- ✔ **When two answers seem very close, consider both answers carefully because they both can't be right — but they both *can* be wrong.** Some answer choices may be very close, and all seem correct, but there's a fine line between completely correct and nearly correct. Be careful. These answer choices are sometimes given to see whether you have really read and understand the material.

- ✔ **Look for opposite answers in the hopes that you can eliminate one.** If two answers contradict each other, both can't be right, but both can be wrong.

- ✔ **Trust your instincts.** Some wrong choices may just strike you as wrong when you first read them. If you spend time preparing for these exams, you probably know more than you think.

Leaving time for review

Having a few minutes at the end of a test to check your work is a great way to set your mind at ease. These few minutes give you a chance to look at any questions that may be troubling. If you've chosen an answer for every question, enjoy the last few minutes before time is called — without any panic. Keep the following tips in mind as you review your answers:

- ✔ **After you know how much time you have per item, try to answer each item in a little less than that time.** The extra seconds you don't use the first time through the test add up to time at the end of the test for review. Some questions require more thought and decision making than others. Use your extra seconds to answer those questions. If you can increase your reading speed without sacrificing comprehension, you can store some extra minutes to answer questions or check answers.

- ✔ **Don't try to change a lot of answers at the last minute.** Second-guessing yourself can lead to trouble. Often, second-guessing leads you to changing correct answers to incorrect ones. If you've prepared well and worked numerous sample questions, then you're likely to get the correct answers the first time. Ignoring all your preparation and knowledge to play a hunch isn't a good idea, either at the race track or on a test.

- ✔ **Use any extra time to review and revise your short answer responses.** You may have written a good response, but you always need to check for typos and grammar mistakes. Your writing is evaluated for style, content, and proper English. That includes spelling and grammar.

Sharpening Your Mental Focus

To succeed in taking the GED Science test, you need to be prepared. In addition to studying the content and honing the skills required, you also want to be mentally prepared. Although you may be nervous, you can't let your nerves get the best of you. Stay calm and take a deep breath. Here are a few pointers to help you stay focused on the task at hand:

- ✔ **Take time to rest and relax.** Rest and relaxation are restorative, revitalizing your body and providing your brain with the downtime it needs to digest all the information you've been feeding it.

✔ **Make sure you know the rules of the room before you begin.** If you have questions about using the bathroom during the test or what to do if you finish early, ask the proctor before you begin. If you don't want to ask these questions in public, call the GED office in your area before test day and ask your questions over the phone. For general GED questions, call 877-392-6433 or check out `www.gedtestingservice.com`. This site has many pages, but the FAQ page is always a good place to start.

✔ **Keep your eyes on your computer screen.** Everybody knows not to look at other people's work during the test, but, to be on the safe side, don't stretch, roll your eyes, or do anything else that may be mistaken for looking at another test. Most of the tests will be different on the various computers, so looking around is futile, but doing so can get you into a lot of trouble.

✔ **Stay calm.** Your nerves can use up a lot of energy needed for the test. Concentrate on the job at hand. You can always be nervous or panicky some other time.

Because taking standardized tests probably isn't a usual situation for you, you may feel nervous. This is perfectly normal. Just try to focus on answering one question at a time, and push any other thoughts to the back of your mind. Sometimes taking a few deep breaths can clear your mind; just don't spend a lot of time focusing on your breath. After all, your main job is to pass this test.

Part II
Honing Your Science Skills and Knowledge

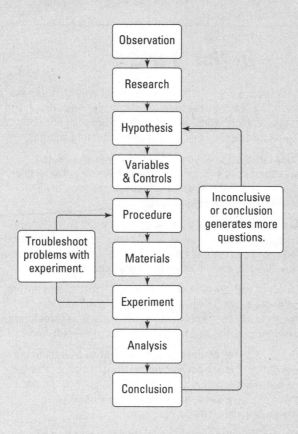

To get the lowdown on topics covered on the GED Science test and tips for where to focus your efforts, head to www.dummies.com/extras/gedsciencetest.

In this part . . .

✔ Make sense of scientific data presented in various formats, including reading passages, graphs, maps, illustrations, and tables; draw reasonable conclusions from scientific data; and correlate scientific evidence from two or more sources.

✔ Tune into the scientific method, identify strengths and weaknesses of scientific investigations, analyze scientific models and theories, and use theories and laws to better understand natural phenomena.

✔ Summarize scientific data using statistics, draw conclusions from data sets, use counting and permutations to solve problems, and calculate the probability of events, as you discover how to apply math to scientific investigations.

✔ Live it up with the life sciences, as you find out what the life sciences cover, how living things are classified, what cell theory is all about, how ecosystems use and transfer energy, and how genetics and heredity play out in the real world.

✔ Get up to speed on physics and chemistry; understand the essentials of energy conservation, transformation, and flow; calculate work, force, and distance; find out how simple machines save effort; and discover more about atoms, molecules, and chemical reactions.

✔ Explore the universe you live in, from galaxies to solar systems, right down to the ground you walk on, along with Earth systems, including air, land, water, and the critters that live here.

Chapter 5

Reading and Writing in a Science Context

- -

In This Chapter

▶ Making sense of scientific presentations

▶ Drawing reasonable conclusions from scientific data

▶ Correlating scientific evidence from multiple sources

- -

To do well on the GED Science test, you need to be able to read and understand science-related content presented in various media — including text, maps, images, charts, and tables — and you must be able to write short essays in response to science-related prompts. In this chapter, we provide guidance on reading and writing in a science context along with plenty of practice to hone your skills.

This chapter contains a few short-answer items that test a different set of skills than do the regular questions. We include these questions to give you practice responding to this type of question and develop a means of self-evaluating your response. If you can do that effectively, you'll have an advantage on the Science test.

Understanding Scientific Presentations

On the GED Science test, you're presented with scientific information in the form of text, maps, images, charts, and tables, and possibly a combination of two or three different formats. Your job is to make sense of the information in various formats so you can answer questions about that information and draw conclusions from it. To answer any science question on the test, I recommend the following process:

1. **Read the passage, if a passage is presented, and/or skim the data that's presented as a map, image, chart, or table, so you have a general idea of what the data is.**

2. **Read the question and any answer choices, so you have a clear idea of what you need to do with the information you're given.**

   Some questions may be fill-in-the-blank or some other format, so you may not have answer choices.

3. **Find the specific information in the passage, map, image, chart, or table that answers the question.**

   For some questions, you may be required to perform mathematical operations, such as calculating an average. If a formula is required, the question gives you the formula you need.

4. Answer the question.

Most questions are multiple-choice, in which case, you identify the choice that's supported best by information in the passage, map, image, chart, or table. Some questions may be fill-in-the-blank or drag-and-drop.

When answering multiple-choice questions, if you don't know the answer, make an intelligent guess. Eliminate obviously wrong answers and then choose from the remaining answers to improve your chances of guessing the correct answer. You're not penalized for wrong answers; you receive a 0 (zero) for a wrong answer, which is what you'd receive for no answer.

In this section, you encounter scientific information presented in a variety of formats, so you'll be familiar with the different formats when you take the test. You may have an easier time understanding information presented in certain formats than in others.

Grasping textual presentations

Much of the scientific information presented on the test comes in the form of reading passages — one or more paragraphs of text. The challenge with these passages is to be able to read and understand the passage and sift through it to find the specific information you need to answer the questions that follow the passage.

Here's a sample reading passage extracted from the booklet "Wetlands" published by the Environmental Protection Agency (`water.epa.gov/type/wetlands/assessment/upload/2000_06_26_98report_chap6.pdf`):

Some wetlands, such as salt marshes, are among the most productive natural ecosystems in the world. Only rain forests and coral reefs come close to matching their productivity. They produce huge amounts of plant leaves and stems that serve as the basis of the food web. When the plants die, they decompose in the water and form detritus. Detritus and the algae that often grow on plants are the principal foods for shrimp, crabs, clams, and small fish, which, in turn, are food for larger commercial and recreational fish species such as bluefish and striped bass.

1. The following diagram represents a typical energy pyramid.

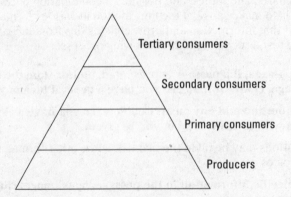

In the energy pyramid, detritus and algae that grow on plants are at which level in the food pyramid?

(A) tertiary consumers

(B) secondary consumers

(C) primary consumers

(D) producers

2. In the energy pyramid, producers convert

(A) nuclear energy into thermal energy

(B) radiant energy into chemical energy

(C) mechanical energy into electrical energy

(D) thermal energy into radiant energy

Check your answers:

1. Detritus and the algae that grow on plants are referred to as the primary foods for smaller animals that larger animals feed on, so the correct answer is Choice (D), producers.

2. Producers are plants that convert radiant energy from the sun into chemical energy in the form of plants, which are comprised of the chemicals carbon, hydrogen, and oxygen, which provide energy to the consumers in the food chain. Choice (B) is the correct answer.

Determining the meaning of scientific symbols, terms, and phrases

The GED Science test expects you to be able to "determine the meaning of symbols, terms, and phrases as they are used in scientific presentations." This means you need to know the language of science, and the only way to know the language of science is to read a lot of science content and look up words, phrases, and any funky symbols you encounter.

The chapters in Part II of this book bring you up to speed on many of the words, phrases, symbols, and concepts you need to know to understand the reading passages and questions. Knowing the basics about energy flow in an ecosystem; the water cycle; the relationship among work, motion, and force; the various states of a chemical element; solar system fundamentals; and so on provides you with the framework to understand scientific symbols, terms, and phrases in context.

Questions such as these require a knowledge of science terminology to answer correctly.

1. How does an endothermic chemical reaction differ from an exothermic reaction?

(A) An exothermic reaction absorbs heat, whereas an endothermic reaction releases heat.

(B) An exothermic reaction requires a great deal of energy to trigger while an endothermic reaction does not.

(C) An endothermic reaction absorbs heat, whereas an exothermic reaction releases heat.

(D) Endothermic reactions proceed much more quickly.

2. The movement of water from an area of high concentration to an area of low concentration is called

   (A) osmosis

   (B) phagocytosis

   (C) respiration

   (D) homeostasis

Check your answers:

1. An *exothermic* reaction gives off heat (*ex* is Latin for "out of"); an *endothermic* reaction absorbs heat. Choice (C) is the correct answer. See Chapter 9 for more about chemistry.

2. The movement of water from an area of high concentration to an area of low concentration is called *osmosis,* Choice (A). To find out more about various cell processes, head to Chapter 8.

Comprehending non-textual presentations

Non-textual presentations are those that present information in the form of maps, graphs, images, and tables. They may not be entirely void of text, but any text they contain is minimal. Here are a few questions based on non-textual science presentations.

1. This illustration from the Centers for Disease Control and Prevention shows how hookworm infections occur.

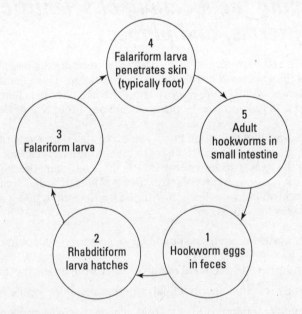

What are the two most effective ways to prevent the spread of hookworm (choose two answers)?

(A) wear tight-fitting clothes

(B) wear shoes when walking outside

(C) provide sanitary treatment of human wastes

(D) wash fruit and vegetables thoroughly before eating

2. This image from the U.S. Geological Survey shows the potential impact area for ground-based hazards during a volcanic event on Mount Rainier, Washington.

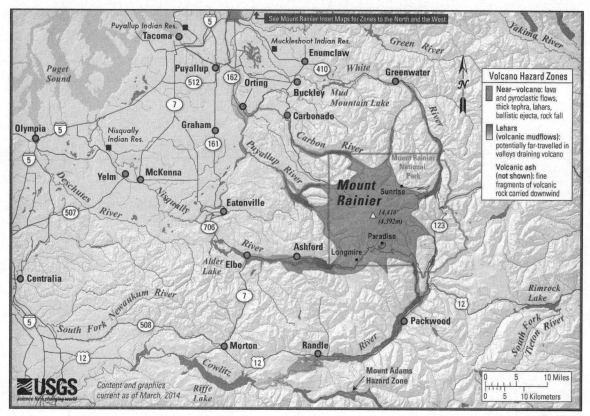

Photo courtesy of USGS

What are the two most dangerous areas to be in the event of a volcanic eruption (choose two answers)?

(A) within 10 miles of the center of Mount Rainier

(B) near any lakes in the vicinity

(C) near valleys in the vicinity

(D) on hills surrounding Mount Rainier

3. This chart shows how the boiling point of water changes at higher elevations.

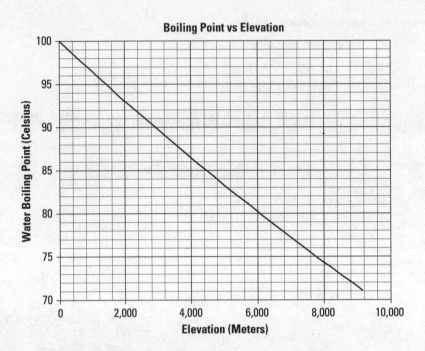

Which of the following cooking instructions would you need to follow when preparing meals at 6,000 meters elevation?

(A) Heat water for a longer period of time to reach its boiling point.

(B) Set the stove top to a higher setting when boiling the water.

(C) Subtract one minute of cooking time for each 1,000 meters of elevation.

(D) Add one minute of cooking time for each 1,000 meters of elevation.

4. According to Newton's second law of motion, *Force = mass × acceleration*, as illustrated in the following table.

Net Force (N)	Mass (kg)	Acceleration (m/s^2)
8	2	4
8	4	2
8	8	1

Which of the following statements best describes the pattern shown in the table?

(A) Increasing force increases acceleration when mass remains constant.

(B) Decreasing acceleration decreases force when mass remains constant.

(C) Decreasing mass increases acceleration when the force remains constant.

(D) Increasing mass increases acceleration when force remains constant.

Check your answers:

1. The illustration shows that hookworm eggs are passed in human feces and enter the body through the skin, so wearing shoes when walking outside and using proper sanitation are the two best ways, according to the image, to prevent hookworm from spreading. Answer Choices (B) and (C) are correct. The other options may help as well, but they're not supported by the image.

2. The shaded portion representing the area near Mount Rainier is approximately 20 miles across according to the scale in the lower-right corner of the illustration, so within 10 miles from the center is the most dangerous area. The valleys where major rivers flow from Mount Rainier are also shaded as high-risk areas because of mudflows. Answer Choices (A) and (C) are correct.

3. Because water has a lower boiling point at higher elevations, you would need to cook your food for a longer period of time at a higher elevation, Choice (D). Choice (A) is wrong; water would boil faster at a higher elevation because its boiling point is lower. Choice (B) is wrong because setting the stove top to a higher setting will make the water boil sooner, but it doesn't make it any hotter. Choice (C) is wrong because decreasing the cooking time is the opposite of what you need to do.

4. The table shows that when mass is decreased and force remains constant, acceleration is increased, as stated in Choice (C). Choice (A) is true, but the table doesn't show mass remaining constant. Choice (B) is also true, but again, the table doesn't show mass remaining constant. Choice (D) is wrong because increasing mass would decrease acceleration if force remained constant.

Demonstrating Your Ability to Reason from Data

If you correctly answered the questions in the previous section, you've already demonstrated your ability to reason from data. Nearly every question on the Science test challenges this ability by presenting data and then asking you to draw a conclusion from that data or apply it to a different situation. For example, if you know that the boiling point of water increases at higher pressures, how does that affect cooking time when you're cooking food in a pressure cooker? (Answer: The food would cook in less time.) You really need to use your noodle to answer the questions; it's not just a matter of reading a passage and picking out facts.

In this section, we explain in greater detail what's required to be able to reason from data. We break this skill down into three sub-abilities: the ability to draw a conclusion based on evidence, the ability to predict an outcome based on evidence, and the ability to cite evidence from a written source to support a conclusion or prediction.

Drawing a conclusion from data or evidence

You may often think that drawing conclusions from scientific data is something done only in science classes, but it's actually more common and important in the real world, where such conclusions can affect health, safety, economic conditions, and the very survival of the planet.

To draw conclusions from evidence, look closely at the data or evidence presented and consider carefully how the evidence was obtained; for example, how an experiment or study was conducted. The data and other evidence along with the question and answer choices lead you to the conclusion.

A poorly designed experiment or study can raise more questions than answers. For example, scientists may hypothesize that global warming is caused primarily by burning fossil fuels, but they draw that conclusion only after evaluating other possible factors, such as farming practices, deforestation, solar variability, and greenhouse gases other than carbon dioxide, such as methane. (See Chapter 6 for more about experimental design.)

Here are a few questions that challenge your ability to arrive at evidence-based conclusions.

1. Oceanographers recently discovered a fish, called an *opah* or *moonfish,* that maintains a constant body temperature. Why does this fish challenge the system for distinguishing classifying vertebrates (animals with a backbone or spinal column)?

    (A) Fish are classified as coldblooded invertebrates.

    (B) Fish are generally classified as coldblooded vertebrates.

    (C) Vertebrates cannot maintain a constant body temperature.

    (D) Invertebrates cannot maintain a constant body temperature.

2. *Photosynthesis* is a process in which plants use energy from the sun to convert carbon dioxide and water into energy-rich carbohydrates and release oxygen as a "waste" product. Plants are considered primary producers. Through respiration, primary consumers eat and digest the plants, converting carbohydrates and oxygen into carbon dioxide, water, and energy.

    Herbivores (animals that eat plants) obtain energy directly from

    (A) the sun

    (B) breathing

    (C) carbohydrates

    (D) water

3. This graph illustrates the effect of different concentrations of engine coolant on the freezing point of water.

    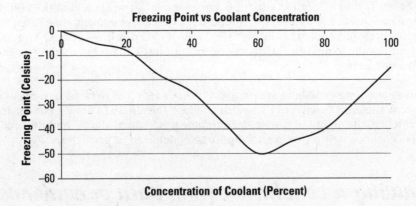

    What is the optimum ratio of coolant to water?

    (A) 50:50

    (B) 100:0

    (C) 60:40

    (D) 40:60

4. According to the Centers for Disease Control (CDC), " . . . cellphones and cordless phones use radiofrequency radiation (RF) to send signals. RF is different from other types of radiation (like X-rays) that we know can be harmful. We don't know for sure if RF radiation from cellphones can cause health problems years later. The International Agency for Research on Cancer (IARC) has classified RF radiation as a 'possible human carcinogen.' (A *carcinogen* is an agent that causes cancer.)"

Based on this information from the CDC, you can conclude that

(A) Cellphones are safe to use.

(B) Cellphones cause cancer.

(C) Cellphones emit X-rays.

(D) Cellphones emit radiofrequency radiation.

Check your answers:

1. To answer this question correctly, you need some information not supplied by the question — the fact that fish are classified as coldblooded vertebrates and that cold-blooded animals can't maintain a body temperature (they're the temperature of their environment). So the opah challenges the classification system because fish are generally classified as coldblooded vertebrates, Choice (B). (Just for the record, other fish, including tuna and sharks, can raise their body temperature temporarily, but they can't maintain a constant body temperature.)

2. Through the process of respiration, herbivores break down carbohydrates to release energy, so Choice (C) is correct. If you picked Choice (A), you're partially right, because the energy originally comes from the sun, but plants convert the radiant energy from the sun into chemical energy stored in carbohydrates, and the question asks where herbivores "obtain energy *directly* from." If you picked Choice (B), you're thinking of a different meaning of "respiration," and Choice (D) is just plain wrong — water doesn't provide energy for animals; it has 0 calories.

3. The graph shows that the freezing point of water/coolant mixture is lowest with 60 percent coolant and 40 percent water, so Choice (C) is correct.

4. Based on the information provided, the only conclusion you can draw is that cellphones emit RF radiation, Choice (D). None of the other answer choices is supported in the passage.

Predicting an outcome based on data or evidence

The greatest benefits of scientific studies can often be attributed to the fact that their conclusions enable people to predict outcomes. (You probably wish science could help you predict your outcome on the test!) You witness science in action every day you check the weather forecast. By observing barometric pressure, humidity, temperature, the movement of high- and low-pressure systems, and other factors, meteorologists can make reasonable predictions about future weather conditions.

In a similar way, the Science test presents you with scientific information and asks you to predict outcomes based on that information. Here are a couple sample questions to help you practice answering such questions:

1. This graph shows the effect that adding salt to water has on water's melting and boiling points. One teaspoon of salt is 6 grams, and 1 kilogram of water is approximately 1 quart.

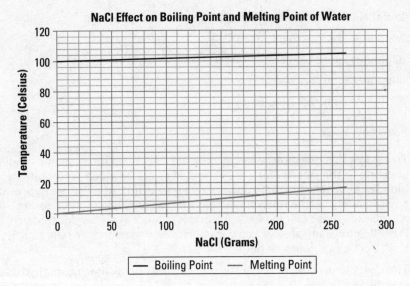

John adds 3 teaspoons of salt (NaCl) to a 6-quart pot of water to boil it at 105° Celsius instead of at the 100° Celsius he is accustomed to, because he read online that adding salt to water increases its boiling point. One teaspoon holds about 6 grams of salt. Did he add enough salt? Yes or No: _____

2. A certain plant species can have curly or flat leaves. The *allele* (gene form) for curly leaves is dominant, and the one for flat leaves is recessive. Two plants of the species are crossed, both with curly leaves. The Punnett square for the breeding looks like this, with "C" representing the allele for curly leaves and "c" representing the allele for flat leaves:

	C	c
C	CC	Cc
c	Cc	cc

What percentage of the offspring is likely to have flat leaves?

(A) 0%

(B) 25%

(C) 50%

(D) 75%

Check your answers:

1. No. According to the chart, John would need to add more than 250 grams of salt to the water to raise its boiling point 5° Celsius. That's more than 41 teaspoons of salt! You may have to do a little math in your head to answer this question.

2. Only 25% of the offspring would be expected to have flat leaves. Because "C" represents the dominant gene, both "CC" and "Cc" offspring would have curly leaves. Only "cc" offspring would have flat leaves.

Answering a scientific question by using sampling techniques

Sampling is a scientific method that enables researchers to draw reasonable conclusions using a relatively small subset of data. For example, researchers may test several different brands of batteries in different devices to determine which battery lasts longest and which devices drain batteries the fastest. On the Science test, you may encounter one or more questions that present sampling data and ask you to draw conclusions from that data. Here are a couple of relatively easy questions to practice on.

Use the data from this table to answer the questions that follow.

Snake Species

Environment	Rat	Milk	Green	King	Fox	Blue Racer
Tree	12	1	22	0	0	3
Forest floor	3	8	3	1	5	7
Farm/meadow	17	23	2	10	15	12
Marsh	2	1	0	25	30	3

1. The snake you are most likely to find in a barn is the

   (A) rat snake

   (B) milk snake

   (C) green snake

   (D) king snake

2. Destruction of wetlands would cause the biggest reduction in which of the following populations?

   (A) green snake and milk snake

   (B) green snake and rat snake

   (C) king snake and milk snake

   (D) fox snake and king snake

Check your answers:

   1. The milk snake, Choice (B), is most prevalent on farms, where barns are common. (Snake trivia: The milk snake gets its name from a folk tale claiming that the milk snake sucks the milk of nursing mothers and cows. Not true.)

   2. Both the fox snake and king snake are found primarily in marsh habitats (wetlands), so Choice (D) is correct.

Citing evidence from a written source to support a finding or conclusion

You're most likely to be asked to cite evidence from a written source to support a finding or conclusion when you encounter a short answer or extended response question on the Science test. To write an effective response, you need to use evidence from the reading passage to support any claims you make. You may include direct quotes from the passage or describe the evidence in your own words. (Remember, these short answer questions are timed as part of the test, not separately. It is up to you to manage your time appropriately.)

> *Read the following passage from NASA, an excerpt from "Dark Energy, Dark Matter," and write a short response to the prompt as directed. Write your answer on a separate piece of paper. This question should take you about 10 minutes to complete.*

In the early 1990s, one thing was fairly certain about the expansion of the Universe. It might have enough energy density to stop its expansion and recollapse, it might have so little energy density that it would never stop expanding, but gravity was certain to slow the expansion as time went on. Granted, the slowing had not been observed, but, theoretically, the Universe had to slow. The Universe is full of matter and the attractive force of gravity pulls all matter together. Then came 1998 and the Hubble Space Telescope (HST) observations of very distant supernovae that showed that, a long time ago, the Universe was actually expanding more slowly than it is today. So the expansion of the Universe has not been slowing due to gravity, as everyone thought, it has been accelerating. No one expected this, no one knew how to explain it. But something was causing it.

Eventually, theorists came up with three sorts of explanations. Maybe it was a result of a long-discarded version of Einstein's theory of gravity, one that contained what was called a *cosmological constant.* Maybe there was some strange kind of energy-fluid that filled space. Maybe there is something wrong with Einstein's theory of gravity, and a new theory could include some kind of field that creates this cosmic acceleration. Theorists still don't know what the correct explanation is, but they have given the solution a name. It is called *dark energy.*

What Is Dark Energy?

More is unknown than is known. We know how much dark energy there is because we know how it affects the Universe's expansion. Other than that, it is a complete mystery. But it is an important mystery. It turns out that roughly 68% of the Universe is dark energy. Dark matter makes up about 27%. The rest — everything on Earth, everything ever observed with all of our instruments, all normal matter — adds up to less than 5% of the Universe. Come to think of it, maybe it shouldn't be called "normal" matter at all, since it is such a small fraction of the Universe.

One explanation for dark energy is that it is a property of space. Albert Einstein was the first person to realize that empty space is not nothing. Space has amazing properties, many of which are just beginning to be understood. The first property that Einstein discovered is that it is possible for more space to come into existence. Then one version of Einstein's gravity theory, the version that contains a cosmological constant, makes a second prediction: "empty space" can possess its own energy. Because this energy is a property of space itself, it would not be diluted as space expands. As more space comes into existence, more of this energy-of-space would appear. As a result, this form of energy would cause the Universe to expand faster and faster. Unfortunately, no one understands why the cosmological constant should even be there, much less why it would have exactly the right value to cause the observed acceleration of the Universe.

What is dark energy and what enables it to accelerate the expansion of the universe?

You have to evaluate your response yourself, but in this case, what's most important is your use of evidence from the reading passage to support whatever claims you made. The Science short-answer questions receive a score between 0 and 3 points. To earn 3 points, you need to provide a clear and detailed answer, along with supporting evidence from the passage. You must ensure you actually answer the question and use facts and data from the passage to support your answer. The answer can be one or two paragraphs, ranging from 50 to 300 words. The answer must be clear and to the point, and your statements justified by the content and your interpretation of that content. Writing style, grammar, and spelling are not part of the evaluation.

If you did that, give yourself a 3. If you simply made claims without citing evidence from the passage, you may want to try writing your response again.

For some samples, with evaluation, go to www.gedtestingservice.com/uploads/ files/89097368525e28544f77607f31391c4f.pdf.

Reconciling Multiple Findings, Conclusions, or Theories

Scientists often must draw conclusions from two or more findings, conclusions, or theories to identify the cause of a certain phenomenon and answer questions. On the test, you may be called on to step into the shoes of a scientist and reconcile results from two or more studies with other data, or you may be asked questions related to incidents in which scientists reconciled other theories or hypotheses.

To answer such questions successfully, examine the data and the question carefully for clues. The information you're given points the way to the correct answer. The following reading passage and questions challenge your ability to evaluate how scientists use existing knowledge from two sources to formulate questions and arrive at a conclusion.

Questions 1–2 refer to the following passage, "What connects fish and maple trees?" from the National Science Foundation.

If we are what we eat, some lake fish, it turns out, are made of maple leaves. These fallen leaves play an integral role in the food webs of lakes.

It has long been thought that aquatic plants form the base of a lake's food web. The energy they contain supports life, from invertebrates to the largest sport fish. Now, a study funded by the National Science Foundation's (NSF) Biological Sciences Directorate shows that aquatic plants are receiving a little help from trees along the shoreline.

Scientists Michael Pace and Jonathan Cole of the Institute for Ecosystem Studies in Millbrook, New York, found that a significant part of the aquatic food chain is supported by organic matter ("food") that originates on shore.

A building block of life, organic carbon is essential to aquatic food webs. In lakes, aquatic plants produce this carbon by harnessing the sun's energy through photosynthesis. Some of the carbon supports the growth of fish and invertebrate populations.

In Lakes Peter and Paul at the University of Notre Dame Research Center, scientists conducted tests to determine whether lake plant production was enough to support resident aquatic life.

The short answer: It's not. Test results show that aquatic plants don't produce nearly enough food to support lake animals. Therefore, to survive and thrive, the lake animals are dependent on inputs from the surrounding shores.

Leaves and other organic matter that enter lakes, it turns out, are ultimately incorporated into aquatic animals. That maple leaves may eventually become perch, and that the vegetation around a lake can have profound impacts on the animal life within that lake, blurs the boundaries between aquatic and land-based ecosystems.

As naturalist John Muir once wrote, tug on one strand of nature, and you'll find it connects to all others.

1. Which of the following conclusions can be drawn from the evidence presented?

   (A) Aquatic plants do not produce enough organic matter to support resident aquatic life, so fish must eat tree leaves.

   (B) Fish cannot obtain sufficient amounts of food from aquatic plants, so they need to eat aquatic invertebrates to survive.

   (C) Aquatic plants do not produce sufficient carbon to support resident aquatic life, so the carbon must be coming from plants along the shoreline.

   (D) Shoreline vegetation supplies sufficient energy to support resident aquatic life without the addition of aquatic plant production.

2. Which of the following is a fact about food chains that caused researchers to question whether aquatic plant production was sufficient to support resident aquatic life?

   (A) All energy in a food chain comes from the sun.

   (B) In lakes, aquatic plants produce all the food required to support resident aquatic life.

   (C) All aquatic animals obtain their energy directly from plants.

   (D) In food chains, secondary consumers eat primary consumers.

Check your answers:

   1. By studying the amount of aquatic plants and animals, researchers concluded that the animal population was greater than the aquatic plant life could support, so additional plant life would need to be added, and the only place it could possibly come from is around the shoreline, Choice (C).

   2. In arriving at their conclusion, scientists needed to reconcile knowledge about food chains and the photosynthetic process. Through photosynthesis, plants convert radiant energy from the sun into chemical energy that animals can eat. A population is limited by the amount of energy plants can harvest from the sun. So the fact about food chains that the researchers used to arrive at their conclusion is that all energy in a food chain comes from the sun, Choice (A).

Chapter 6

Analyzing Experimental Design and Scientific Theories

*I*n an attempt to understand and explain natural phenomena, scientists engage in inquiries that involve asking questions, making observations, formulating *hypotheses* (educated guesses), conducting experiments to test hypotheses, analyzing results, asking more questions, and so on. To keep themselves honest and obtain the most accurate information possible, they follow a specific procedure when conducting these inquiries, called the *scientific method.*

On the GED Science test, you're likely to encounter a few questions that test your understanding of the scientific method, so in this chapter, we explain the basics and provide sample test questions for practice.

Getting a Bird's-Eye View of the Scientific Method

The *scientific method* is a step-by-step approach to answering science questions and solving problems. It ensures the credibility and reproducibility of experimental evidence.

Now you'd think that for a scientific method to be scientific, all scientists would agree on the steps involved. They sort of do agree, but if you search online for "scientific method," you'll find a variety of scientific methods (plural). Our version of the scientific method goes like this, with a couple loops, as shown in Figure 6-1:

1. **Observe and wonder.** Many of the most important scientific discoveries start with an observation — information obtained primarily through the senses (seeing, hearing, touching, and so on). Alexander Fleming discovered penicillin when he was cleaning up petri dishes in his lab and noticed that around the edges of a patch of mold growing in one of the dishes, infectious staph bacteria had been killed. He wondered, "Why?"

2. **Research.** Another scientist may have answered the question or solved the problem already. Research provides insight into what's already been done to answer the question or solve the problem. The research may show that plenty of work has been done and the question or problem remains.

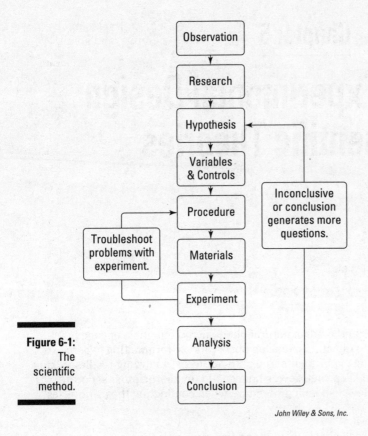

Figure 6-1:
The
scientific
method.

John Wiley & Sons, Inc.

3. **Formulate a hypothesis.** A *hypothesis* is a proposed explanation for a condition or occurrence that can be tested and either proved or disproved. A hypothesis can usually be phrased as an if/then question; for example, "If you warm a cup of water, it will dissolve more sugar."

4. **Define variables and controls.** Establishing variables and controls is the first step toward designing an experiment:

   • **Variables:** Conditions that are changed to determine the effects of those changes. In the water/sugar example, heat is the variable being changed.

   • **Controls:** Conditions that remain unchanged, to prevent them from influencing the results. In the water/sugar example, using water from the same source and making sure the same amount of water is used for each test are controls.

5. **Create a procedure.** A *procedure* is a step-by-step process for conducting the experiment or study, including specifics about the data that will be collected and how it will be recorded.

   The procedure is very important because it enables other researchers to evaluate the process used to create and gather data. If the experiment or study is done right, anyone should be able to follow the same steps and get the same results. A poorly designed experiment or study produces unreliable data.

6. **List and gather the required materials.** Before starting an experiment or study of any sort, the scientist needs to gather all the supplies needed, including, in some cases, participants for the experiment or study.

7. **Conduct the experiment or study.** It's show time! Scientists conduct the experiment or study and record the results.

8. **Analyze the data.** Analysis can be as simple as looking at the data or it may involve plugging it into a spreadsheet, rearranging it, using it to create graphs, and so on.

9. **Draw conclusions or not.** The results may lead to certain conclusions, may be inconclusive, or may bring up other questions that need to be answered first. In some cases, the conclusions reveal a problem in the design of the experiment or study or the way it was performed.

Certain steps in the scientific method may vary slightly. For example, if a scientist stumbles on something very unusual, research may not be necessary. The scientist can skip ahead to the hypothesis and then plan an experiment to test it. Likewise, if the results of an experiment are inconclusive, the scientist doesn't necessarily jump back to hypothesis. She may be able to trace the reason for the inconclusive results to a problem in the variables and controls, the procedure followed, the materials used, mistakes in conducting the experiment, or the analysis. In addition, sometimes results lead to observations that may take the scientist down another path.

1. A scientist traveling in Kenya has suffered terribly with nasal allergies for decades. He discovers a group of people who don't have any allergies. Most of the people are infected with hookworm. He hypothesizes that hookworms may cure his allergies, so he introduces the parasite into his system. Which step(s) in the scientific method did he skip?

(A) observation, research, and hypothesis

(B) research and variables and controls

(C) research, hypothesis, variables and controls, and procedure

(D) hypothesis, variables and controls, procedure, and materials

2. Janice is testing two different fertilizers to see which works better. She uses Fertilizer A on the vegetable garden in her backyard and Fertilizer B on her flower garden in the front of her house. The plants in the vegetable garden grow three times faster and larger than the plants in her flower garden. She concludes that Fertilizer A is the better product. What is wrong with the design of Janice's experiment?

(A) It has no well-defined variables.

(B) She did not propose a hypothesis.

(C) It has no well-defined controls.

(D) Janice forgot to do her research.

3. Patsy Sherman, a chemist at 3M, was working on developing a rubber substance that would not deteriorate when exposed to jet aircraft fuels. She mistakenly splashed some on her shoe and noticed several weeks later that the areas on her shoe that had the substance on them looked nearly new, while areas without the substance were dirty and stained. She assumed the substance must have been responsible for preserving the shoe. To confirm her suspicions, Patsy needed to conduct

(A) research

(B) experiments

(C) observation

(D) analysis

4. After gathering results and conducting a thorough analysis, a scientist concludes that the results are inconclusive. Which step should he go back to in the process?

(A) research

(B) hypothesis

(C) procedure

(D) it depends

Now check your answers:

1. The scientist made an observation and a hypothesis, so you can eliminate Choices (A), (C), and (D). Choice (B) is the only correct answer. The scientist did no research and didn't establish variables and controls. He tested only on himself, so his results are likely to be unreliable. If his allergies disappear, he may want to find more participants for his next experiment, assuming he can find people to volunteer to be infected with hookworm.

2. The problem is that Janice failed to use controls, Choice (C). To perform a controlled experiment, every factor other than the fertilizer needs to be the same in the two groups being tested. The two fertilizers would need to be tested on the same plant type, growing in the same soil with the same amount of sunshine and water.

3. Patsy would need to conduct controlled experiments, Choice (B), to determine whether the substance or something else was responsible for protecting her shoe. Choice (A) is a good second choice, but because Patsy was the chemist developing the substance, she would probably have little or no research available to help her.

4. It depends, Choice (D). In most cases, scientists can revise the hypothesis and start over from that point. However, if the scientist can pin down the reason for the inconclusive results and attribute it to a problem in the design or execution of the experiment, she can go back to that point in the process instead of having to return to almost the beginning.

Evaluating the Design of Scientific Investigations

When science people, including medical professionals, read and publish studies, they're concerned not only with the results of a scientific investigation but also with the methods followed, which include everything from how participants are chosen to the number of participants, the length of the study, and even whether the people conducting the study may have a biased perspective. For example, when prescription medications are tested, the researchers are generally required to disclose whether they have any financial ties to the pharmaceutical company that manufactures the medication, so that anyone evaluating the study can take that into consideration.

Finding and eliminating sources of error

If scientists were perfect, then every experiment would prove the hypothesis and be reproducible by any other scientist at any time. Unfortunately, scientists are human, and errors may creep into the observations, leading to results that can't be reproduced. In a proper and valid experiment, all errors and potential errors should be documented and analyzed to help researchers in the future reproduce the experiments without repeating the errors. Errors are generally divided into two groups:

> ✔ **Systematic errors:** Flaws in the experimental procedure from faulty calibration of measuring instruments, faulty use or reading of an instrument *(parallax error),* using faulty equipment, or using equipment that was designed for some other purpose. Properly documenting systematic errors helps future researchers avoid them.
>
> Systematic errors are typically *one-sided errors* (consistently high or consistently low).

> ✔ **Random errors:** These arise when those conducting the experiment have trouble reading measurements; for example, when a needle moves when taking a reading or a needle is between two lines on a meter. Such errors affect measurement precision and can be reduced through repeating the measurement or refining the measurement method or technique.
>
> Random errors are typically *two-sided errors* (results fluctuate above and below the true or accepted value).

1. Why is documenting errors in experiments or studies so important?

   (A) It enables researchers to repeat the experiment without repeating the errors.

   (B) Any error can affect the conclusions reached.

   (C) Errors may shed light on the reliability of the data.

   (D) All of the above.

2. Why is the documentation of errors in an experiment important for consumers, as well as for scientists?

   (A) Attorneys can use the information to sue drug companies.

   (B) You may want to become a scientist one day.

   (C) Errors reflect the reliability of evidence about consumer products.

   (D) Consumers may want to conduct the studies themselves.

3. Scientists record the procedures they followed to conduct an experiment for which of the following reasons?

   (A) to enable others to evaluate the experiment and its conclusions

   (B) to inform the scientific community of recent discoveries

   (C) to document their accomplishments

   (D) to encourage other scientists to reproduce the experiment

Check your answers:

1. All the answer choices, Choice (D), explain why documenting errors in an experiment is important.

2. Scientists aren't the only ones who need to evaluate the reliability of data from studies. Consumers, Choice (C), can also benefit from knowing about errors in studies.

3. Disclosing the procedures followed enables others to evaluate the experiment and its conclusions, Choice (A).

Identifying the strengths and weaknesses of a scientific investigation

Scientific investigations should be *empirical;* that is, conclusions should be based on verifiable observation, experience, and experimental evidence. For a scientific investigation to produce reliable results, it must meet all the following criteria:

✔ Participants/subjects must be chosen randomly.

✔ Controls must be in place to reduce or eliminate variables not being tested.

✔ Only one variable can be manipulated and tested. (More than one may be used, but that makes statistical analysis difficult.)

✔ Results must be *quantifiable* — size, number, weight, or something else that can be measured. For example, the number of hairs on a cat is *quantifiable,* although they would be very difficult to count, whereas the softness of the cat would be *qualitative* — a judgment call, unless you could figure out some way to quantify it.

✔ Participants/subjects must be assigned randomly to either the experimental or control group.

✔ Participants/subjects may also be retested, so they're tested in both the experimental and the control group. This "repeated measure" technique produces more uniform results. When repeated measures are done, *counterbalancing* may also be done to reduce the effects of the order in which participants are tested in either the experimental or control group.

✔ All evidence must be reported, even if — and perhaps especially if — it doesn't support the hypothesis. If evidence is excluded, the reason for the exclusion must be provided.

Controls are particularly important. When pharmaceutical companies conduct tests on medications, they commonly use the following three types of controls:

✔ **Control group:** A group that establishes a baseline from which results are measured. The control group receives no treatment or a neutral treatment. Results from the treated and untreated (control) groups are compared to determine whether treatment had any effect.

✔ **Placebo:** Untreated participants in a study often respond differently if they think they received treatment. To account for this *placebo effect,* researchers provide a neutral treatment (such as a "sugar pill") that has no real effect.

✔ **Blinding:** Those conducting the study hide the fact that some participants are receiving a placebo and some aren't, because when people know they're getting a placebo, they're less likely to respond to it. In a double-blind test, neither the researcher nor the participant is aware of who's getting the placebo, so nobody involved can inadvertently influence the results by what they say or do.

Another factor that determines the quality of a scientific study is its size. A study that involves a large number of experiments, participants, or measurements is likely to produce a more accurate body of data than does a smaller study. When testing products, researchers often refer to each experiment as a *trial*.

1. The number of variables that should be changed in a properly designed and well-controlled experiment is

   (A) 0

   (B) 1

   (C) 2

   (D) depends on what is being tested

2. When planning and conducting an experiment, one should

   (A) carefully choose participants

   (B) test as many variables as possible

   (C) establish controls to eliminate as many variables as possible

   (D) try to prove the hypothesis

3. Which of the following evidence should be reported in the results of a scientific study?

   (A) results from only one selected trial

   (B) results from only those trials that prove the hypothesis

   (C) results from only those trials that falsify the hypothesis

   (D) results from all trials

4. Which of the following is *not* quantifiable data?

   (A) beauty

   (B) height

   (C) weight

   (D) speed

Check your answers:

1. Ideally, you test only one variable in any given experimental trial, Choice (B).

2. When conducting an experiment, you should establish controls to limit variables so the only variable is the one you're changing/testing, Choice (C).

3. When publishing the results of a scientific study, you should report all results, Choice (D), even those that are excluded from your analysis.

4. You can measure height, weight, and speed, but not beauty, Choice (A).

Read the following excerpt from "Science Fair Fun: Designing Environmental Science Projects for Students Grades 6–8" (www.epa.gov/osw/education/pdfs/sciencefair.pdf) and write a short response to the prompt that follows it.

Give your project a title

Choose a title that describes what you are investigating. Make it catchy, yet descriptive.

State the purpose of your project

Ask yourself: "What do I want to find out? Why am I designing this project?" Write a statement that answers these questions.

Develop a hypothesis

Make a list of answers to the questions you have. This can be a list of statements describing how or why you think the subject of your experiment works. The hypothesis must be stated in a way that will allow it to be tested by an experiment.

Design an experiment to test your hypothesis

Make a step-by-step list of what you will do to test the hypothesis. Define your variables, the conditions that you control or in which you can observe changes. The list is called an *experimental method* or *procedure*.

Obtain materials and equipment

Make a list of items you need to perform the experiment. Try to use everyday, household items. If you need special equipment, ask your teacher for assistance. Local colleges or businesses might be able to loan materials to you.

Perform the experiment and record data

Conduct the experiment and record all measurements made, such as quantity, length, or time.

Record observations

Record all your observations while conducting your experiment. Observations can be written descriptions of what you noticed during an experiment or the problems encountered. You can also photograph or make a video of your experiment to create a visual record of what you observe. Keep careful notes of everything you do and everything that happens. Observations are valuable when drawing conclusions and are useful for identifying experimental errors.

Do calculations

Perform any calculations that are necessary to turn the data from your experiment into numbers you can use to draw conclusions. These numbers may also help you make tables or graphs summarizing your data.

Summarize results

Look at your experimental data and observations to summarize what happened. This summary could be a table of numerical data, graphs, or a written statement of what occurred during your experiment.

Draw conclusions

Use your results to determine whether your hypothesis is correct. Now is the time to review your experiment and determine what you learned.

Document your findings in a report, display, and presentation

Record your experiment and the results in a report, a display, and, if required, a presentation. Your report should thoroughly document your project from start to finish. If you can choose the report format, it should include a title; background or introduction and purpose; hypothesis; materials and methods; data and results; conclusions; acknowledgement of people who helped; and bibliography. You may want to prepare a poster or three-dimensional display to give your audience an overview of your project. You can use charts, diagrams, or illustrations to explain the information. Bring a computer with a slide show or video of your experiment and the results. Your display should include a descriptive title; photos, charts, or other visual aids to describe the project and the results; the hypothesis; and a project report near the display.

Some science fairs require oral presentations. In preparing your presentation, ask yourself, "What is most interesting about my project, what will people want to know about, and how can I best communicate this information?" Use an outline or note cards to help you in your presentation. Be sure to check the rules for the presentation. You will probably need to introduce yourself and your topic; state what your investigation attempted to discover or prove; describe your procedure, results, and conclusions; and acknowledge anyone who helped you. Practice your presentation before delivering it.

Use this checklist to help you walk through the steps to a good science fair project:

- Select a topic.
- Conduct background research and prepare a bibliography.
- Formulate a testable hypothesis.

- Write a step-by-step experimental procedure.
- Develop a list of items and equipment for the experiment.
- Prepare a project schedule.
- Conduct the experiment, make observations, collect data, and document everything.
- Prepare visual aids (such as charts and graphs).
- Develop a report outline.

Using the material in the preceding passage, write a short response to the following prompt:

> Why would students benefit from doing a science project following the procedure of the scientific method?

This question should take you about 10 minutes to complete.

Ask a friend or a family member to read your response to determine whether you've answered the prompt in sufficient detail, citing evidence from the passage. Your response should be written in proper English in an acceptable essay style with no spelling or grammatical errors.

Interpreting independent and dependent variables

Variables are anything that changes during the course of an experiment, and they come in the following two varieties:

- ✔ **Independent:** An *independent variable* is the condition that the researcher chooses to change. If you're testing how temperature affects pressure in a pressure cooker, the temperature of the water is the independent variable that you manipulate.

- ✔ **Dependent:** A *dependent variable* is the result from manipulation of the independent variable. If you crank up the temperature of water in a pressure cooker, the dependent variable is the pressure, which rises accordingly.

For example, suppose a scientist designs an experiment to test how high different quantities of helium will lift his cat into the air. He buys balloons, string, helium, and a suitable harness for his cat. He ties the harness to his cat and starts filling the helium balloons and tying them to the harness. In this case, the independent variable is the amount of helium, and the dependent variable is the height his cat is lifted off the ground.

Here are some other examples of dependent and independent variables in scientific experiments.

1. A scientist studies the impact of a medication on symptoms of the common cold. What is the dependent variable?

2. To test her hypothesis that tasteless food will curb appetite, a scientist divides 40 chimpanzees into two groups and feeds one group a normal diet while feeding the other the same food with the taste removed. What is the dependent variable?

3. An automobile manufacturer is designing a flex-fuel vehicle that can run on gasoline or E85 ethanol fuel and needs to know the difference in distance it can travel on a tank of gasoline or a tank of E85 ethanol. What is the dependent variable?

Check your answers:

1. The cold symptoms — specifically whether the symptoms improve, worsen, or remain unchanged — are the dependent variable.

2. Appetite, which would probably be measured by the quantity of food the two groups consumed, is the dependent variable.

3. Distance is the dependent variable. The independent variable is the type of fuel.

The relationship between independent and dependent variables is often plotted on a graph, with each axis of the graph representing a different variable. On the test, you may be presented with a graph and asked to identify the dependent and independent variable.

An airplane manufacturer needs to test the effect of airspeed on lift. The test pilot increases the airspeed and records data from the instrument panel that indicates the change in altitude.

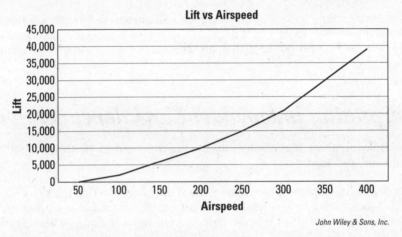

John Wiley & Sons, Inc.

The independent variable is ⬜, and the dependent variable is ⬜.

The independent variable is the condition that the test pilot is changing, which is the airspeed of the plane. The dependent variable is the lift, measured in altitude.

Digging into Scientific Theories and Supporting Evidence

The general public often dismisses scientific theories as irrelevant hunches that scientists have. In the world of science, however, a *theory* is an interpretation of the facts. Although the theory is subject to change, it's not a willy-nilly guess. So when you see something like the "Big Bang theory" or the "theory of global warming," you can rest assured that scientists have invested a great deal of study, thought, and debate in coming up with that particular theory. Think of hypotheses, theories, and laws as a hierarchy of truth:

✓ **Hypothesis:** An explanation of a limited number of observations based on experience, background knowledge, and logic.

✔ **Theory:** An explanation of a wide range of observations presented in a concise, coherent, systematic, predictive, and broadly applicable statement. A theory explains why a certain thing or condition is the way it is. A theory can't be considered to have been proven by the results of a single experiment. Repeated experimentation makes the conclusions reached more acceptable and credible.

✔ **Law:** An explanation of a wide range of observations that will most likely not be proven wrong. A law is less likely than a theory to be proven wrong. However, a law doesn't necessarily describe why something is the way it is. A law is more useful at predicting outcomes. For example, Newton's laws of motion don't explain how forces work but do provide a practical means for making calculations related to mass and force.

Any theory that has been proven repeatedly with consistent results may become a scientific law until disproven, in which case its status returns to that of a theory. Advances in equipment leading to more accurate measurement can lead to this change in status.

You may also hear the term *model,* which is a concept that has some validity and can be used to formulate predictions that are accurate only under certain limited conditions. Meteorologists often use different models to predict the weather.

Science can be described as an ongoing debate between evidence and conclusions. As new evidence is discovered, it may challenge or add support to conclusions that were previously made or even to well-established theories.

In the following sections, we explain how to determine whether evidence supports or challenges a theory; how to apply scientific models, theories, and processes; and how to apply formulas that have been developed from scientific theories.

Determining whether evidence supports or challenges a theory or conclusion

You can read about challenges to scientific theories in the news. Nearly every day, someone challenges the theory of global warming, questioning whether Earth really is heating up, whether the problem really is related to the amount of carbon in the atmosphere, and whether human activities really are the primary cause. And perhaps that theory itself will continue to evolve as technological advances reveal more about ecology and the effects of the potential life of living, breathing creatures on Earth.

However, many people dismiss theories more out of ignorance than anything else. Global warming skeptics, for example, point out that Earth has experienced numerous cycles of warming and cooling over its 4.5 billion years of existence, failing to recognize that the current warming trend doesn't follow the same pattern as those other cycles. We're not saying that all global warming skeptics are ignorant. We're just saying that if you're going to question or challenge a theory or conclusion, you need solid evidence to dispute it. Scientist are pursuing various avenues through their experiments to disprove or prove the theories.

On the test, you may encounter questions that involve making a judgment call on whether evidence supports or challenges a theory or conclusion or what theory or conclusion can be drawn from a particular data set.

1. Which of the following pieces of evidence does *not* support the conclusion that H. pylori bacterium causes peptic ulcers in humans?

    (A) Nine out of every 10 participants in a study who were infected with H. pylori bacterium developed peptic ulcers.

    (B) Antibiotics that kill H. pylori bacterium have proven 90 percent effective in treating peptic ulcers.

    (C) Eight out of every 10 animals infected with H. pylori bacterium developed peptic ulcers.

    (D) Thirty to fifty percent of the population is infected with the H. pylori bacterium.

2. Which conclusion can be drawn from the following data?

Sugar Consumption (% of calories)	Increase in Systolic Blood Pressure (mm Hg)
10	0.0
20	2.0
30	6.2
40	10.4

    (A) Increased sugar consumption raises blood pressure.

    (B) People should stop consuming sugar.

    (C) Blood pressure is not affected by sugar consumption.

    (D) Results are inconclusive.

3. Medical researchers are beginning to believe that cholesterol-lowering medications used to treat patients with heart disease may cause dementia. Which of the following pieces of evidence would provide the best support for this conclusion?

    (A) Several doctors reported that patients of theirs who had been prescribed cholesterol-lowering medication suddenly developed problems with thinking and memory.

    (B) A double-blind, placebo-controlled study involving 200 participants demonstrated cognitive decline in patients taking a cholesterol-lowering medication.

    (C) One patient reported cognitive difficulties while taking a cholesterol-lowering medication.

    (D) In several trials, rats given high doses of cholesterol-lowering medications developed cognitive difficulties, as measured by their performance in navigating complex mazes.

Check your answers:

1. The fact that a certain percentage of the population is infected with H. pylori bacterium, Choice (D), doesn't mean that it causes peptic ulcers. If you chose Choice (A), (B), or (C), then you are confusing correlation with causation.

2. The higher the percentage of calories from sugar, the higher the blood pressure, so Choice (A) is the correct answer.

3. A well-controlled study, Choice (B), provides better evidence than clinical evidence from doctors, Choice (A), or patients, Choice (C). Choice (D) represents good evidence, but the fact that high doses of medications cause a certain side effect in rats doesn't necessarily mean that a standard dose of the medication in humans will cause the same side effect.

Applying scientific models, theories, and laws

While evidence may support or challenge a scientific theory, you can go the other way and use scientific models and theories to explain natural phenomena and to predict the outcome of certain experiments or natural occurrences. On the test, questions may challenge your ability to apply scientific models and theories.

Matter has three phases: gas, liquid, and solid. In gases, molecules are separated with no regular arrangement. In liquids, molecules are close together with no regular arrangement. In solids, molecules are tightly packed in a regular pattern.

John Wiley & Sons, Inc.

This illustration represents which of the following?

(A) gas

(B) liquid

(C) solid

(D) cannot be determined from the information provided

The illustration shows molecules packed closely in a pattern, representing a solid, Choice (C).

Using formulas from scientific theories and laws

Scientists often develop mathematical formulas to describe natural phenomena. Scientific theories and laws provide formulas that have a wide range of uses in fields ranging from engineering to medicine. Engineers, for example, apply the formulas to design buildings and machines that actually do what they're expected to do and to perform calculations that enable great accomplishments, such as landing people on the moon and land rovers on Mars.

Ohm's law is an example. It states that the current through a conductor between two points is directly proportional to the difference across the two points to arrive at the mathematical formula that describes this relationship: $V = I \times R$ where V is the voltage, I is the amperage, and R is the resistance. To answer questions on the test that involve formulas such as this, you don't need to memorize the formulas. The test presents the formula to use, and you just need to figure out which numbers to plug in and how to do the math.

1. Using the equation from Ohm's law, $V = I \times R$, the resistance of a circuit that draws 0.9 amperes when 12 volts is applied is [   ]. Round your answer to the nearest hundredth.

2. According to Newton's second law of motion, acceleration is produced when a force acts on a mass. The greater the mass, the greater the amount of force needed to accelerate the object. The mathematical formula that expresses this relationship is $F = m \times a$, where F is force (typically measured in newtons), m is mass (typically measured in kilograms), and a is acceleration in meters per second squared.

   The force required to accelerate a 4,000-kilogram car at a rate of 40 meters per second squared is [   ].

   Check your answers:

   1. V is 12 volts and I is 0.9 amperes, so plug in the numbers and solve for R:

   $$V = I \times R$$
   $$12 = 0.9R$$
   $$R = 12 \div 0.9 = 13.33$$

   2. m is 4,000 and a is 40 meters per second squared, so plug in the numbers and solve for F:

   $$F = 4,000 \times 40$$
   $$F = 160,000$$

Chapter 7

Applying Mathematical Reasoning to Science Problems

*A*lthough you're not using this book to prepare for the GED Math test, science relies a great deal on mathematical data and calculations. Physics and chemistry, in particular, involve the use of formulas to solve problems and draw conclusions from raw data. In addition, you may be presented with data that you must analyze by calculating percentages, averages, or other statistical representations of the data. Some questions may also require that you calculate the mathematical probability of one or more events occurring.

In this chapter, we offer the information and guidance to help you deal effectively with the math you're likely to encounter on the GED Science test.

Describing a Data Set Statistically

You can often summarize a collection of data (from an experiment, observations, or surveys, for example) by using *descriptive statistics,* numbers used to summarize and analyze the data and draw conclusions from it. Descriptive statistics for a collection of data include the following:

✔ **Frequency:** The number of individuals in a group or the number of times a value occurs in a data set. For example, in a community of 360 children, 240 of them have brown, curly hair, so the frequency is 240.

✔ **Relative frequency:** The number of individuals in a group or the number of times a value occurs in a data set relative to the total number of individuals in the group or the total number of values in the data set. For example, the relative frequency of children with brown, curly hair from the preceding bullet would be $\frac{240}{360} = \frac{2}{3}$.

✔ **Cumulative frequency:** The running total of frequencies, which is often represented in a linear graph. For example, if you're tracking the appearance of a full moon, you have 1 occurrence roughly every 29.5 days, so at the end of 29.5 days, the cumulative frequency would be 1. At the end of 59 days, it would be 2; at the end of 88.5 days, it would be 3; and so on.

✔ **Measures of the center:** The midpoint of the data set, which may be any of the following:

- *Mean* is the *average*. To calculate the mean, total the values and divide by the number of values; for example, the mean of 3, 4, and 5 is $(3 + 4 + 5) \div 3 = 12 \div 3 = 4$.

- *Median* is the middle value in the set when the values are arranged sequentially. Half of the numbers in a data set lie below the median and half lie above the median. If a data set contains an even number of values, average the two in the middle to find the median. For example, the median of 3, 4, 5, and 6 is $(4 + 5) \div 2 = 9 \div 2 = 4.5$.

- *Mode* is the value that appears most often in the set.

✔ **Measures of the spread:** How spread out the values are in a data set, which includes the following:

- *Range:* The difference between the highest and the lowest value in the data set.

- *Interquartile range:* The range of the middle 50 percent of the values in the data set. Think of this as the midrange.

Here are a few sample questions to help you warm up for statistics questions you're likely to encounter on the GED Science test.

Researchers tested soil samples to estimate levels of soil compaction on a farm. The data are shown in the following table. To answer the questions, note that density = mass/volume.

Sample	Soil Mass (grams)	Soil Volume (cm³)
1	8.9	15.9
2	7.4	11.54
3	12.2	20.3
4	11.7	19.7
5	9.3	16.5

1. The average soil density for all the samples is closest to which of the following?

   (A) 5.9

   (B) 0.06

   (C) 0.59

   (D) 1.696

2. The median soil density for all the samples is closest to which of the following (rounded to 2 decimal places)?

   (A) 0.59

   (B) 0.594

   (C) 0.564

   (D) 0.6

3. The range of soil density is closest to which of the following?

   (A) 0.814

   (B) 8.76

   (C) 4.8

   (D) 0.081

Now check your answers:

1. To calculate the average soil density, total the mass for all soil samples, total the volume of all soil samples, and then divide the mass total by the volume total:

$$(8.9 + 7.4 + 12.2 + 11.7 + 9.3) \div (15.9 + 11.54 + 20.3 + 19.7 + 16.5) =$$
$$49.5 \div 83.94 = 0.589707$$

which rounds up to 0.59, answer Choice (C). Another way to find the answer is to calculate the density of each soil sample and then calculate the average of those densities.

2. To find the median soil density, calculate the soil density for each sample, arrange the soil densities from smallest to greatest, and choose the one in the middle, Choice (B), 0.594.

3. The range of soil densities is the difference between the greatest and smallest soil density, so calculate the soil density for each sample and subtract the smallest from the largest to get 0.081, Choice (D).

Graphs, especially line and bar graphs, are often used to display data graphically, as explained in Chapter 5. In most cases, when you see a question with a graph, the task of describing the data statistically has been done for you. The graph displays the data in a meaningful format, so you can visualize the mean, median, mode, and distribution of data. However, even if a question includes a graph, you may be asked to identify a statistical aspect of the data displayed. To answer such questions, you may need to convert the visual data into an actual value. Here are a couple questions for practice.

1. The Centers for Disease Control (CDC) released the graph shown here:

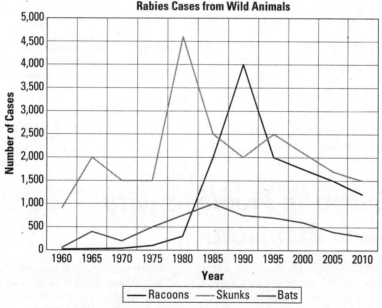

Rabies Cases from Wild Animals

Racoons ———— Skunks ———— Bats

John Wiley and Sons, Inc. (Source material courtesy of Centers for Disease Control [www.cdc.gov/rabies/ resources/publications/2010-surveillance/rabid-wild-animals.html])

Which of the following statements best summarizes the data displayed in the graph?

(A) Rabies in raccoons is a growing problem.

(B) Incidents of rabies overall has been declining since 1993.

(C) Raccoons are primarily responsible for infecting people with rabies.

(D) Bats pose the greatest rabies risk to humans.

2. Which of the plants in the following graph grows best with an average amount of sunshine?

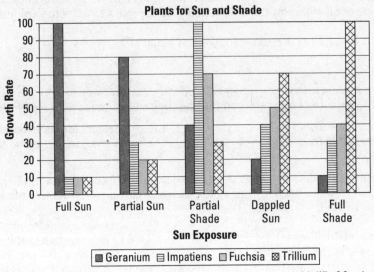

John Wiley & Sons, Inc.

(A) geranium

(B) fuchsia

(C) impatiens

(D) trillium

Check your answers:

1. You can rule out Choices (C) and (D) because the graph shows no correlation between rabies in animals and in humans. You can rule out Choice (A) because the incidents of rabies in raccoons actually declined from 1993 to 2010, which is also the reason that Choice (B) is the correct answer.

2. The average (mean) amount of sunshine is between Full Sun and Full Shade, which is labeled Partial Shade on the graph. The plant shown to grow best in partial shade is impatiens, Choice (C).

Solving Scientific Problems with Counting and Permutations

If you encounter a problem on the test asking you to determine the number of ways two or more items can be combined or arranged, you're looking at a question that requires the use of a *counting technique* to answer. The counting technique you use depends on whether the problem involves a *combination* or a *permutation*. With combinations, order doesn't matter; for example, you can combine oranges, apples, and lemons in any order. With permutations, order does matter; for example, if 5 spaceships race to Mars as part of a contest to see which spaceship can land first on the planet's surface, and 3 of them land on the surface first, second, and third, order matters — otherwise, the winner of the contest can't be determined.

Calculating combinations

You may encounter various situations in science that require the use of combinations. One situation is when you're designing an experiment to study the effects of different variables on different subjects. For example, suppose you want to determine the effects of pressure and temperature on different liquids. You have 5 liquids you want to test at 3 different temperatures and 2 different pressures. How many different experiments do you need to run? This is a combination problem because the order in which you run the experiments doesn't matter.

You could solve the problem by counting the different combinations. For example, each liquid will need to be tested at temperature A and pressure X and Y, temperature B and pressure X and Y, and temperature C and pressure X and Y. That's 6 different temperature/pressure combinations for 5 different liquids, so you're looking at 30 different experiments. You could also arrive at the answer by drawing a table, like this:

Liquid	Temperature	Pressure
1	A	X
	A	Y
	B	X
	B	Y
	C	X
	C	Y
2	A	X
	A	Y
	B	X
	B	Y
	C	X
	C	Y
3	A	X
	A	Y
	B	X
	B	Y
	C	X
	C	Y
4	A	X
	A	Y
	B	X
	B	Y
	C	X
	C	Y
5	A	X
	A	Y
	B	X
	B	Y
	C	X
	C	Y

Fortunately, there's an easier way that comes in quite handy when you're dealing with larger numbers. According to the *counting principle,* if one event has *m* possible outcomes and another event has *n* possible outcomes, then together the two events have $m \times n$ outcomes. So, if you're testing 5 liquids at 3 temperatures and 2 pressures, the number of combinations is $5 \times 3 \times 2 = 30$. The same is true of any number of items in combination.

A researcher wants to test the effects of water, temperature, and fertilizer on 5 different plants. She plans to test 3 different amounts of water, 4 different temperatures, and 2 different fertilizers. How many of each type of plant will she need to conduct the experiments necessary to test every combination of factors on each plant? [   ]

To answer this question, simply multiply all the numbers. In this case, however, you omit the number of plants because that's the number you're trying to determine. You're not trying to determine the total number of plants that must be tested but the total number of each plant that must be tested: $3 \times 4 \times 2 = 24$.

In some problems that involve the counting principle, you may be asked to determine the number of different combinations of items that can be selected from a group. For example, suppose you have 15 frogs, and you need to choose 5 of them for an experiment. How many different combinations of 5 frogs can be formed out of that group of 15 frogs? To solve such a combination problem, use the following formula:

$$C_r^n = \frac{n!}{r!(n-r)!}$$

where *C* is the number of combinations you're trying to determine, *n* is the total number of objects or events, and *r* is the number of objects or events you're choosing. The exclamation point (!) is the factorial symbol, which is a convenient way to represent the product of integers up to and including a specific integer, so 5!, which stands for "5 factorial," is $5 \times 4 \times 3 \times 2 \times 1 = 120$. (0! breaks the rule. 0! = 1.)

To determine how many different groups of 5 frogs can be selected from a total of 15 frogs, the equation looks like this:

$$C_5^{15} = \frac{15!}{5!(15-5)!} = \frac{15!}{5!(10!)} = \frac{\cancel{15}^3 \times \cancel{14}^7 \times 13 \times \cancel{12}^1 \times 11 \times \cancel{10!}}{\cancel{5} \times \cancel{4} \times 3 \times \cancel{2} \times 1 (\cancel{10!})} = 3,003$$

When order matters: Permutations

If the order in which items are arranged or events occur matters, use the permutations formula to solve the problem: $_nP_r = \frac{n!}{(n-r)!}$, where *P* stands for permutations, *n* is the total number of things to choose from, and *r* is the number chosen. For example, suppose 5 spaceships race to Mars as part of a contest to see which spaceship can be the first to land on the planet's surface:

1. Five spaceships have a chance to land first.

2. After 1 spaceship lands, only the 4 remaining have a chance to land second.

3. After 1 of those 4 spaceships lands second, only 3 are left to land third.

4. You have 5 different spaceships that can land first, 4 four that can land second, and 3 that can land third, so you have $5 \times 4 \times 3 = 60$ different ways the spaceships can finish first, second, and third.

Try the permutations formula on the spaceships problem:

$$_nP_r = \frac{n!}{(n-r)!} = \frac{5!}{(5-3)!} = \times\frac{5\times4\times3\times\cancel{2\times1}}{\cancel{2\times1}} = 60$$

Combinations also come into play when analyzing arrangements, as the following example shows.

A simple protein called *vasopressin* contains 8 amino acids that must be arranged in a specific sequence. If you were to arrange the amino acids randomly, what are the chances of arranging them in the proper sequence?

You could reason this out as follows:

1. Any of the 8 amino acids can be placed first, leaving 7 options for filling the next position.

2. Any of the 7 remaining amino acids can be placed next.

3. Any of the 6 remaining amino acids can be placed next.

4. Any of the 5 remaining amino acids can be placed next.

5. Any of the 4 remaining amino acids can be placed next.

6. Any of the 3 remaining amino acids can be placed next.

7. Any of the 2 remaining amino acids can be placed next.

8. The 1 remaining amino acid must be placed last.

9. You have 8 amino acids that can be placed first, 7 second, 6 third, 5 fourth, 4 fifth, 3 sixth, 2 seventh, and 1 last, so you have $8\times7\times6\times5\times4\times3\times2\times1 = 40,320$ different ways that the amino acids can be arranged. So, you have a 1 in 40,320 chance of arranging the amino acids in the correct sequence.

A quicker way is to use the permutations formula:

$$_nP_r = \frac{n!}{(n-r)!} = \frac{8!}{(8-8)!} = \times\frac{8\times7\times6\times5\times4\times3\times2\times1}{0!} = \frac{40,320}{1}$$

Determining the Probability of Events

Probability is the likelihood of one or more events occurring. The probability of the sun rising tomorrow morning is almost a certainty. The probability of your winning the lottery tomorrow is much less likely (and is zero if you didn't buy a ticket). In this section, we explain how to calculate probability for *simple* (one-time) events and *compound* (two or more) events.

Simple events

Simple events are independent. No matter how many coins you toss or how many times you flip a coin, with each toss of the coin, you have a 1 in 2 chance of it landing on heads.

To calculate probability, divide the number of ways the desired outcome can happen by the total number of outcomes possible. For example, a die has 6 sides marked with dots representing the numbers 1 through 6, so the total number of outcomes possible is 6. The chances of rolling a 5 (desired outcome) are 1 in 6 or $\frac{1}{6}$, because it can happen only 1 way — if the die shows a 5. A 52-card deck of playing cards has 4 aces, so there are 4 ways to draw an ace (desired outcome) and 52 possible outcomes when you draw a card from the deck, so the possibility of drawing an ace is $\frac{4}{52} = \frac{1}{13}$.

To calculate the probability of either of two or more events occurring, add the probabilities of the two events. For example, what are the chances of rolling a die and having it come up a 2 or a 5? Each event has a 1 in 6 chance, so add the probabilities:

$$\frac{1}{6} + \frac{1}{6} = \frac{2}{6} = \frac{1}{3}$$

Compound events

Compound events are two or more events occurring at the same time or sequentially. For example, what are the odds of a coin landing on tails 6 times in a row? To calculate probability for compound events, multiply the probabilities of each event occurring. For example, each time you toss a coin, you have a $\frac{1}{2}$ chance it'll land on tails, so the chance of tossing 6 tails in a row is:

$$\frac{1}{2} \times \frac{1}{2} \times \frac{1}{2} \times \frac{1}{2} \times \frac{1}{2} \times \frac{1}{2} = \frac{1}{64}$$

Calculating probability of compound events becomes more complicated when an event changes the odds for the next event. For example, to determine the probability of drawing 4 hearts from a standard 52-card deck of playing cards, you need to subtract the number of cards drawn from the total. The odds of drawing a heart on the first draw is 13 in 52 (or 1 in 4). Assuming you drew a heart with your first draw, there are now 12 hearts and a total of only 51 cards in the deck, so the chance of drawing a heart on the second draw is 12 in 51. On the third draw, you have an 11 to 50 chance.

Chapter 8

Living It Up with Life Science

· ·

In This Chapter

▶ Brushing up on what the life sciences cover

▶ Getting to know the system used to classify living things

▶ Understanding cells and cell theory

▶ Investigating human anatomy, physiology, and health

▶ Connecting life functions to energy intake and tracing the flow of energy in ecosystems

▶ Discovering the basics of heredity and evolution

· ·

The life sciences study all forms of life, from single-cell organisms all the way up to the creatures comprised of tens of trillions of cells arranged to form organs that function as parts of a complex system to enable the organism to live, breathe, think, move, and so much more. Although the GED Science test provides all the information you need to know to answer the questions, having a firm understanding of basic life science concepts and vocabulary enables you to more easily read and understand the passages and their accompanying questions.

Life sciences cover a lot of ground — everything from microscopic, single-cell organisms up to giant redwoods and animals like whales, all with numerous cell types and complex biological systems. We would need several volumes to cover all the life sciences in any detail, and you couldn't possibly cram everything into your brain in such a short amount of time. Fortunately on the GED Science test, all you have to do is read passages and answer questions about them. If you understand the vocabulary, then you'll understand the passages and be able to answer the questions correctly. This chapter brings you up to speed on the fundamentals and gives you practice answering questions.

Recognizing What Life Sciences Cover

To do well on the Science test, you have to be familiar with science vocabulary. Start by getting to know the names of the different life sciences and what each one covers, as presented in Table 8-1.

Table 8-1	The Life Sciences and What They Cover
Life Science	*What It Covers*
Anatomy	The structures of living organisms
Biology	Living organisms and how they live
Botany	Plants
Ecology	The interaction of organisms with their environment
Genetics	Heredity
Physiology	The function of living systems
Zoology	Animals

Here's a little quiz to see how much you know about life sciences. Don't peek at the table, or better still, cover it with a piece of paper and answer each of the questions with one of the areas of life sciences listed here:

    a. Anatomy

    b. Biology

    c. Botany

    d. Ecology

    e. Genetics

    f. Physiology

    g. Zoology

Which area of life science would you look up to find out

    1. why you look so much like your father? [   ]

    2. more about bone structure from looking at an X-ray of your arm? [   ]

    3. about the effect pollution or global warming has on marine life? [   ]

    4. how the brain communicates with muscles to make you move? [   ]

    5. more about armadillos? [   ]

Check your answers:

    1. e

    2. a

    3. d

    4. f

    5. g

Classifying All Living Things

In an attempt to organize nature, humans have developed a system of classifying all living things called a _taxonomy._ The most widely accepted taxonomy divides all living things into broad categories, or _kingdoms,_ based on their structure. Following is a list of the five kingdoms with a brief description of each:

✔ **Monera:** Simple, single cells that don't have membrane-bound nuclei, such as parasitic bacteria and photosynthesizing blue-green algae.

✔ **Protista:** Complex, single-cell organisms that have distinct nuclei, including slime molds, protozoa, and single or multiple cell algae. Members of this group are distinguished from one another by whether they feed off of other organisms or feed themselves through _photosynthesis_ — a process by which an organism uses sunlight to synthesize foods from carbon dioxide and water.

✔ **Fungi:** Immobile, multicellular organisms that can't perform photosynthesis and must decompose other dead organisms for food. Fungi include mushrooms, yeasts, and molds.

✔ **Planta:** Multicellular organisms, such as mosses and plants, that can perform photosynthesis to create food.

- ✔ **Animalia:** Mobile, multicellular organisms that feed on other organisms (plant or animal) for food. The main division within this kingdom is between *vertebrates* and *invertebrates* (with or without a backbone).

Kingdoms are the broadest category for classifying plants and animals. Six more categories further subdivide the *kingdoms.* Each subcategory contains a progressively smaller number of different organisms. Here's a complete list of categories in increasing specificity:

- ✔ **Kingdom** contains several related phyla.
- ✔ **Phylum** contains several related classes.
- ✔ **Class** contains several related orders.
- ✔ **Order** contains several related families.
- ✔ **Family** contains several related genera.
- ✔ **Genus** contains several related species.
- ✔ **Species** contains organisms so similar that they can reproduce together.

For human beings, it goes like this: kingdom: *Animalia;* phylum: *Chordata* (vertebrate); class: *Mammalia;* order: *Primate;* family: *Hominidae;* genus: *Homo;* species: *Sapiens.*

All You Need to Know about Cells and Then Some

Among living things, a cell is the smallest, but the body of information that surrounds it is huge. The following sections present the vocabulary you should recognize and understand and information to make it all clearer. Remember that you need a general knowledge of the subject but a good understanding of the words.

Passing the life test

Cells are the most basic form of life, which leads to the question: What exactly is life? Something is considered to be living only if it has the following characteristics:

- ✔ **Adaptation:** The ability to adjust to a changing external environment.
- ✔ **Growth:** The ability to increase in size in all or some of its parts, not just acquiring more matter.
- ✔ **Homeostasis:** The ability to regulate its own internal environment to maintain a cell or body at a relatively constant state.
- ✔ **Metabolism:** The transfer of energy by consumption of matter or chemicals or through photosynthesis.
- ✔ **Organization:** Being composed of one or more cells.
- ✔ **Reproduction:** The ability to reproduce either sexually or asexually (without sex).
- ✔ **Response to stimuli:** The ability to react to external stimuli, including light, sound, and heat. Responses may vary from the most basic chemical response of a single-cell organism to motion resulting from the perception of a complex sensory system.

Viruses straddle the line between living and nonliving organisms. Because they require a host cell to reproduce (instead of cell division), don't grow, and don't have energy metabolism or produce waste products, many scientists consider them nonliving organisms that deserve a class of their own — *infectious agents*.

Viruses are not included in the classification of living organisms because

(A) they're too small.

(B) they infect other organisms.

(C) they can't reproduce without a host cell.

(D) they rely on other organisms for their survival.

Viruses aren't considered to be living organisms because they lack many of the properties shared by living organisms, such as the ability to reproduce through cell division, to metabolize energy, to grow, and to produce waste products. If you were tempted by Choices (B) or (D), realize that these answer are wrong because bacteria and parasites can infect other organisms and may rely on other organisms for their survival, as well.

Understanding cell theory

Cell theory is one of the principle theories in modern biology and was made possible by the invention of the microscope. According to *cell theory,*

✔ All known living things are comprised of cells.

✔ The cell is the structural and functional unit of all living things.

✔ All cells come from other cells through the process of cell division.

✔ Cells contain the hereditary information that's passed from one cell to another when the cell divides.

Multicellular (many celled) organisms have various levels of organization within them. Although individual cells may perform specific functions, they also work together for the good of the entire organism and become dependent on one another.

Multicellular organisms have the following five levels of organization, ranging from simplest to most complex:

1. *Cells* are the basic unit in living organisms.

2. *Tissue* is composed of similar structural and functional cells working together for a specific purpose.

3. *Organs* are composed of tissues working together.

4. *Organ systems* are two or more organs working in concert to perform a specific function.

5. *Organisms* are composed of organ systems. An organism is an entire entity capable of all basic life processes.

Which of the following is not one of the main principles of cell theory?

(A) To exist, a cell must be a part of a larger organism.

(B) Cells are the basic units that comprise all living things.

(C) All cells are created through the process of cell division.

(D) Every living thing is composed of cells.

Choice (A) is the correct answer. Some microscopic organisms consist of a single cell. All the other choice are principles of cell theory.

Recognizing cell parts

Although cells are tiny, they're comprised of even tinier parts. The following list, along with Figure 8-1, should help you pick the parts out of a lineup:

- ✔ **Cytoplasm:** The fluid membrane that holds and supports all of a cell's components.

- ✔ **Endoplasmic reticulum (ER):** An extensive network of sac-like structures that synthesize proteins and lipids and assist in folding and transporting manufactured proteins.

- ✔ **Golgi body (Golgi apparatus):** Layers of membrane-bound structures that modify, sort, and package complex molecules (macromolecules) to be used within the cell or to be secreted by the cell.

- ✔ **Lysosome:** Cube-shaped structures that contain enzymes to help break down cell waste and prepare it for excretion. These structures are found only in animal cells.

- ✔ **Vacuoles:** Plant cells' equivalent to lysosomes.

- ✔ **Membrane (wall):** The protein layer that surrounds the cell, giving it form and protecting it from its external environment. The membrane is *selectively permeable* to allow food and other desirables into the cell, while keeping harmful matter outside. (*Permeable* means water or gas can pass through it, like a coffee filter.)

- ✔ **Mitochondrion:** Commonly described as the cell's "power plants," the mitochondrion is a membrane-enclosed structure where cell respiration occurs. The activity of mitochondrion within a cell and the number of mitochondria determine the cell's metabolism.

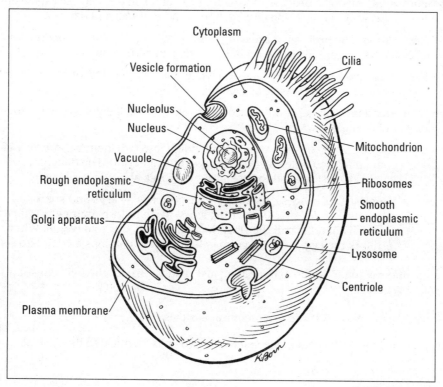

Figure 8-1: Cell parts.

Illustration by Kathryn Born

- **Chloroplast:** Plant cells' equivalent to the mitochondrion. Chloroplasts capture light energy and convert it into free energy within the cell.

- **Nucleus:** The part of a cell that contains its DNA and controls reproduction.

- **Organelles:** Any of the many subunits within a cell, including ribosomes, mitochondria, and lysosomes.

- **Ribosome:** Components within a cell that form proteins from amino acids.

Knowing how cells survive and thrive

Cells live, breathe, and procreate by engaging in various *cellular processes*. You may encounter questions that require you to know what a specific process is all about based on a passage. Following are the names of the different cellular processes, along with a brief description of each:

- **Metabolism:** Chemical reactions within living cells that maintain the cell's life. Metabolism is broken down into two functions:

  - *Catabolism* breaks down organic matter to create energy.

  - *Anabolism* uses energy to build complex molecules out of smaller chemical units.

- **Osmosis:** The movement of water molecules across a partially permeable membrane. Osmosis enables cells to "take a drink."

- **Phagocytosis:** The process of a cell ingesting a particle. In simple terms, the cell is eating. The cell senses a particle or another cell near its membrane and then surrounds the particle. After surrounding the particle, the *phagocyte* (the cell ingesting the particle) breaks down its own outer membrane, bringing the particle inside itself.

- **Photosynthesis:** The process by which plants and some single-cell organisms use light to convert water and carbon dioxide into carbohydrates and oxygen.

- **Respiration:** The process of breaking down nutrients to produce energy for a cell. The byproducts of respiration are carbonic acids and carbon dioxide.

- **Fermentation:** A metabolic process in which bacteria, yeasts, or other microorganisms convert sugar to acids, gases, or alcohol.

- **Reproduction:** Cells reproduce through *cytokinesis* (cell division), which occurs in one of the following two ways:

  - **Mitosis:** Most cells reproduce by dividing into two identical *daughter cells,* each containing a complete set of DNA (genetic material). The daughter cells also happen to be identical to the parent cell. Talk about a close family!

  - **Meiosis:** This process, used to create sex cells — eggs and sperm used to reproduce — consists of splitting a cell twice to form four cells *(gametes),* each of which contains half the DNA the organism needs to develop. When the sperm fertilizes the egg, a cell *(zygote)* is formed that contains a complete set of DNA.

Use the information from the material you just read to answer the following questions about cellular processes.

1. The movement of water through a membrane is called [   ].

2. The cellular process by which one cell forms two cells identical to itself is called [   ].

3. Which of the following is not an example of cellular metabolism?

   (A) converting the food you eat into energy

   (B) a plant using sunlight, carbon dioxide, and water to create glucose

   (C) a weight lifter building muscle mass

   (D) an amoeba eating a bacterium

4. The metabolic process used to break down nutrients to produce energy for a cell is called [____].

   Check your answers:

   1. osmosis

   2. mitosis

   3. Choice (D): An amoeba eating a bacterium is an example of *phagocytosis.* Choices (A) and (B) are examples of *catabolism* (breaking down organic matter to create energy), while Choice (C) is an example of *anabolism* (using energy to build complex molecules out of smaller chemical units).

   4. respiration

Exploring the Human Body, Nutrition, and Disease

You don't need to graduate from medical school to pass the GED Science test, but knowing a little about human anatomy, physiology, nutrition, and disease can make some of the reading passages easier to comprehend. In this section, we cover the basics.

Read this section carefully because you'll be tested on it (in a fun way) at the end.

Understanding human anatomy as a collection of systems

The human body is like a large metropolitan area complete with its own infrastructure. Several complex systems work simultaneously 24/7 to maintain existence and enable the body to engage in various activities.

The outer shell: The integumentary system

You don't hear much about it, but the most obvious system in the human body is the *integumentary system,* comprised of skin, hair, and nails, which acts as a barrier to protect the rest of the body from injury and from loss of fluid and heat.

No bones about it: The skeletal system

The *skeletal system* is the frame that gives your body its shape, the structure that supports you and everything beneath your skin. Without your skeleton, you would be little more than a big bag of organs. The skeletal system is comprised of bones, hard and rigid, and *cartilage* — the softer, more flexible material found in places like your nose and ears.

Oh, and just in case you're asked what connects the knee bone to the hipbone, that would be the *ligament* — special tissue that forms the connections between bones.

Putting some muscles on them bones

Your *muscular system* enables you to move. *Tendons* attach muscles to bones, and muscles come in two basic types, depending on their function:

- **Voluntary:** You consciously contract or relax the muscle, as you might do when you smile.

- **Involuntary:** Your brain instructs the muscle to contract or relax without any conscious intervention on your part, as in the case of your heart muscle.

Getting around with the circulatory system

Think of the *circulatory system* as a vast transportation system inside your body that's in charge of pickups and deliveries. The central hub is the heart, which pumps the blood to deliver essential nutrients to cells and carry waste products from them. Blood has several components: *plasma* is the liquid part, *red cells* carry oxygen, *white cells* fight infections, and *platelets* make blood clot — to stop a wound from bleeding.

Arteries carry blood *away* from the heart, when it is rich and bright red with oxygen. *Veins* carry blood *to* the heart, when it is darker because of a lack of oxygen. *Capillaries* are cells with thin walls that facilitate the exchange of nutrients between your blood and cells.

Breathing easy with the respiratory system

Your *respiratory system* teams up with your circulatory system to deliver oxygen to cells throughout your body. It begins when you inhale through your nose, which filters, warms, and moistens the air. Air travels down your *trachea* (throat) and divides between your left and right *bronchi,* leading into your left and right *lungs.*

Inside your lungs are even smaller branches of bronchioles that have small sacs at their ends called *alveoli,* which contain the capillaries where oxygen enters the bloodstream. Your *diaphragm* is a large muscle that forces you to breathe in and out by relaxing and contracting beneath your lungs.

Nervous? That's your nervous system talking

The *nervous system* is the body's communication network, transporting messages throughout your body even faster than email. The *central nervous system* includes the brain and spinal cord. *Peripheral nervous systems,* comprised of nerve cells *(neurons),* are located throughout the rest of the body.

Knowing the four parts of the central nervous system may come in handy as background knowledge:

- **Cerebrum:** This largest part of your brain controls senses and thoughts.

- **Cerebellum:** The lower, back side of your brain controls balance and movement through communications with muscles.

- **Medulla or brain stem:** Located in front of the cerebellum, the medulla controls involuntary functions such as breathing and heartbeat. It is quite literally the stem that connects your brain to your spinal cord.

- **Spinal cord:** Running vertically up and down your spine, the spinal cord functions as the main highway for messages between your brain and the neurons located all over your body. The spinal cord also controls simple reflexes, like those the doctor tests when banging on your knee with that rubber hammer.

Feeding your curiosity about the digestive system

The *digestive system* is in charge of squeezing energy and nutrients out of all that stuff you eat and drink and then expelling any and all waste products. Your digestive system is hard at work right now. As it does its job, introduce yourself to the various parts of the digestive system so you have a clearer understanding of what's going on inside you this very minute:

- **Mouth:** This is where it all begins, starting with your teeth that slice, dice, and mash the food into small particles and mix it with saliva. Saliva contains enzymes that help break down the starches.

- **Esophagus:** This muscular tube connects your mouth to your stomach; contractions in the muscle push the contents from your mouth downward into your stomach.

- **Stomach:** A muscular bag in which food collects after being swallowed. Your body releases gastric acids and pepsin into the stomach to digest the proteins in the food and prepare it for its move into the intestines.

- **Small intestine:** The place where the majority of digestion occurs. It breaks down food, using enzymes from your pancreas and bile from your liver and gallbladder, before absorbing the nutrients through capillaries that line its walls.

- **Large intestine:** This absorbs any water, vitamins, or minerals that remain in solid waste after leaving the small intestine.

- **Rectum:** The last leg of the journey and the last length of the large intestine, this is where your body stores solid waste until it's ready to exit the body. Your body stores liquid waste in the bladder.

- **Anus:** The place where solid waste exits the body. Liquid waste exits through the urethra.

The endocrine system: It's a hormone thing

The *endocrine system* consists of numerous glands that release hormones into the body. *Hormones* are chemicals that act as messengers in the body, regulating metabolism, growth, tissue function, and reproductive needs. The main glands to be familiar with are the following:

- **Adrenal:** Located at the top of the kidneys, the adrenal gland produces *adrenaline,* which controls heart rate, blood pressure, and other important bodily functions.

- **Ovaries** (in women) and **testes** (in men): Located in the lower part of the abdomen, these are responsible for reproductive functions.

- **Pancreas:** Located behind the stomach, this gland produces enzymes to digest food and regulate blood sugar and insulin levels in your body.

- **Pituitary:** A pea-sized gland located at the bottom of the brain that helps control blood pressure and growth.

- **Thymus:** Located at the back of the chest, this gland is part of the immune system.

- **Thyroid:** Located at the front of the throat, this gland is mainly responsible for producing hormones that regulate the body's metabolism.

Making babies: The reproductive system

The *reproductive system* is what separates men from women. As covered in the preceding section, women have ovaries and men have testes, so what else do you need to know? Every 28 days or so, a woman's ovaries release an egg that travels down the fallopian tube to the uterus. During the reproductive act, the male's penis ejaculates sperm into the female's vagina. The sperm cells travel up into the uterus. If the timing is right (or wrong, depending on the situation), a single sperm cell penetrates the egg, fertilizing it, which results in pregnancy.

Flushing the system: The urinary system

The *urinary system* consists of only a few organs that filter, store, and eliminate liquid waste from the human body in the form of urine. Urine is the sterile fluid excreted from the body. It consists primarily of water with small amounts of chloride, sodium, and potassium.

The main organs and parts to be familiar with are the following:

- ✔ **Kidneys:** These fist-sized organs, located just below the rib cage on both sides of your spine, filter blood to separate wastes and toxins from the circulatory system.

- ✔ **Ureter:** These tubes carry the filtered waste from the kidneys to the bladder.

- ✔ **Urinary bladder:** A hollow, muscular organ located in the center of your pelvis, the bladder stores urine prior to excretion.

- ✔ **Urethra:** The tube connected to the bladder that carries urine out of the human body.

- ✔ **Sphincter:** This muscle located at the bottom of the bladder controls the excretion of urine from the body. This muscle holds the urethra closed to store urine and relaxes to excrete urine. If the bladder becomes 100 percent full, the voluntary muscle becomes involuntary and immediately ejects the urine.

Immune system

The *immune system* teams up with the lymphatic system (discussed next) to prevent and purge the body of *pathogens* — disease-causing agents, including harmful bacteria, viruses, and parasitic worms. The immune system has *innate immunity* (defenses that every human being is born with), including the skin (part of the integumentary system discussed earlier), which prevents pathogens from entering the body; mucous membranes in the nose and mouth that trap bacteria, viruses, and other pathogens; gastric acid in the stomach that kills bacteria in food; saliva that rinses off your teeth and mouth; and enzymes in tears and skin oils that kill pathogens.

The immune system also has *acquired immunity,* which develops over time as the body is exposed to infectious agents. The immune system constantly monitors antigens (usually proteins) on the surface of cells and viruses, and when it identifies unfamiliar antigens, it launches an attack on those cells or viruses to kill and expel the alien invaders. This immune response typically results in inflammation, as the body increases blood flow to the infected areas. Increased blood flow brings more white blood cells to the area to attack the pathogens and then to "wash" the damaged and dead cells and viruses out of the body.

Allergies occur when the immune system wrongly identifies a harmful or beneficial substance as an alien invader, triggering an immune response. An *autoimmune disease,* such as rheumatoid arthritis, occurs when the immune system wrongly identifies a part of the body itself as an alien invader and triggers an immune response.

Fighting infection with the lymphatic system

The *lymphatic system* consists of numerous glands, capillaries, and nodes. The system's primary functions are to trigger immune system response, transport immune cells to and from the lymphatic system into bones, remove swelling and fluid from tissues, and absorb and transport fatty acids. This system is critical for the body's immune system response to infection and also helps eliminate swelling and in some cases tumors and cancerous cells. The main components to be familiar with are the following:

✔ **Lymph:** A clear liquid containing white blood cells, including the killer cells that attack and destroy invading pathogens.

✔ **Lymphatic vessels:** Located throughout the body, lymphatic vessels transport lymph to lymph nodes and to almost every organ and tissue.

✔ **Lymph nodes:** Glands located throughout the body where lymph is filtered free of infection before returning to the circulatory system to maintain the hydration of the system. These glands are located throughout the body and are in particularly high concentration in the chest, neck, throat, and abdominal regions. Lymph nodes are the battleground where the immune system fights off many infections.

✔ **Tonsils:** Located in the back of the throat, these glands are the body's first line of defense against infections that enter the body through ingestion or inhalation.

✔ **Thymus:** Located in the upper chest, between the lungs, the thymus holds the body's *T cells,* which are responsible for the body's acquired immune response.

✔ **Spleen:** Located in the upper-left quadrant of the abdomen, the spleen not only stores extra blood for the circulatory system but also removes antibody-coated bacteria and blood cells from the circulatory system. The spleen essentially is a gigantic lymph node that also stores extra blood for the body.

Getting your fill of nutrition

The human body is a complex machine that requires fuel to keep it going and provide the essential components to build cells. You don't need to be a nutritionist to handle the one or two nutrition questions you may encounter on the exam, but you do need a general understanding of the macro- and micronutrients required by the human body. Start with the *macronutrients:*

✔ **Carbohydrates:** Starches and sugars that supply energy and usually make food taste a whole lot better. Breads, cereals, pastas, potatoes, beans, and baked desserts are the primary sources of carbohydrates. The body converts any excess starches and sugars into fat, which is why many modern diets recommend limiting consumption of carbohydrates.

✔ **Fiber:** Fiber teams up with water to form a bulky mass that helps move nutrients through your intestines and eventually enables your body to rid itself of waste. Your body needs enough fiber for this process to work properly. Good sources of fiber are raw vegetables, nuts, fruit, whole grains, and beans.

✔ **Lipids (fats):** Fats have a bad reputation, but they're essential for energy, growth, and absorption of fat-soluble nutrients. You find fats in lots of foods, including bacon and eggs, dairy products, nuts, avocados, and cooking oils. An interesting fact is that sugar and starchy (simple) carbohydrates, such as bread and baked goods, are more likely than dietary fat to increase body fat.

✔ **Proteins:** Present in almost every part of the human body, proteins are used in repairing and growing cells. You find protein in animal products, including meat, eggs, milk, and cheese, as well as in beans, nuts, grains, and some vegetables.

✔ **Water:** Water is a vital nutrient. By weight, it is the most prevalent nutrient in the human body, and it's required by every component of the human body. Water is contained in almost all foods and in all beverages.

Micronutrients are essential but in smaller amounts. They include the following:

- **Vitamins:** Organic compounds that also aid in proper bodily functions.

- **Minerals:** Chemical compounds that your body needs to function properly. Some of the more familiar minerals are calcium, potassium, sodium, iron, fluoride, chlorine, iodine, magnesium, and zinc.

Recognizing how the body self-regulates: Homeostasis

Homeostasis is the tendency of an organism to maintain a particular internal state in the midst of external changes. For example, the human body maintains an internal temperature of approximately 98.6°F regardless of exposure to warmer or colder air. Liver and muscle contractions, along with the activities of other organs, including the brain, generate a great deal of heat. Excess heat is released through the skin and through the evaporation of perspiration. The body also maintains homeostasis in relation to fluid pressure, blood sugar, and levels of various vitamins and minerals.

Grasping the basics of disease and prevention

Bacteria, viruses, fungi, and parasites cause *infectious* diseases — diseases caused by microscopic germs. Your body is the habitat of many varied organisms that are normally harmless and often helpful or even essential. In fact, bacteria cells outnumber the cells of the human body by about 10 to 1, and most of them are essential in breaking down food in the digestive system. (They're much smaller than the cells of the human body.)

Some infectious diseases, such as the common cold and chickenpox, are *contagious* — they can be passed from person to person. While vaccinations get all the press these days for preventing infectious diseases, sanitation is actually one of the most effective methods. Having clean water and sanitation facilities, practicing proper hygiene, and eating safe food that's prepared properly are all very useful in preventing disease.

The human body is also equipped with an immune system that is very effective in ridding the body of *pathogens* — microorganisms, such as bacteria and viruses, that cause illness.

Testing your knowledge

Although you won't be asked to solve crossword puzzles on the GED Science test, we figured we'd give you something fun to do to break up the intensity of having to read through all this heavy stuff about the human body while testing your ability to read, comprehend, and retain information. Play along and solve this crossword puzzle.

Across

1 An effective means to prevent infectious disease
6 System that includes skin
8 Macronutrient consumed for energy
11 System responsible for making babies
12 Clear liquid containing white blood cells
13 The tendency of the body to self-regulate
14 Muscular tube that carries food to stomach

Down

2 System responsible for allergies
3 Disease-causing microbes and parasites
4 Soft bone
5 Muscle that helps you breathe
7 Gland that regulates metabolism
8 Largest part of the brain
9 Carry blood away from the heart
10 Gland that regulates blood sugar

Answers

Across: 1 Sanitation, 6 Integumentary, 8 Carbohydrate, 11 Reproductive,
12 Lymph, 13 Homeostasis, 14 Esophagus.

Down: 2 Immune, 3 Pathogens, 4 Cartilage, 5 Diaphragm, 7 Thyroid,
8 Cerebrum, 9 Arteries, 10 Pancreas.

Examining Ecosystems

An *ecosystem* is a community of plants, animals, and other living things that interact with one another and their physical environment. For example, in a forest, plants capture sunlight and use water and other nutrients in the soil and air to grow; insects and other animals eat the plants and fruits and nuts that the plants produce; other animals may eat the insects and animals that eat the plants, fruits, and nuts; and every living thing in the system produces waste products that return water and other nutrients to the environment to replenish the system.

You're likely to encounter one or more questions on the Science test that deal with ecosystems and may include short reading passages, illustrations, charts, and other information on which the questions are based. Having a background knowledge of the inner workings of ecosystems can help you understand this information and answer the questions.

Tracking energy flow in ecosystems

Every living thing requires energy to live, grow, and reproduce, so energy is a key component in ecosystems. The sun generates nearly all the energy that flows through an ecosystem. Plants *(producers)* capture the sun's energy and use it to grow and reproduce; *consumers* eat the plants, berries, nuts, and fruit (and/or other consumers); and *decomposers* break down the waste products to return nutrients to the ecosystem that plants require to continue to produce.

Energy flows through the system by passing from one trophic level to the next. A *trophic level* represents an organism's position in a food chain or food pyramid, with plants at the bottom and omnivores at the top:

1. *Primary producers* (plants, algae, and some bacteria) use solar energy to produce organic plant material through photosynthesis.

2. *Primary consumers* are *herbivores* (animals that feed exclusively on plants).

3. *Secondary consumers* eat primary consumers and may eat primary producers, as well. Animals that eat primary consumers are *carnivores*. Those that eat consumers and producers are *omnivores*.

4. *Tertiary consumers* eat secondary consumers and may eat at lower trophic levels, as well.

Most land-based ecosystems have as many as five trophic levels. Marine-based systems tend to have more — as many as seven.

Consumers obtain a small fraction (about 10 percent) of the energy captured by the organisms they consume at lower trophic levels. The other 90 percent of the energy is used by the organism that's consumed to fuel its growth, survival, and reproduction or is converted to heat. So, for example, if you eat a salad, you're getting about 10 percent of the energy that the plants in your salad captured from the sun. If you eat a hamburger, the cow obtained 10 percent of the energy captured by the plants it ate, and you're getting 10 percent of the energy from the cow, so you're only getting 1 percent of the energy captured by the plants the cow ate.

Conservation of energy

According to the law of *conservation of energy,* energy can't be created or destroyed; it can only be transformed. Plants, for example, use solar energy to fuel photosynthesis, which converts energy in the form of light into chemical energy in the form of the molecules created from water, carbon dioxide, and other nutrients. These molecules form the substance of a plant. When an animal eats and digests the plant, those molecules are broken down, releasing energy that fuels growth, movement, and reproduction. Some of the energy is said to be "lost" in the form of heat, but it's never really lost as in "gone for good." The energy isn't recycled and pumped back into the ecosystem, but it rises into the atmosphere. The important point to remember is that energy is never destroyed. (See Chapter 9 for more about the law of conservation of energy.)

Forms of energy

Although energy is never destroyed in an ecosystem, it can be converted into other forms of energy:

- **Chemical:** Through photosynthesis, plants use water and nutrients from the soil to convert solar energy into chemical energy that's stored in the molecules that comprise the plant and fuel its growth.

- **Electrical:** Some of the energy animals obtain from the food they eat is converted to electrical energy that's used in communication systems within the body. For example, your body essentially has its own electronic pacemaker that keeps your heart beating, which explains why you need to replenish electrolytes after exercise.

- **Mechanical:** Much of the energy animals obtain from the food they eat fuels internal mechanical processes and movement.

- **Nuclear:** Nuclear energy is stored in the nucleus of an atom. The sun converts nuclear energy into massive amounts of radiant energy.

- **Radiant:** Radiant energy is electromagnetic energy that flows into the ecosystem from the sun.

- **Thermal:** Thermal energy (heat) is released as animals digest plant material, breaking down the molecules in the plant material.

Following the flow of nutrients in ecosystems

Unlike energy that flows through an ecosystem and eventually dissipates in the form of heat, nutrients are recycled. For example, plants use the inorganic elements (nutrients) hydrogen, oxygen, and carbon dioxide to create organic molecules (carbohydrates). An animal that eats the plant breaks down the carbohydrates and, through the respiration process, uses them to fuel growth, movement, and reproduction. Waste products return unused matter to the ecosystem, and when plants and animals die, they're returned to the ecosystem, as well. Decomposers, including bacteria and fungi, break down the waste products and dead organisms to return the nutrients to the soil, where they can be reused by growing plants.

Although nutrients are generally recycled in an ecosystem, this is not always the case. For example, if a farmer harvests a crop and ships it to a city, the nutrients locked inside that crop are not returned to the soil and are likely to be spread far and wide.

Grasping the carrying capacity concept

Any environment can maintain only a finite number of organisms. Each has a *carrying capacity,* or the maximum population it can maintain. This carrying capacity depends on the amount of food, habitat, water, and other necessities available within the environment. On land, ecosystems that are warm and humid, such as the tropics, have a much higher carrying capacity than do hot, dry areas, such as deserts, and extremely cold areas, such as Antarctica.

Increases in population or decreases in food, habitat, water, or other necessities within an environment can decrease the carrying capacity of the environment.

Exploring relationships among organisms

Organisms in an ecosystem develop various types of relationships, either living together in harmony or not:

✔ **Predator-prey:** In predator-prey relationships, one organism (the predator) eats the other (the prey); for example, a bear eating a salmon. The relationship isn't all that bad for the prey because it thins out the population, preventing them from starving, and it strengthens the genetic pool, making the prey evolve into stronger, faster, and smarter creatures over time. (For more about genetics, see the later section "Digging into the Theory of Evolution.")

✔ **Symbiosis:** In symbiotic relationships, organisms live together in one of the following three ways:

  • **Mutualism:** Both organisms benefit from the relationship; for example, a flower and a bee. The bee gathers pollen it can use to make honey and the flower is pollinated by the bee carrying pollen from one flower to the next as it gathers pollen, helping the flower reproduce.

  • **Commensalism:** One organism benefits from the relationship, and the other is neither harmed nor helped. For example, some barnacles attach themselves to whales to obtain transportation and greater access to food without harming or helping the whale in any way.

  • **Parasitism:** One organism (the *parasite*) benefits, and the other (the *host*) is harmed in the process. For example, if a tapeworm becomes attached to a host (human or animal), the tapeworm benefits, and the human is harmed. (Interestingly, however, scientists are beginning to wonder whether certain critters considered parasites truly are; for example, people infected with pinworms or hookworms tend to have a lower risk of developing autoimmune disorders, such as allergies and asthma, which is a definite benefit.)

Tipping the scales: Ecosystem disruptions

Ecosystems can become disrupted or destroyed by a number of factors, including invasive species (plants or animals that are carried into an ecosystem instead of evolving as a member of it), flooding, habitat destruction, desertification (productive land turning into desert), and extinction. The causes are both natural and human, but only one has the ability to reduce their effect on the ecosystem.

Testing your knowledge

Use the information from the material you just read to answer the following questions about ecosystems.

1. A grasshopper eats a plant, a frog eats the grasshopper, a snake eats the frog, and an eagle eats the snake. Which animal is the tertiary consumer?

(A) grasshopper

(B) frog

(C) snake

(D) eagle

2. Through the process of photosynthesis, plants convert ⬚ energy into ⬚ energy.

3. Which of the following group of organisms returns nutrients to the ecosystem?

   (A) producers

   (B) decomposers

   (C) carnivores

   (D) herbivores

4. Aphids (tiny insects) are causing extensive crop damage, so a farmer releases thousands of ladybugs, which are known to eat aphids without damaging the crops. The relationship of the ladybugs to the crops is best classified as which of the following?

   (A) mutualism

   (B) commensalism

   (C) parasitism

   (D) predator-prey

5. Needing to get rid of snakehead fish imported from China and not wanting to kill them, an aquarium owner releases them into a nearby river. After several years, ecologists discover that the snakeheads are outcompeting native species for food and other resources. This situation is an example of which of the following?

   (A) energy flow

   (B) predator-prey relationship

   (C) symbiosis

   (D) ecosystem disruption

Check your answers:

1. The grasshopper is the primary consumer, the frog is secondary, and the snake is tertiary, Choice (C). That makes the eagle a quaternary consumer.

2. Through the process of photosynthesis, plants convert <u>radiant</u> energy into <u>chemical</u> energy.

3. Choice (B), decomposers, break down dead plant and animal matter and waste products to return nutrients to the ecosystem.

4. The crop benefits by being rid of the aphids, and the ladybugs fatten up on a diet of aphids, so the answer is Choice (C), mutualism. If the question asked about the relationship between the ladybugs and aphids, that's a predator-prey relationship. Aphids living off the crops and damaging them is an example of a parasite-host relationship.

5. In this example, the snakeheads are an invading species that have been introduced into the ecosystem instead of having evolved with it. As a result, the ecosystem has not yet adapted in a way to keep the system in balance. The answer is Choice (D), ecosystem disruption.

Looking at the Molecular Basis for Heredity

Heredity is the passing of traits from parents to offspring, and this passing of traits occurs at the molecular level within cells. Every cell in your body contains DNA, genes, and chromosomes that serve as a blueprint for how you're made:

✔ **Deoxyribonucleic acid (DNA)** is a self-replicating macromolecule that carries the genetic information that defines an organism's unique traits. DNA is a long chain of nucleic acid molecules — hundreds of millions in human DNA. Differences in the nucleic acid molecules and the order in which they're arranged define the organism.

✔ **Genes** are sections of DNA, each containing specific instructions for a particular protein or function.

✔ **Chromosomes** are packages of DNA tightly coiled many times around proteins called *histones*. Every human being has 46 chromosomes: 23 from each parent. The egg (from the mother) and the sperm (from the father) each contains 23 chromosomes. When a sperm cell fertilizes an egg, it creates a zygote, which contains 46 chromosomes.

Read the following passage from Genetics Home Reference (http://ghr.nlm.nih. gov/handbook/basics/chromosome) and answer the questions that follow. Check your answers and, if any of them is incorrect, reread the passage to figure out the correct answer. If your error was related to not knowing or understanding a word or idea, look it up, makes notes about it, and save them for study before the test.

What Is a Chromosome?

In the nucleus of each cell, the DNA molecule is packaged into thread-like structures called *chromosomes*. Each chromosome is made up of DNA tightly coiled many times around proteins called *histones* that support its structure.

Chromosomes are not visible in the cell's nucleus — not even under a microscope — when the cell is not dividing. However, the DNA that makes up chromosomes becomes more tightly packed during cell division and is then visible under a microscope. Most of what researchers know about chromosomes was learned by observing chromosomes during cell division.

Each chromosome has a constriction point called the *centromere,* which divides the chromosome into two sections, or "arms." The short arm of the chromosome is labeled the "p arm." The long arm of the chromosome is labeled the "q arm." The location of the centromere on each chromosome gives the chromosome its characteristic shape, and can be used to help describe the location of specific genes.

1. What is DNA?

   (A) a thread-like structure

   (B) part of a chromosome

   (C) only visible under a microscope during cell division

   (D) all of the above

2. Chromosomes are part of the cell's [   ].

3. Each chromosome has a constriction point called the *centromere* that divides it into [   ] sections, or "arms."

   (A) two

   (B) three

   (C) four

4. The arms are called [   ] and [   ].

Check your answers:

1. Choice (D), all of the above

2. nucleus

3. two

4. p-arm and q-arm

In the following sections, we explain heredity and how genes affect the characteristics and function of organisms.

Grasping the basics of genotypes, phenotypes, and inherited traits

To understand inheritance, you first need to recognize the difference between genotype and phenotype:

- ✔ **Genotype** is the genetic blueprint for each individual organism.

- ✔ **Phenotype** is the physical manifestation of the genotype in the organism, such as the size and color of a horse.

At a basic level, certain genes and their associated physical traits are considered _dominant_ or _recessive_. In people, for example, brown eyes are dominant, and blue eyes are recessive. Scientists commonly use a Punnett square (see Figure 8-2) to illustrate the relationship between dominant and recessive genes. Dominant genes are represented by uppercase letters; recessive genes, by lowercase letters. Each person has two _alleles_ (genes) for each trait — one from the mother and one from the father. A person inherits the recessive trait only if he receives the recessive allele from both parents. Otherwise, he inherits the dominant trait.

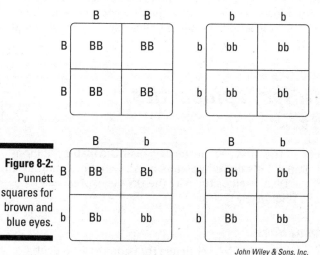

Figure 8-2: Punnett squares for brown and blue eyes.

John Wiley & Sons, Inc.

The Punnett squares in Figure 8-2 show how this works for brown and blue eyes:

- ✔ If either parent has two copies of the dominant allele (BB), all their children will receive at least one copy of the dominant allele, and all will have brown eyes, regardless of the eye color of the other parent.

✔ If both parents have blue eyes, each has two copies of the recessive allele (bb), so all their children will get two copies of the recessive allele, and all will have blue eyes.

✔ If one parent has a dominant and recessive allele (Bb) and the other parent has two copies of the recessive allele (bb), each child has a 50/50 chance of inheriting brown or blue eyes.

✔ If each parent has one dominant and one recessive allele (Bb), each child has a 75 percent chance of inheriting brown eyes and a 25 percent chance of inheriting blue eyes.

When both alleles are identical (both are dominant or both are recessive, as in BB and bb), the organism is considered *homozygous* for that trait. If the organism contains one dominant and one recessive allele (as in Bb), it is considered *heterozygous* for that trait.

Inheritance doesn't always follow a neat pattern. Partial dominance is also a possibility. For example, with some flowers, if you cross a white and a red variety, some offspring may have red flowers, some may have white flowers, and others may have flowers that are various shades of pink. And if you cross the pink-flowered plants, you may get some offspring that produce red or white flowers.

In a family, both grandparents have brown eyes, all their children have brown eyes, but two of their many grandchildren have blue eyes. Which of the following could be the genotypes of the grandparents?

(A) Both grandparents are BB.

(B) One grandparent is BB, and the other is bb.

(C) One grandparent is BB, and the other is Bb.

(D) One grandparent is Bb, and the other is bb.

Because both grandparents have brown eyes, neither can have the bb genotype, so you can rule out answer Choices (B) and (D). All their children have brown eyes, so the grandparents could both have the BB or Bb genotype, or one could have the BB and the other could have the Bb genotype. Because at least one grandchild has blue eyes, at least one of the grandparents has the recessive allele, so either both grandparents have the Bb genotype or one has the BB genotype and the other has Bb, Choice (C). Choice (A) is wrong because if they both had the BB genotype, their children would all have the BB genotype, and their children (the grandchildren) would have at least one dominant allele, so they would all have brown eyes.

Brushing up on mutation, epigenetics, and related concepts

Although DNA is very stable (think of all the monarch butterflies over the history of monarch butterflies that all look pretty similar), it's not completely fixed. Genetic mutations and other changes can occur that affect the DNA itself or the way the DNA is expressed — how it shows up in a particular organism's phenotype.

Getting up to speed on genetic mutations

A *genetic mutation* is a permanent change in the DNA sequence that comprises a gene, making the organism differ in some way from other organisms of the same species. Mutations are classified as hereditary, acquired, or new:

Studying identical twins and adopted siblings

To make sense of the interaction of genes and the environment, scientists often study identical twins and adopted siblings. Identical twins, even when raised apart, tend to have similar traits, such as intelligence, and often live through similar events in their lives. By studying similarities and differences between identical twins, scientists have developed a clearer understanding of which environmental factors influence gene expression, mutation, and epigenetics.

Adopted siblings also demonstrate the influence of the environment. Children of the same parents who grow up with different adopted parents have similar genotypes. Similarities and differences between the children help to shed light on the influence environment has on their development.

✔ **Hereditary (germline)** mutations are passed from parents to offspring and are present in every cell in the body. These mutations are present in the germ cells (sperm or egg) of the parent.

✔ **Acquired (somatic)** mutations arise at some point during an organism's life and only affect some cells. For example, if a person smokes a lot of nicotine cigarettes, a mutation may occur that converts healthy cells into cancer cells.

✔ **New (de novo)** arise in some stage of reproduction, such as when the egg or sperm are created or after the zygote is formed and cells begin to divide. These newly developed mutations may explain instances of a child being born with a genetic disorder that neither parent has a gene for.

Short answer practice

Read the following passage and write a short answer to the question, "Why is genetic diversity important in our present agricultural communities?"

This question should take about 10 minutes to answer. It is part of the 90 minutes you have to complete the test, so manage your time carefully. When you're finished, read it over and ask a friend to look at it to make sure you've answered the question. If you haven't, look over the passage again to see whether you can trace the weakness in your essay to a specific problem, such as not reading carefully enough, not understanding the vocabulary, or being unfamiliar with the subject. You can fix a reading problem by reading more carefully and through practice. Vocabulary can be learned. If the subject is unfamiliar to you, read some more about it either in books or on the Internet.

Genetic Diversity Helps Organisms Cope with Current Environmental Variability

Organisms exist in environments that vary in time and over space. Such variation is often described in terms of the *natural* or *historic range of variability* (NRV, HRV) in environmental conditions such as weather, disturbance events, resource availability, population sizes of competitors, and so on. (White and Walker, 1997). If a group of organisms (say, a population of species X) were to live in a completely stable physical and biological environment, then a relatively narrow range of phenotypes might be optimally adapted to those conditions. Under these circumstances, species X would benefit more by maintaining a narrow range of genotypes adapted to prevailing conditions, and allele frequencies might eventually attain equilibrium. By contrast, if the environment is patchy, unpredictable over time, or includes a wide and changing variety of diseases, predators, and parasites, then subtle differences among individuals increase the probability that some individuals and not others will survive to reproduce — that is, the traits are "exposed to selection." Since differences among individuals are determined at least partly by genotype, population genetic theory predicts (and empirical observation confirms) that in variable environments, a broader range of genetic variation (higher heterozygosity) will persist (Cohen, 1966; Chesson, 1985; Tuljapurkar, 1989; Tilman, 1999).

Examples of traits with a genetic basis for tolerance of environmental variation important in restoration work include tolerance of freezing, drought or inundation, high or low light availability, salinity, heavy metals, soil nutrient deficiencies, and extreme soil pH values in plants; resilience to fluctuating temperature, dissolved oxygen, and nutrient availability in aquatic organisms; and resistance to novel diseases in all groups of organisms (Huenneke, 1991). For example, if all individuals in a population are the same genotype with limited drought tolerance, then a single climatic event may destroy the entire population. Plant populations often include individuals with a range of flowering or emergence times. For instance, Great Basin shrub populations include individuals that leaf out and flower over a period of weeks, increasing the likelihood of persistence of the population through periods of unusually early or late growing conditions. Knapp et al. (2001) documented flowering periods in a population of individual blue oak trees and found that trees initiated flowering over a period of a month in the spring. Such variability could potentially be adaptive, since it is more likely that at least some trees in the population will flower during warm sunny periods when wind pollination is most successful.

A diverse array of genotypes appears to be especially important in disease resistance (Schoen and Brown, 1993; McArdle, 1996). Genetically uniform populations (such as highly inbred crops) are famously vulnerable to diseases and pathogens, which can (and do) decimate populations in which all individuals are equally vulnerable. Such uniformity also predisposes a population to transmit disease from one individual to another: Instead of having isolated diseased individuals, nearly every individual may be exposed to disease by direct contact or proximity. More diverse populations are more likely to include individuals resistant to specific diseases; moreover, infected individuals occur at lower density, and thus diseases or pathogens may move more slowly through the population.

Finally, genetic variation is a factor in competition among individuals in real ecological communities. Traits with a genetic basis such as flower size are key factors in competition among individuals. Among animals, behavioral traits may regulate interspecific competition. Since organisms make energetic or life history tradeoffs among traits (for example, allocating energy between growth and reproduction), genetic variability is an important factor in how populations function (Koyama and Kira, 1956; Thompson and Plowright, 1980; Fowler, 1981; Gurevitch, 1986; Goldberg, 1987; Manning and Barbour, 1988; Welden, Slauson, and Ward, 1988; Grace and Tilman, 1990; Tilman and Wedin, 1991; Pantastico-Caldas and Venable, 1993; Wilson and Tilman, 1993; Delph, Weinig, and Sullivan, 1998).

From "Why is genetic diversity important?" www.nps.gov/plants/restore/pubs/restgene/1.htm

This article, like many other scientific articles, includes citations in the body of the text. You can ignore the citations unless you're absolutely fascinated by the subject, in which case look them up in your favorite search engine.

If you had trouble writing the response or if you're worried about how it will be marked on the test, look at http://www.gedtestingservice.com/uploads/files/8909736852 5e28544f77607f31391c4f.pdf. This booklet was written for teachers, but it does have some useful information for you as a test-taker.

Digging into the Theory of Evolution

Evolution is a scientific theory that explains how the diversity of living things developed in response to various environmental factors and how they adapt to changing conditions over time. But evolution itself is more fact than theory. You can observe it taking place in the field of medicine, for example, as bacteria develop resistance to antibiotics. Exterminators witnessed evolution at work in the 1980s when a certain poison that had been very effective in killing cockroaches stopped working. The cockroaches had developed a genetically pro-grammed aversion to the corn syrup used to attract them to the poison.

Scientists are still uncertain of how, specifically, evolution occurs. *Darwinism* is the most accepted theory today. Darwin's theory is that genetic mutations occur randomly. Through a process of *natural selection* or *survival of the fittest,* mutations that are beneficial to the organism's survival are passed along to future generations, while those that are detrimental fail to survive. Selective pressures include disease, competition for food and other resources, and environmental factors. For example, near the equator, genes for dark skin have an advantage over those for light skin because dark skin has more melanin to protect against damage from intense ultraviolet (UV) radiation. In colder areas with less intense sunlight, genes for lighter skin have an advantage because lighter skin allows more sunlight to penetrate, which drives the production of vitamin D, which is needed for strong teeth and bones.

Investigating common ancestry

Common ancestry is the scientific theory that all known living organisms arose from a common ancestor. By closely examining DNA, scientists can determine how closely related two species are and estimate the time when the two species diverged. These relationships are often illustrated in the form of a *cladogram,* as shown in Figure 8-3.

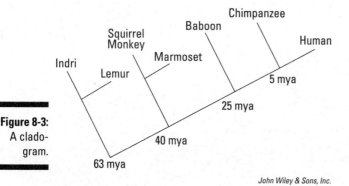

Figure 8-3:
A clado-gram.

John Wiley & Sons, Inc.

Exercise

Crocodiles and birds are related. They're not sibling related but are very distantly related, both sharing a common ancestor that lived around 240 million years ago. Using the Internet for research, perhaps starting with news.ucsc.edu/2014/12/crocodile-genomes. html:

1. Develop an outline of information on the topic of "Guess who was in the family a long, long time ago?"

2. From your outline, write a one- to two-page essay.

3. Based on your essay, develop four or five questions that can be answered from the information in your essay and some general knowledge. Develop answer choices and make sure the correct answer is based on information in your essay and not something you remembered from your research.

This exercise is similar to the process an examiner would use to develop questions for a test. Now that you can see a process that's not magical or mystical, relax; with preparation, you can do well on these tests.

Chapter 9

Getting Physical with Physical Science

• •

In This Chapter

▶ Looking into energy conservation, transformation, and flow

▶ Measuring work, motion, and forces and their impact on objects

▶ Mastering chemistry basics

• •

The *physical sciences* are those that study inanimate substances and forces in the world. For the purposes of this book, we classify chemistry and physics as the two physical sciences. The physical sciences also include earth and space science, but we cover that separately in Chapter 10.

In this chapter, we bring you up to speed on energy and matter; work, motion, and forces; and chemistry basics. With fundamental knowledge and skills in these areas, you should have no trouble answering the chemistry and physics questions you're likely to encounter on the GED Science test.

Grasping Energy Basics: Conservation, Transformation, and Flow

Energy powers everything in the universe, and you don't even have to flip a switch or turn a key in the ignition to turn it on. And what's even more amazing about energy is that it can't be created or destroyed, which may make you wonder why you need to pay for gas or electricity, but more about that later in this section.

Here, we introduce you to the various energy forms and sources, explore the unique qualities of heat, distinguish between exothermic and endothermic reactions, and explain how waves transfer energy. Along the way, we present sample questions, so you can practice answering energy-related questions you're likely to encounter on the test.

Exploring energy types and transformation

Energy is power that has the capacity to do work or effect change, and it comes in many forms that can be broken down into two main categories:

> ✔ **Kinetic:** Energy in motion, including the following forms of energy:
>
> • **Electrical:** Electrical energy is the flow of *electrons,* negatively charged particles in atoms.
>
> • **Electromagnetic (radiant):** Various forms of light, including the visible light you're most familiar with, microwaves, and X-rays, are all forms of electromagnetic energy.

- **Motion:** Anything in motion carries energy that's a product of its mass and velocity.

- **Sound:** Sound energy causes vibration and is a relatively small source of energy.

- **Thermal:** Although you can't always see heat move, you can feel it flow from an object or cause steam to rise from water.

✔ **Potential:** Energy at rest, stored in an object by virtue of its position, electrical charge, or other factor(s). Potential energy includes the following forms of energy:

- **Chemical:** Energy stored in the bonds among atoms in a compound. When bonds are formed or broken through chemical reactions, energy can be released.

- **Gravitational:** Energy exerted on objects by the gravitational field surrounding them. If you do a push-up, you experience gravitational energy acting on your body.

- **Nuclear:** Energy stored in the nucleus (core) of an atom. When an atom is split (a process referred to as *fission*) or two atoms combine *(fusion)*, energy is released. Nuclear power plants use fission to produce energy. Fusion is responsible for most of the energy produced by the sun and other stars.

- **Elastic:** The energy stored in a stretched rubber band is elastic energy. If you release the rubber band, the energy is converted into mechanical (motion) energy.

According to the law of *conservation of energy,* the total energy in a system remains constant; in other words, energy can't be created or destroyed, although it can be converted from one type of energy to another. For example, when you flip a switch to turn on the lights, electrical energy is converted into electromagnetic energy in the form of light and into heat energy. The electrical energy doesn't just disappear.

You're probably most familiar with energy that's used every day for heating, refrigeration, light, or performing mechanical work to operate machines.

1. A screw becomes warm when unscrewed from a board using an electric screwdriver. Which of the following best describes the type of energy conversion taking place?

   (A) mechanical to thermal to electrical

   (B) electrical to mechanical to thermal

   (C) gravitational to mechanical to thermal

   (D) chemical to mechanical to thermal

2. Trees are damaged when struck by lightning, but the lightning is nowhere apparent afterward. Because lightning is a form of energy, what would explain the apparent disappearance of the energy in the lightning?

   (A) The energy in the lightning disappears.

   (B) The tree absorbs the lightning and stores the energy for future use.

   (C) The energy in the lightning is converted to mechanical and thermal energy.

   (D) Lightning striking the tree creates new energy, which damages the tree.

Now check your answers:

1. Electrical energy is converted into mechanical energy to turn the screw, which is then converted into thermal energy in the form of heat, so Choice (B) is correct.

2. Electrical (and light) energy from the lightning is converted into mechanical energy that causes the tree to split and thermal energy in the form of heat, Choice (C). Based on the law of the conservation of energy, you can instantly rule out Choices (A) and (D) because energy can neither be created nor destroyed. Choice (B) would be a good second guess, but it's wrong because the tree has no means to store the electrical energy in order to release it later.

Recognizing energy sources

Energy sources are natural resources that can be used or harnessed to provide power for light, heat, and operating machinery. The most common energy sources include the following:

- **Biomass:** Wood and other plants contain tremendous amounts of chemical energy formed through photosynthesis (see Chapter 8). These may be burned directly or converted into other forms of fuel, such as ethanol (commonly added to gas for automobiles) and biodiesel.

- **Fossil fuels:** Coal, oil, and natural gas are all fossil fuels obtained from the accumulated remains of prehistoric plants and animals that have been compressed and heated over many thousands of years. Burning these fuels converts chemical energy into thermal energy for heating, into mechanical energy to operate machinery (as in a car), or into mechanical energy to produce electrical energy (such as turning a turbine to produce electricity).

- **Geothermal:** The core of the Earth is extremely hot. Geothermal energy harnesses this heat directly for heating homes and businesses and for producing electricity.

- **Hydroelectricity:** The movement of water in the form of rivers and waves (mechanical energy) is often harnessed to produce electrical energy to supply homes and businesses.

- **Hydrogen:** Hydrogen can be burned or used in fuel cells to produce vast amounts of electricity. NASA has used liquid hydrogen since the 1970s as rocket fuel. It's a clean-burning fuel that releases only water into the environment. However, hydrogen requires a great deal of energy to produce, so it's not yet economically efficient to use.

- **Nuclear:** Certain chemical elements, especially uranium, have an incredible amount of potential energy. In fact, one gram of the rare uranium isotope U-235 contains approximately the same energy as three tons of coal. Splitting the atoms of these elements releases the energy, or at least a portion of it.

- **Sun:** Most of our energy — whether it's in the form of fossil fuels, biodiesel, biomass (wood, for example), or solar energy — comes from the sun. Solar energy is commonly harnessed using photovoltaic cells that convert the sun's radiant energy into electrical energy. Solar energy is also used in passive heating systems in homes and businesses to allow energy from the sun to penetrate buildings through windows, where the windows also serve to hold in the heat.

- **Wind:** Wind is commonly harnessed in a variety of ways, especially through the use of windmills, to produce electricity.

Using details from the following table, write a short essay explaining the possible challenges of transitioning from fossil fuels to cleaner, renewable energy sources. Write your essay on a separate sheet of paper and spend no more than 10 minutes writing your response.

Energy Source	Advantages	Drawbacks
Biomass	Abundant Lower emissions than fossil fuels Can be used as fuel in diesel- and gas-powered vehicles	Air pollutant Uses fossil fuels in harvest, conversion, and transportation
Coal	Abundant Inexpensive Reliable Generates large amounts of power	Emits greenhouse gases High environmental impact Dangerous for miners
Geothermal	Clean Efficient Low cost after initial investment	Limited availability Expensive to start up Wells could be depleted over time
Hydroelectric	Clean Reliable Can generate large amounts of electricity Output can be regulated to meet demand	Expensive to build May be affected by drought Impacts environment and fish migration, if not mitigated
Natural gas	Plentiful Relatively clean fossil fuel	High transportation costs Emits some pollution Nonrenewable
Oil/gas	Efficient fuel for transportation Economical Easy to transport	High greenhouse gas emissions Environmental impact from drilling and transporting Nonrenewable
Sun	Clean Abundant	High initial investment Unreliable, depends on sunny weather Requires large physical space for solar panels
Uranium	No greenhouse gas or CO_2 emissions Efficient Abundant	High investment costs Long-term storage of dangerous radioactive waste Environmental impact of heated waste water released in nearby river or lake Potentially harmful to environment and humans
Wind	Clean Affordable High energy output	Unreliable, relies on presence of wind Limited availability based on location High building and maintenance costs Extensive land use Environmental impact of bird kill

Heating up the discussion

Heat is a form of energy present in an object because of the movement of the atoms that the object is made of. The greater the amount of heat, the faster the atoms jiggle, and vice versa. At *absolute zero*, the lowest theoretical temperature, no heat remains in an object, and all atoms stop moving. Heat is an interesting form of energy and has certain qualities that you need to know about for the test, as explained in the following sections.

Heat transfer

Heat transfers from hotter objects to cooler objects and never in the opposite direction. When you pour coffee into a standard ceramic mug, for example, you can see heat transfer to the air as steam rises from the mug. If you hold the mug, you can feel that heat has been transferred from the coffee to the mug and now into your hands. Heat transfers in three ways:

- ✔ **Conduction:** Heat transfer between particles (for example, the coffee and the mug) without the displacement of the particles themselves. Conduction occurs when heat is transferred from one solid to another, as in the case of heat traveling through a mug and into your hands.

- ✔ **Convection:** Heat transfer through the movement of particles as hotter, lighter particles rise and displace cooler, heavier particles. Convection enables a space heater to heat an entire room, as hot air continuously rises from the heater, displacing the cooler air until all the air in the room reaches a certain temperature.

- ✔ **Radiation:** Heat transfer through electromagnetic waves. Radiation is how the sun transfers energy to the Earth. You also feel radiant heat when you're near a fire. A unique property of radiant heat is that it requires no medium to carry it, so it can travel through a vacuum, as radiant heat from the sun travels through the vacuum of space.

1. If an incandescent light bulb is made of a filament inside a glass enclosure from which all air has been exhausted, what method(s) of thermal transfer would cause your fingers to warm up if you touched the glass enclosure?

   (A) conduction

   (B) convection

   (C) radiation

   (D) radiation and conduction

2. If an LED light bulb produces 98 percent less heat than an incandescent light bulb for the same amount of light, why would it be a more energy-efficient source of light?

   (A) The LED bulb costs less.

   (B) The incandescent bulb converts more electricity into heat energy.

   (C) The LED bulb is brighter.

   (D) The LED bulb lasts longer.

3. Why is a convection oven called a "convection oven"?

   (A) It has a fan that moves air during the cooking process.

   (B) All ovens are convection ovens.

   (C) A conventional oven uses radiant heat.

   (D) A conventional oven heats with conduction.

   Check your answers:

   1. Because air has been removed, the inside of the bulb has no medium to carry the heat, so the heat is transferred by radiation to the glass. The glass then conducts the heat to your fingers. The correct choice is (D).

2. A light-emitting diode (LED) is more efficient at converting electricity into light, so less is converted into heat, making Choice (B) the correct answer. An incandescent bulb releases 90 percent of its energy in the form of heat, so only 10 percent is used to produce light. You can eliminate Choice (C) because the question states that both bulbs produce the same amount of light. Choices (A) and (D) have more to do with cost efficiency than energy efficiency, and Choice (A) happens to be wrong, although you couldn't tell that without reading the question carefully.

3. A convection oven has a fan that moves air during the cooking process, so Choice (A) is the best answer. Choices (B) and (C) are also correct; conventional ovens do use radiant heat, and convection is involved as the air inside the oven heats up, but neither explains the reason for the name "convection oven." Choice (D) is wrong because ovens don't heat with conduction, although stove tops certainly do.

Heat and temperature

Don't confuse the terms *heat* and *temperature*. *Heat* is the energy in the molecular motion of particles. *Temperature* is a measure of the average heat in a substance. To grasp the difference, consider the fact that a swimming pool at 80°F contains far more heat than does a pot of boiling water at 212°F. Even though the boiling water has a higher temperature, it contains less heat because it contains far fewer water molecules.

Endothermic and exothermic reactions

Chemical reactions involve a transfer of energy as bonds among atoms are created or broken. These reactions are commonly classified as one of the following two types depending on whether the reaction absorbs or releases heat:

- **Endothermic:** Requires heat. A good example of an endothermic reaction is photosynthesis, where the energy from the sun is used by plants to convert carbon dioxide and water into glucose and oxygen.

- **Exothermic:** Releases heat. Burning wood is an exothermic reaction that requires some initial energy input to get started.

Endothermic and exothermic reactions are commonly measured by the change in *enthalpy* (the measure of heat content) that results. In an exothermic reaction, the change in enthalpy, represented as ΔH, is a negative value because the heat content of the resulting substance is less than that of the *reactants* (chemicals involved in the reaction). In an endothermic reaction, the resulting substance draws heat from the surroundings, so the change in enthalpy is positive.

Getting a little wave action

A *wave* is a disturbance that travels through a medium, transferring energy from one point to another without any net movement of the medium. Particles that make up the medium may move up and down or back and forth as the wave energy passes through the medium, but they ultimately return to their original positions.

Waves transfer energy, not matter.

In this section we describe different wave types and the parts of a wave while presenting some sample wave questions like those you may encounter on the test.

Recognizing different wave types

Waves are classified by the direction the particles move as the wave energy passes through the medium (see Figure 9-1):

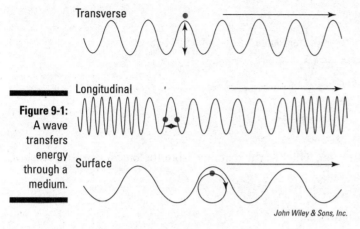

Figure 9-1:
A wave
transfers
energy
through a
medium.

John Wiley & Sons, Inc.

 ✔ **Longitudinal wave:** Particles move back and forth, parallel to the direction of the
   wave.

 ✔ **Surface wave:** Particles move in a circular motion.

 ✔ **Transverse wave:** Particles move up and down, parallel to each other but
   perpendicular to the direction of the wave.

You can also categorize waves as mechanical and electromagnetic:

 ✔ **Mechanical waves** require a medium, such as air or water. They can't transmit energy
   through a vacuum. Sound waves are an example of mechanical waves.

 ✔ **Electromagnetic waves** transmit energy through the vibration of electrical and
   magnetic fields and can transmit energy through a vacuum. Types of electromagnetic
   waves include radio waves, microwaves, infrared rays, visible light, ultraviolet radiation, X-rays, and gamma rays. Many types of electromagnetic waves can't be seen.

1. Waves transmit which of the following?

   (A) energy

   (B) matter

   (C) energy and matter

   (D) neither energy nor matter

2. Ocean waves are classified as which of the following wave type?

   (A) transverse

   (B) longitudinal

   (C) surface

   (D) electromagnetic

Check your answers:

   1. Waves transmit energy, Choice (A), not matter.

   2. Ocean waves are surface waves, Choice (C).

Inspecting a wave's characteristics

A wave has the following characteristics, as shown in Figure 9-2:

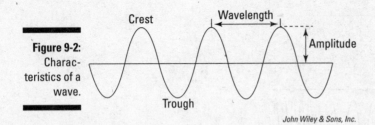

John Wiley & Sons, Inc.

Figure 9-2:
Charac-
teristics of a
wave.

- ✔ **Amplitude:** Size of the vibration, which is the distance from the baseline to the crest or baseline to trough.

- ✔ **Crest:** Highest point of the wave.

- ✔ **Trough:** Lowest point of the wave.

- ✔ **Wavelength:** Distance between corresponding points on consecutive waves.

All waves have these features, although they may appear different in the different types of waves. They're easiest to grasp in terms of a transverse wave, as shown in Figure 9-2.

The speed at which a wave travels is typically measured in frequency or period, as shown in Figure 9-3:

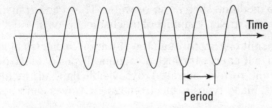

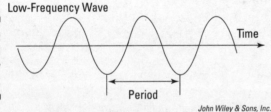

John Wiley & Sons, Inc.

Figure 9-3:
Wave
frequency
and period.

- ✔ **Frequency:** The speed of the vibration — the number of waves that pass a fixed point in a given amount of time.

- ✔ **Period:** The duration of time for one wave, from crest to crest, to pass a fixed point.

EXAMPLE

1. Shortening a wavelength has which of the following effects?

    (A) decreases the amplitude

    (B) increases the amplitude

    (C) increases the frequency

    (D) shortens the period

2. A sound is made louder or softer by changing which of the following characteristics of the sound wave?

   (A) amplitude

   (B) frequency

   (C) period

   (D) wavelength

Check your answers:

   1. A shorter wavelength results in more waves over a shorter distance, resulting in an increase in frequency, Choice (C).

   2. A sound is made louder by an increase in amplitude or the size of the vibration, Choice (A). A change in frequency makes the pitch higher or lower.

> *Read the following excerpt (from* http://www.fda.gov/Radiation-EmittingProducts/
> ResourcesforYouRadiationEmittingProducts/ucm252762.htm#Microwave_Ovens_and_
> Health *and answer the questions that follow.*

Microwave Ovens and Health

Much research is underway on microwaves and how they might affect the human body. It is known that microwave radiation can heat body tissue the same way it heats food. Exposure to high levels of microwaves can cause a painful burn. The lens of the eye is particularly sensitive to intense heat, and exposure to high levels of microwaves can cause cataracts. Likewise, the testes are very sensitive to changes in temperature. Accidental exposure to high levels of microwave energy can alter or kill sperm, producing temporary sterility. But these types of injuries — burns, cataracts, temporary sterility — can only be caused by exposure to large amounts of microwave radiation, much more than the 5mW limit for microwave oven leakage.

Less is known about what happens to people exposed to low levels of microwaves. Controlled, long-term studies involving large numbers of people have not been conducted to assess the impact of low-level microwave energy on humans. Much research has been done with experimental animals, but it is difficult to translate the effects of microwaves on animals to possible effects on humans. For one thing, there are differences in the way animals and humans absorb microwaves. For another, experimental conditions can't exactly simulate the conditions under which people use microwave ovens. However, these studies do help us better understand the possible effects of radiation.

The fact that many scientific questions about exposure to low levels of microwaves are not yet answered requires the FDA to continue enforcement of radiation protection requirements. Consumers should take certain common sense precautions.

1. If you look through the window of a microwave oven, you can see the food cooking but not the microwaves doing the cooking. Why is that?

   (A) The windows are designed to hide microwaves.

   (B) Microwaves are invisible waves.

   (C) Microwaves can harm your eyes.

   (D) The window is too small.

2. Why are scientists concerned about the effects of microwaves on human beings?

   (A) Even small amounts of microwave radiation can harm humans.

   (B) Microwaves harm other animals.

   (C) People may leave microwave doors open when cooking.

   (D) Microwaves can transfer energy to tissues and organs.

   Check your answers:

   1. You can't see the microwaves because they're invisible, Choice (B).

   2. The first paragraph establishes the fact that high levels of exposure to microwaves can damage tissues and organs, Choice (D). The rest of the passage questions whether low-level exposure also poses health risks.

Appreciating Force, Motion, and Work

A great deal of basic physics involves the study of forces that act on objects to move them: how much work is required to move an object, and how simple machines, such as levers and ramps, affect the amount of force required to lift or move objects. You don't need to be a physicist or know a lot about machines to answer the work, motion, and forces questions you may encounter on the test, but answering the questions is much easier if you have a general understanding of the concepts involved. In this section, we bring you up to speed on basic physics.

Calculating distance, speed, and displacement

In physics, motion is measured in terms of distance, speed, displacement, velocity, and acceleration:

- **Acceleration:** Rate of change in velocity, typically measured in meters per second per second (m/s/s or m/s^2).
- **Displacement:** The net change in an object's position and direction.
- **Distance:** The space between two positions.
- **Speed:** The rate (typically average rate) at which an object moves.
- **Velocity:** Speed in a certain direction.

Note the difference between scalar and vector quantities. Distance is a *scalar* quantity indicating how far an object has traveled, whereas displacement is a *vector* quantity indicating the change in an object's position. If you run one lap around a quarter-mile track, you run a distance of 0.25 miles, but your displacement is 0 because you're back where you started. Likewise, speed is scalar, whereas velocity is vector. If you run a 6-minute mile on that same oval track, you ran 10 miles per hour, but your velocity is 0 because you're back where you started.

To calculate distance, average speed, or time when given the other two values, use the following formula:

$$s = \frac{d}{t}$$

1. An eagle flies due east 40 miles per hour for 1 hour and 30 minutes and then 10 miles in the opposite direction at 20 miles per hour. How far did it fly? ☐ miles

2. What is the eagle's displacement? ☐ miles

3. Which of the following represents the eagle's velocity?

    (A) 40 mph

    (B) 40 mph east

    (C) 25 mph

    (D) 25 mph east

Check your answers:

1. The eagle flew 40 miles in 1 hour plus 20 miles in a half-hour plus 10 miles, for a total distance of 70 miles.

2. The eagle flew 40 miles east in 1 hour plus another 20 miles east in a half-hour minus 10 miles west, so its displacement is $60 - 10 = 50$ miles.

3. The eagle's net change in position is 50 miles east, and it was flying for 2 hours, so its velocity is $50 \div 2 = 25$ miles per hour east, Choice (D).

Wrapping your brain around vectors

According to Newton's first law of motion:

> An object at rest stays at rest, and an object in motion stays in motion with the same speed and in the same direction unless acted upon by an unbalanced force.

By *force,* Newton is referring to a push or pull on an object. Forces are measured in newtons (N) in a certain direction; for example, 20N forward or 15N up. Vector diagrams, such as those shown in Figure 9-4, indicate such forces. Vectors (arrows) are typically used to demonstrate the direction and magnitude of the force, with the arrow head showing the direction and the length of the arrow representing the relative magnitude of the force.

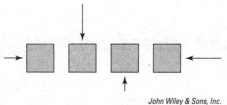

John Wiley & Sons, Inc.

Understanding how mass, force, and acceleration are related

According to Newton's second law of motion:

> Acceleration is produced when a force acts on a mass. The greater the mass [of the object], the greater the force needed [to accelerate it].

This law gives rise to one of the most important physics formulas you may encounter on the test, which explains the relationship of mass, force, and acceleration:

- ✔ **Mass** is the amount of matter an object has. Don't confuse mass with weight. Weight varies depending on gravity; for example, you weigh much less on the moon than you do on Earth because gravity is much stronger on Earth. However, your mass is the same regardless of gravity.

- ✔ **Force** is any energy that changes the motion or direction of an object.

- ✔ **Acceleration** is the rate of change of velocity of an object. (Velocity is speed in a given direction.)

The relationship among mass, force, and acceleration is expressed in the formula $F = ma$ or _Force = mass × acceleration_. You can use this formula or other versions of it to calculate force, mass, or acceleration when given values for the other two variables.

To answer questions related to mass, force, and acceleration, you don't need to memorize the formula. If a question requires that you perform a calculation, the formula will be provided.

According to Newton's second law of motion, _Force = mass × acceleration_.

1. If you keep the force the same and double an object's mass, what will be the effect on acceleration?

    (A) Acceleration will be doubled.

    (B) Acceleration will be halved

    (C) Acceleration will remain the same.

    (D) Not enough information.

2. If the net force on a 4-kilogram object is 20 newtons, what is its acceleration? ⬚

Check your answers:

1. If the force is kept the same and you double the object's mass, the acceleration will be cut in half, Choice (B).

2. $F = ma$, so $20 = 4 \times a$, so $a = 20 \div 4 = 5$.

Investigating gravity and related concepts

According to Newton's third law of motion:

> For every action there is an equal and opposite reaction.

In other words, whenever you push or pull anything, it pushes or pulls you in the opposite direction. For example, if you tie a rope to an elephant and try to pull the elephant when he would prefer to remain where he is, you'd probably end up pulling yourself forward and fall flat on your face.

You can also observe Newton's third law of motion in action as you're sitting in a chair reading this book. Gravity is a force that pushes down on you. On Earth, the force is $9.8 \frac{m}{s^2}$.

As gravity pushes you down into the chair, the chair pushes up with an equal force. If the force were less than that of gravity, you would fall through the chair. If the force were greater than that of gravity, the chair would lift you.

This brings up Newton's law of universal gravitation:

> Any two bodies in the universe attract each other with a force that is directly proportional to the product of their masses and inversely proportional to the square of the distance between them.

The formula representing this relationship is $F_{grav} = \dfrac{m_1 \times m_2}{d^2}$, where F_{grav} is the force of gravity, m_1 is the mass of one object, m_2 is the mass of the other object, and d is the distance between them. By looking at the formula, you can tell that gravity increases when mass increases, and it decreases when the distance between the two objects increases. This explains why people tend to float on the space station — because they're relatively small in terms of mass, and the distance from the Earth is much greater.

1. Why does a pistol recoil (push back) when it is fired?

   (A) The force projecting the bullet forward has an equal force that projects the gun backward.

   (B) The explosion of the gunpowder emits a force in all directions, including a force that projects the gun backward.

   (C) As the bullet accelerates through the barrel, it pushes the gun back.

   (D) When the shooter pulls the trigger, he forces the gun down, which requires an equal and opposite force to push up on the gun.

2. Based solely on mass, on which of the following planets would you expect surface gravity to be the greatest?

   (A) Venus, 4.87×10^{24} kg

   (B) Earth, 5.97×10^{24} kg

   (C) Mars, 0.642×10^{24} kg

   (D) Uranus, 568×10^{24} kg

Check your answers:

1. The recoil is an example of Newton's third law of motion, which states that for every action, there must be an equal and opposite reaction. In this example, the force of the explosion that sends the bullet forward sends the gun back in the opposite direction, Choice (A).

2. The force of gravity on the surface of a planet is proportional to its mass and inversely proportional to its distance. Because the question instructs you to ignore any factors other than mass, you would expect Uranus to have the strongest surface gravity, Choice (D), and that answer would be correct. However, Uranus is comprised mostly of gas, so the distance from the center of the planet to its surface is much greater than that of the other planets listed; its actual surface gravity ($8.69 \frac{m}{s^2}$) is less than that of Earth ($9.8 \frac{m}{s^2}$).

Grasping the basics of momentum

An object in motion has *momentum* (mass in motion). Its momentum depends on its mass and velocity and can be expressed using the following equation: $p = m \times v$, where p is the momentum ($kg \times \frac{m}{s}$), m is the mass (kg), and v is velocity ($\frac{m}{s}$).

Momentum explains why you shouldn't cross the tracks when a train is coming. A train has incredible mass, and even if it's traveling relatively slowly, it has enormous momentum. Whether you're on foot, on a bicycle, in a car, or in a truck, you're not likely to have much effect on the momentum of the train.

According to the law of *conservation of momentum,* in an isolated system, the total momentum before a collision is equal to the total momentum after the collision. If you've ever played billiards, you've seen conservation of momentum in action. When you strike the cue ball and it hits a ball at rest, much of the cue ball's momentum is transferred to the ball it collided with, setting the other ball in motion.

A pitcher throws a fastball. The batter swings and knocks the ball out of the park for a home run. Which of the following principles applies here?

(A) conservation of mass

(B) conservation of energy

(C) conservation of momentum

(D) Newton's first law of motion

Both the bat and the ball have momentum. When the two collide, the momentum is conserved, but the ball is sent in a different direction. The actual physics involved are complicated by numerous advanced factors but are not necessary for your success on the test.

Understanding work, simple machines, and power

When a force applied to an object moves that object, work has been done and can be calculated with the equation *Work = force × distance* or $W = fd$. Any mechanical device that changes the magnitude or direction of a force is a *simple machine.* All simple machines function by increasing the distance over which the force is applied, so less force is required to perform the work. During the Renaissance, scientists defined six simple machines:

- ✔ **Lever:** A teeter-totter is an example of a lever in action, allowing a lighter person on one end of the teeter-totter to lift a heavier person on the other end. Levers are also the machinery behind scissors, hammers (for removing nails), nail clippers, and pliers.

- ✔ **Wheel and axle:** Wheels reduce the force of friction, enabling heavy loads to move more easily. Wheels also reduce the force required to rotate the axle by increasing the distance over which the force is applied.

- ✔ **Pulley:** A pulley increases the distance to reduce the force required to move an object. With a one-wheel pulley, for example, you must pull twice as much rope to move an object the same distance.

- ✔ **Inclined plane:** An inclined plane (a ramp) makes it easier to "lift" an object; it increases the distance, so less force is required to perform the work necessary to lift the object. For example, in Figure 9-5, the block requires a force of 4 newtons to lift it straight up 2 meters. By doubling the distance over which the block is moved, you require only half as much force to move it.

- ✔ **Wedge:** A wedge, such as an ax or a knife, transfers a downward force into sideways forces to split an object.

- ✔ **Screw:** A screw is essentially a wedge wrapped around a shaft.

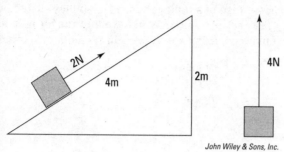

Figure 9-5:
An inclined plane reduces the force required to lift an object.

John Wiley & Sons, Inc.

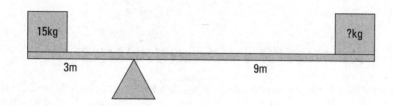

How much weight would need to be placed on the right end of this lever to keep it balanced?

One third of the weight would be required because the distance is three times as far from the point at which the lever pivots.

The *mechanical advantage* of a machine is a ratio of its output force to its input force and can be expressed as $MA = \dfrac{output\ force}{input\ force}$. Using this formula, you can calculate mechanical advantage, output force, or input force if you know the two other values.

The mechanical advantage of a pulley is 2*n*, where *n* represents the number of pulleys being used.

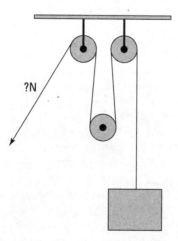

If a 12-newton force were required to lift an object straight up, how much force, in newtons, would be required to lift the object using a 3-pulley system as shown here?

You're told that the mechanical advantage of a pulley is 2*n*, so a 3-pulley system would have a mechanical advantage of $2 \times 3 = 6$. Plug the numbers you have into the formula for mechanical advantage and solve for the unknown, using *x* to represent the unknown input force:

$$MA = \frac{output\ force}{input\ force}$$

$$6 = \frac{12N}{x}$$

$$6x = 12N$$

$$x = \frac{12N}{6} = 2N$$

Grasping Chemistry Fundamentals

Chemistry is the study of substances, the matter that comprises those substances, and the properties of substances and matter. You don't need to take a course in advanced placement (AP) chemistry to answer chemistry questions on the GED Science test, but having a general understanding of substances, matter, and their properties can help you answer any chemistry questions you encounter correctly and in less time. In this section, we explain the basics and provide some sample practice questions.

Noting the structure of atoms

Anything that has mass and volume (occupies space) is matter and is composed of *elements* (pure substances composed of one type of atom). An *atom* comprises a nucleus at its center containing *protons* (positively charged particles) and *neutrons* (uncharged particles) surrounded by *electrons* (negatively charged particles), as shown in Figure 9-6. The electrons maintain their position around the nucleus through electric forces, while nuclear forces hold the nucleus together.

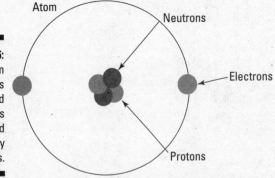

Figure 9-6: An atom contains protons and neutrons surrounded by electrons.

John Wiley & Sons, Inc.

The graphic representation of atoms provides a conceptual model only. In reality, electrons are more like a cloud that surrounds the nucleus than like particles that orbit the nucleus.

All known naturally occurring elements are listed in the Periodic Table of the Naturally Occurring Elements, as shown in Figure 9-7.

PERIODIC TABLE OF THE ELEMENTS

	1 IA	2 IIA	3 IIIB	4 IVB	5 VB	6 VIB	7 VIIB	8 VIIIB	9 VIIIB	10 VIIIB	11 IB	12 IIB	13 IIIA	14 IVA	15 VA	16 VIA	17 VIIA	18 VIIIA
1	1 H Hydrogen 1.00797																	2 He Helium 4.0026
2	3 Li Lithium 6.939	4 Be Beryllium 9.0122											5 B Boron 10.811	6 C Carbon 12.01115	7 N Nitrogen 14.0067	8 O Oxygen 15.9994	9 F Fluorine 18.9984	10 Ne Neon 20.183
3	11 Na Sodium 22.9898	12 Mg Magnesium 24.312											13 Al Aluminum 26.9815	14 Si Silicon 28.086	15 P Phosphorus 30.9738	16 S Sulfur 32.064	17 Cl Chlorine 35.453	18 Ar Argon 39.948
4	19 K Potassium 39.102	20 Ca Calcium 40.08	21 Sc Scandium 44.956	22 Ti Titanium 47.90	23 V Vanadium 50.942	24 Cr Chromium 51.996	25 Mn Manganese 54.9380	26 Fe Iron 55.847	27 Co Cobalt 58.9332	28 Ni Nickel 58.71	29 Cu Copper 63.546	30 Zn Zinc 65.37	31 Ga Gallium 69.72	32 Ge Germanium 72.59	33 As Arsenic 74.9216	34 Se Selenium 78.96	35 Br Bromine 79.904	36 Kr Krypton 83.80
5	37 Rb Rubidium 85.47	38 Sr Strontium 87.62	39 Y Yttrium 88.905	40 Zr Zirconium 91.22	41 Nb Niobium 92.906	42 Mo Molybdenum 95.94	43 Tc Technetium (99)	44 Ru Ruthenium 101.07	45 Rh Rhodium 102.905	46 Pd Palladium 106.4	47 Ag Silver 107.868	48 Cd Cadmium 112.40	49 In Indium 114.82	50 Sn Tin 118.69	51 Sb Antimony 121.75	52 Te Tellurium 127.60	53 I Iodine 126.9044	54 Xe Xenon 131.30
6	55 Cs Cesium 132.905	56 Ba Barium 137.34	57 La Lanthanum 138.91	72 Hf Hafnium 179.49	73 Ta Tantalum 180.948	74 W Tungsten 183.85	75 Re Rhenium 186.2	76 Os Osmium 190.2	77 Ir Iridium 192.2	78 Pt Platinum 195.09	79 Au Gold 196.967	80 Hg Mercury 200.59	81 Tl Thallium 204.37	82 Pb Lead 207.19	83 Bi Bismuth 208.980	84 Po Polonium (210)	85 At Astatine (210)	86 Rn Radon (222)
7	87 Fr Francium (223)	88 Ra Radium (226)	89 Ac Actinium (227)	104 Rf Rutherfordium (261)	105 Db Dubnium (262)	106 Sg Seaborgium (266)	107 Bh Bohrium (264)	108 Hs Hassium (269)	109 Mt Meitnerium (268)	110 Ds Darmstadtium (269)	111 Rg Roentgenium (272)	112 Uub Ununbium (277)	113 Uut §	114 Uuq Ununquadium (285)	115 Uup §	116 Uuh Ununhexium (289)	117 Uus §	118 Uuo Ununoctium (293)

Lanthanide Series	58 Ce Cerium 140.12	59 Pr Praseodymium 140.907	60 Nd Neodymium 144.24	61 Pm Promethium (145)	62 Sm Samarium 150.35	63 Eu Europium 151.96	64 Gd Gadolinium 157.25	65 Tb Terbium 158.924	66 Dy Dysprosium 162.50	67 Ho Holmium 164.930	68 Er Erbium 167.26	69 Tm Thulium 168.934	70 Yb Ytterbium 173.04	71 Lu Lutetium 174.97
Actinide Series	90 Th Thorium 232.038	91 Pa Protactinium (231)	92 U Uranium 238.03	93 Np Neptunium (237)	94 Pu Plutonium (242)	95 Am Americium (243)	96 Cm Curium (247)	97 Bk Berkelium (247)	98 Cf Californium (251)	99 Es Einsteinium (254)	100 Fm Fermium (257)	101 Md Mendelevium (258)	102 No Nobelium (259)	103 Lr Lawrencium (260)

§ Note: Elements 113, 115, and 117 are not known at this time but are included in the table to show their expected positions.

John Wiley & Sons, Inc.

Figure 9-7: The Periodic Table of the Naturally Occurring Elements.

The Periodic Table organizes the chemical elements in accordance with the following rules:

- *Periods* are the rows from left to right.
- Elements that share similar chemical and physical properties are grouped accordingly.
- The *atomic number* above each element's abbreviation represents the number of protons in the element; for example, hydrogen (H) has a single proton, whereas oxygen (O) has eight.
- The *atomic mass* is displayed below each element's abbreviation and is determined by the number of protons and neutrons the atom contains.

EXAMPLE

1. The number of protons in the nucleus of a calcium atom is ______.
2. The symbol for the element manganese is ______.

Check your answers:

1. A calcium atom has 20 protons, which is its atomic number as presented in the Periodic Table of the Elements.
2. The symbol for manganese is Mn.

Investigating molecules and compounds

When atoms bond to one another, they form *molecules* that share electrons, as shown in Figure 9-8. Because they share electrons, the bond is referred to as *covalent*. Many elements exist naturally in a molecular form, which is more stable than existing as separate atoms. The oxygen you breathe, for example, exists as O_2 — a molecule consisting of two oxygen molecules bonded covalently.

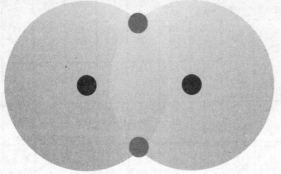

Figure 9-8:
A molecule consists of two or more chemically bonded atoms.

John Wiley & Sons, Inc.

Compounds are molecules that contain more than one type of element, such as water, H_2O, which contains two hydrogen molecules bonded to one oxygen molecule. A compound is commonly illustrated using a structural formula, such as the formula for H_2O shown in Figure 9-9. The dots above the O indicate that four electrons of the oxygen atom are unshared. In many cases, the dots aren't shown.

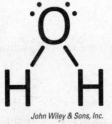

Figure 9-9:
Structural formulas for H_2O (water molecules).

John Wiley & Sons, Inc.

Compounds can also be created when atoms form *ionic bonds,* transferring electrons instead of sharing them. When one atom gives up an electron, it takes on a positive charge, and the atom that receives the electron takes on a negative charge. An *ion* is an atom or molecule that has a positive or negative charge because of its taking on or giving up an electron. For example, K^+ represents a positively charged potassium atom, an atom that has given up one of its electrons.

1. Sodium perborate ($NaBO_3$) contains which of the following?

    (A) one sodium atom and three boron atoms

    (B) one nitrogen atom, one bromine atom, and three oxygen atoms

    (C) one nitrogen atom, one barium atom, and three oxygen atoms

    (D) one sodium atom, one boron atom, and three oxygen atoms

2. When sodium chloride is dissolved in water, the sodium and chloride atoms ionize, forming Na^+ and Cl^-. What type of bond is at work in sodium chloride? ☐ bond

Check your answers:

1. Sodium perborate (solid bleach) contains one sodium atom (Na), one boron atom (B), and three oxygen atoms (O_3), Choice (D).

2. Because two ions are formed when sodium is dissolved in water, the type of bond that holds them together in table salt is an *ionic* bond.

Examining matter's characteristics

Every type of matter has certain characteristics that distinguish it from other types, including how hard it is, its melting and freezing points, how reactive it is with other types of matter, and so on. In this section, we explain the various characteristics of matter.

Physical properties

Physical properties of matter are those that can be observed and measured without changing the nature of the matter. These properties are categorized as intensive and extensive:

- ✔ **Intensive properties** are those that don't depend on the amount of matter, including color, odor, luster, malleability, ductility, conductivity, hardness, melting/freezing/boiling points (see the later section "Changes of state" for details), and density (mass per unit volume).

- ✔ **Extensive properties** depend on the amount of matter and include mass, weight, volume, and length.

Chemical properties

Chemical properties can be seen and measured only when matter undergoes a chemical change or reaction. Chemical properties include reactivity, toxicity, *flammability* (how easily a substance ignites), *heat of combustion* (the amount of energy released when a substance is burned in the presence of oxygen), and *half-life* (the amount of time for half of the original substance to decay).

Changes of state

Common physical properties that scientists often study and refer to are *changes of state*, when a substance changes from its solid to its liquid form or from its liquid to its gas form or vice versa. These changes of state occur at certain points relative to pressure and temperature. For example, water generally turns from a liquid into a solid (ice) at 0°C or 32°F and from water to gas (steam) at 100°C or 212°F. Changes in pressure affect the melting and (even more so) the boiling point of water.

Changes of state occur when energy is added or removed. Generally speaking, when energy is added to a substance, the motion of the molecules and the distance among molecules increases, and when energy is removed from a substance, the motion of the molecules and the distance among them decreases. We say "generally," mostly because water doesn't comply; when it changes from water to ice, the distance among molecules actually increases because of the way water molecules are structured when they crystallize. For most substances, the solid is denser (less volume) than the liquid form.

Scientists commonly use a *heating curve* to represent a substance's changes of state. Figure 9-10 shows the heating curve for water. Note that the curve flattens at the melting point of 0°C and boiling point of 100°C. At these points, energy is added without causing a rise in temperature because the energy is being used to fuel the change of state.

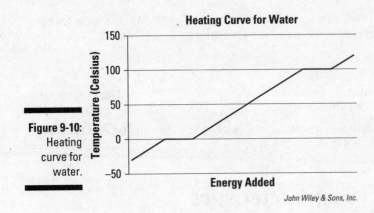

Figure 9-10:
Heating
curve for
water.

Changes of state occur in either direction. Adding heat, for example, changes water from a solid (ice) to a liquid (water) to a gas (steam). Removing heat changes water from a gas to a liquid through condensation and from a liquid to a solid through freezing.

Some substances change directly from a gas to a solid, skipping the liquid phase (a process referred to as *deposition*) and change directly from a solid to a gas *(sublimation)*. Solid carbon dioxide (dry ice), for example, passes from a solid into a gas.

1. Which of the following processes occurs when a solid turns directly into a gas?

   (A) melting

   (B) condensation

   (C) vaporization

   (D) sublimation

2. Which of the following most clearly describes the difference between boiling and evaporation?

   (A) There is no difference.

   (B) Boiling breaks the bonds between atoms, while evaporation does not.

   (C) When a liquid boils, its temperature remains constant, while evaporation may occur at different temperatures.

   (D) During evaporation, temperature remains constant, while boiling may occur at different temperatures.

Check your answers:

1. When a solid skips the liquid stage and turns directly into a gas, the process is called *sublimation,* Choice (D).

2. As shown in Figure 9-10, water boils at a constant temperature as it turns from a liquid into a gas, but the temperature of the steam (droplets of water) can continue to rise. Choice (C) is correct.

Brushing up on chemical equation basics

Certain molecules and compounds react with one another to form other molecules and compounds. For example, burning coal (carbon) in the presence of oxygen produces CO_2. Such reactions are often represented in the form of chemical equations, such as this:

$$C(s) + O_2(g) \rightarrow CO_2(g)$$

C represents carbon, O_2 is oxygen, and CO_2 is carbon dioxide. The (s) and (g) represent the states of the substances involved, (s) indicating solid and (g) indicating gas.

Two key (related) concepts to remember about chemical reactions and equations are these:

✔ According to the *law of conservation of mass,* in a closed system, mass (of matter and energy) can't be gained or lost.

✔ Chemical equations must be balanced. If you start with two atoms of oxygen on one side of the equation, you need to end with two atoms of oxygen on the other side of the equation. Bonds between atoms can be broken and formed to create new arrangements, but no existing atoms can be destroyed, and no new atoms can be created as a result of the reaction.

Chemical reactions are often classified by the type of reaction:

✔ **Combination:** Two or more reactants form one product, which is always a compound.

✔ **Combustion:** Commonly referred to as *burning,* this is when one compound combines with another to form one or more compounds and release heat.

✔ **Decomposition:** A compound breaks down into two or more compounds (the opposite of a combination reaction).

✔ **Double displacement:** Two more reactive elements replace two less reactive elements.

✔ **Redox:** Short for *reduction-oxidation,* a reaction in which electrons are exchanged.

✔ **Single displacement:** A more reactive element replaces a less reactive element. For example, if you add zinc metal to a copper sulfate solution, the zinc replaces the copper.

You also need to be aware of the concepts of limiting and excess reactants:

✔ **Limiting reactant:** A reactant that's present in an insufficient quantity to use up all the other reactants.

✔ **Excess reactant:** A reactant that's left over after all the other reactants are consumed.

1. Which of the following chemical equations is incorrect?

(A) $C + O_2 \rightarrow CO_2$

(B) $4\,FeS + 7\,O_2 \rightarrow 2\,Fe_2O_3 + 4\,SO_2$

(C) $C_2H_4O + 3\,O_2 \rightarrow 2\,CO_2 + 3\,H_2O$

(D) $TiCl_4 + 2\,H_2O \rightarrow TiO_2 + 4\,HCl$

2. Which of the following categories best describes the chemical reaction $C(s) + O_2(g) \rightarrow CO_2(g)$?

(A) decomposition

(B) combustion

(C) single displacement

(D) redox

Check your answers:

1. In the equation shown for Choice (C), four hydrogen atoms are on the left side of the equation, but six hydrogen atoms are shown on the right, breaking the balanced chemical equations rule.

2. Early in this section, $C(s) + O_2(g) \rightarrow CO_2(g)$ was presented as the chemical equation for the burning of coal, which makes it a combustion reaction, Choice (B).

Looking at chemicals in solution

When a chemical is dissolved in another substance, a *solution* (homogenous mixture) is formed with properties that differ from those of either substance — the *solute* (the dissolved substance) or the *solvent* (the substance into which the solute is dissolved). For example, if you dissolve salt in water, the salt is the solute, and the water is the solvent. The properties of the saltwater differ from those of plain water and of salt. The freezing point of the saltwater, for example, is lower than that of plain water.

A solution differs from a mixture. In a mixture, each substance retains its physical and chemical properties.

When you encounter solution questions on the test, keep the following terminology in mind:

✓ **Concentration:** The more solute you add to a solution, the more concentrated it becomes, until the point at which no more of the solute will dissolve in the solvent.

✓ **Dilution:** The more solvent you add to a solution, the more diluted (less concentrated) it becomes.

✓ **Saturation:** The point at which no more solute will dissolve in the solution is the *saturation point.*

Solutes differ in how they behave in a solution. When you dissolve sugar in water, for example, the sugar molecules retain their molecular structure. On the other hand, when you dissolve salt (sodium chloride or NaCl) in water, the ionic bonds that hold the sodium and chloride atoms together are broken, forming sodium and chloride ions (Na^+ and Cl^-).

1. You mix up a batch of lemonade from scratch, and no matter how long and fast you stir it, you can't get the sugar crystals at the bottom to dissolve. Which of the following most accurately describes the concentration of this solution?

(A) concentrated

(B) diluted

(C) ionized

(D) saturated

2. Randy reasons that if a 50/50 mixture of coolant and water will protect his car from freezing temperatures, using pure coolant would be even better.

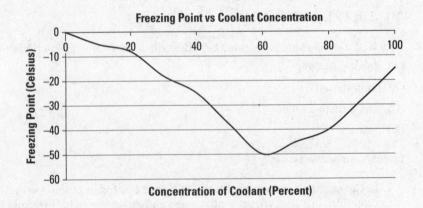

Based on the graph shown here and what you just read, what conclusion can be drawn about Randy's logic?

(A) He is correct. Using 100 percent coolant would provide superior protection from freezing temperatures.

(B) He is wrong because the freezing point of the solution of water and coolant is lower than the freezing point of coolant alone.

(C) He is wrong because water has a lower freezing point than does coolant.

(D) He is correct because coolant has a lower freezing point than does water.

Check your answers:

1. If excess solute does not dissolve in the solvent, the solution is saturated, Choice (D).

2. Randy is wrong because, as the graph shows, a solution of 60 percent coolant and 40 percent water has the lowest freezing point. Choice (B) is the correct answer.

Chapter 10

Cosmic, Dude! Investigating Earth and Space Science

- -

In This Chapter

▶ Getting to know Earth's parts

▶ Touring Earth's systems and how they interact

▶ Stargazing: Turning your eyes to the cosmos

- -

*T*he folks who develop the GED Science test expect you to have a general understanding of the universe in which you live and the planet Earth you call home. You're not required to have in-depth knowledge of astronomy or a mastery of meteorology or other earth sciences, but knowing that you live in a universe and, more specifically, in a particular solar system and on the planet Earth, along with some additional details, gives you the contextual framework required to understand reading passages and answer questions.

An understanding of basic earth science and astronomy concepts also helps, including knowledge of the Big Bang theory, continental drift, the water cycle, atmospheric conditions that drive the weather patterns, forces that control the ocean tides, renewable and nonrenewable natural resources, and so on.

In this chapter, we provide the contextual framework required to read and comprehend earth science and astronomy reading passages and questions. Along the way, we present questions similar to those you're likely to encounter on the test, so you gain experience tackling such questions.

Exploring Earth's Systems and the Ways They Interact

If you ever start to think that there's nothing to do on a Saturday night, realize that a whole lot of activity is going on all around you and around the planet Earth that you may not even be aware of. Tectonic plates are shifting, vast amounts of water are being transported above and below you, the atmosphere is in constant motion and transformation, and life is plentiful both inside your body and all around you as the great cycle of life marches on. All these activities can be attributed to the four earth science systems:

✔ **Atmosphere:** Various layers of gas that contain the air you breathe, protection from the sun, and insulation to prevent heat from escaping

✔ **Biosphere:** All life forms

✔ **Geosphere:** Earth's core, mantle, and crust

✔ **Hydrosphere:** Water in all its forms

You can also look at these systems as air (atmosphere), land (geosphere), water (hydrosphere), and life (biosphere).

In this section, we explore the four earth science systems and then look at a few ways these systems interact.

Digging down into Earth's layers and landforms

Earth's layers and landforms are the earthy parts of Earth — everything that's not water, air, or a living thing. Begin your exploration of Earth's layers and landforms by taking a look at the big picture. The planet Earth comprises the following three layers:

- **Core:** At the center of the Earth is a very hot, dense core thought to be made mainly of a metal alloy (mixture) of nickel and iron. The core contains most of Earth's mass and is its primary source of internal heat, emitting heat as radioactive materials within the core decompose into more stable elements. The core is subdivided into two layers:

  - **Inner core:** The inner core is solid because of the pressure exerted by the other layers and the force of gravity, which compacts the atoms so tight that they can't pass into a liquid state. (See Chapter 9 for more about the different states of matter.)

  - **Outer core:** The outer core is liquid because of the intense heat at the center of the Earth. The pressure in the outer core isn't sufficient to prevent the hot metal from turning to liquid.

- **Mantle:** The mantle that surrounds the core is estimated to be approximately 2,000 miles (3,000 kilometers) thick and is made of two layers of rock:

  - **Upper mantle:** The upper mantle is made of cooler, brittle rock that can break when subjected to stress. The breaking and shifting of this rock is responsible for earthquakes.

  - **Lower mantle:** Hot, soft rock composes the lower mantle. This rock flows when subjected to stress.

  Activity in the mantle is responsible for creating mountains and producing earthquakes and volcanoes.

- **Crust:** The crust is the very thin layer that surrounds the Earth, and it differs depending on its location:

  - **Oceanic crust:** The crust below the oceans is relatively thin (3 to 4 miles) and is composed mainly of *basalt* (a low-density rock).

  - **Continental crust:** The crust beneath the continents is approximately 20 to 30 miles thick and is composed primarily of *granite* (a relatively high-density rock).

The crust and the upper mantle form the *lithosphere,* a layer of brittle rock that floats atop the lower mantle. The lithosphere is broken up into several major and many minor *tectonic plates* that move, causing many of the geological events that can be observed on Earth's surface. *Plate tectonics* is the scientific theory that explains the movements of tectonic plates and the various geological events that occur as a result. Plate tectonics is responsible for the following:

- **Continental movement:** The various continents on Earth (Africa, Antarctica, Asia, Australia, Europe, North America, and South America) were thought to be one super-continent commonly referred to as *Pangea.* As soft rock oozes up from the lower mantle, it pushes apart the plates on which the continents rest, causing them to "drift" apart over long periods of time. (The early theory was referred to as *continental drift.*)

✔ **Earthquakes:** Moving tectonic plates cause earthquakes as they drift apart, press against each other, or the edge of one plate slides below another.

✔ **Mountains:** As plates push into each other, the rock has nowhere to go but up, creating mountains.

✔ **Tsunamis:** When the edge of one tectonic plate slips beneath the edge of another at the bottom of the ocean, massive amounts of water are displaced, forming a wave that can be very destructive when it washes up on land.

✔ **Volcanoes:** Molten rock flows up between plates to create volcanoes. When the heat and pressure reach a certain point, the volcano erupts, sending rock and ash into the atmosphere and creating lava (molten rock) flows. The heat from a volcano may also melt snow and ice, creating mud flows.

Figure 10-1 shows the three types of tectonic plate boundaries:

✔ **Convergent:** When two tectonic plates move toward or against each other, they form a convergent boundary characterized by mountain ranges, ocean trenches, volcanoes, and earthquakes. If the edge of one plate slips beneath the edge of another, the lower plate is referred to as a *subducting plate,* which is typically responsible for creating ocean trenches. When the edge of the subducting plate reaches a certain depth, it is absorbed back into the lower mantle.

✔ **Divergent:** When two tectonic plates move away from each other, a divergent boundary is formed characterized by frequent earthquakes, lava flows, and *geysers* (a gushing column of superheated water and steam). Under all this, a layer of molten rock flows slowly into the gap and hardens to form solid rock.

✔ **Transform:** Two plates sliding past each other form a transform plate boundary. Natural or human-made structures that straddle such a boundary can be split into pieces and carried in opposite directions. At these boundaries, rocks are pulverized as the plates grind along, creating a linear fault valley or undersea canyon. As the plates alternately jam and jump against each other, earthquakes rattle through a wide boundary zone. In contrast to convergent and divergent boundaries, no magma is formed. Thus, crust is cracked and broken at transform margins, but isn't created or destroyed.

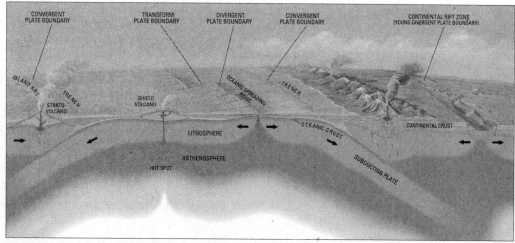

Figure 10-1:
Tectonic
plate
boundaries.

1. What are the three layers of Earth's geosphere?

    (A) inner core, middle core, outer core

    (B) core, mantle, lithosphere

    (C) core, mantle, crust

    (D) core, mantle, tectonic plates

2. Plate tectonics help scientists explain which of the following?

    (A) continental movement

    (B) what causes volcanoes and tsunamis

    (C) how mountains are formed

    (D) all of the above

3. Which type of plate boundary is most likely responsible for the movement of continents away from each other?

    (A) divergent

    (B) convergent

    (C) transform

    (D) subducting

4. The crust is part of which of the following?

    (A) the upper mantle

    (B) the lower mantle

    (C) the lithosphere

    (D) the atmosphere

5. Which of the following is *not* a characteristic of a subduction zone?

    (A) The leading edge of one plate is bent downward.

    (B) The leading edge of the subducting plate is absorbed into the lower mantle.

    (C) The leading edge of one plate slides over another plate.

    (D) The leading edges of two plates are bent upward.

    Now check your answers:

    1. The three layers that compose Earth's geosphere are the core, mantle, and crust, Choice (C).

    2. Plate tectonics help scientists explain continental movement along with the formation of mountains, volcanoes, and tsunamis, Choice (D), all of the above.

    3. A divergent plate boundary, Choice (A), would be most responsible for causing continents to drift apart.

    4. The crust is part of the lithosphere, Choice (C). The other part of the lithosphere is the upper mantle.

    5. In a subduction zone, the leading edge of one plate slides below the edge of another plate, so both can't possibly bend upward. Choice (C) is the correct answer.

Soaring through Earth's atmosphere

Earth's atmosphere is composed of gases surrounding the planet and retained by Earth's gravity. Although the composition of gases in Earth's atmosphere is subject to change, the current mix is about 78 percent nitrogen, 21 percent oxygen, 0.9 percent argon, 0.03 percent carbon dioxide, 0.0 to 0.4 percent water vapor, and trace amounts of other gases.

In addition to providing the oxygen that humans and other animals breathe and the carbon dioxide that plants require for photosynthesis, the atmosphere protects plants and animals by screening out a considerable amount of ultraviolet radiation, retaining heat from the sun, reducing temperature extremes, and facilitating the transportation of water via clouds.

Like the geosphere, Earth's atmosphere has several layers: five to be exact, as shown in Figure 10-2. The following list names and describes all five atmospheric layers from the ground up:

✔ **Troposphere:** This is where you live and breathe. The troposphere begins at the Earth's surface and extends up to the stratosphere. It contains roughly 80 percent of the mass of the entire atmosphere and is where most familiar weather patterns form.

✔ **Stratosphere:** The stratosphere is best known for the company it keeps. This is where the ozone layer hangs out. The ozone layer is comprised of *triatomic oxygen* (O_3), meaning each molecule consists of three oxygen atoms instead of the standard two in the normal *diatomic oxygen* (O_2) that you breathe. The ozone layer is great for blocking ultraviolet radiation from space, but this form of oxygen is toxic closer to the Earth's surface as it is harmful to breathe and can burn plants. In the stratosphere, temperature increases the higher you fly.

✔ **Mesosphere:** This extends up from the stratosphere, and the temperature decreases as altitude increases. Most meteors burn up in the mesosphere before they have a chance to crash into the Earth because the density of the atmosphere rises considerably closer to the Earth's surface.

✔ **Thermosphere:** This layer is toasty — up to 1200°C. It has a higher temperature at higher altitudes, but due to the lower pressure and the fact that molecules are so far apart, the "air" doesn't feel as hot as it would at lower altitudes.

✔ **Exosphere:** This far-out layer contains mostly hydrogen and helium atoms — not somewhere you'd want to spend a lot of time.

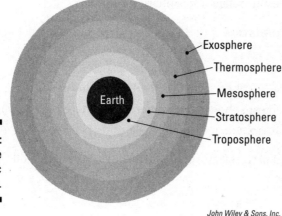

Figure 10-2:
Earth's five atmospheric layers.

Exosphere
Thermosphere
Mesosphere
Stratosphere
Troposphere

John Wiley & Sons, Inc.

Weather events occur in the troposphere and are typically triggered by *fronts* — the leading edges of air masses that differ in temperature and pressure. To understand the weather, you need to understand the four types of fronts:

- **Cold front:** Cold fronts occur where colder, denser air pushes under warmer, thinner air. Cold fronts travel faster than warm fronts and usually form more violent storm conditions and higher amounts of precipitation.

- **Warm front:** Warm fronts occur where warmer air forms a wedge over the colder air and slowly advances, pushing the cold air out. Warm fronts sometimes have thunderstorms on their leading edge, but more often form fog.

- **Stationary front:** When fronts stop moving, they're said to be stationary, and you experience little if any change in the weather until another front pushes it out of the way.

- **Occluded front:** Occluded fronts form when cooler or warmer air is behind the front. When cooler air is behind the front, the cooler air moves under the cool air ahead of it, and the occluded front behaves very similar to a cold front. When warmer air is behind the front, the warmer air rises above the air that's in front of it, and the occluded front acts very much like a warm front. In both cases, the boundaries between the warmer and cooler air are well-defined.

Hurricanes, tornadoes, and other violent storms usually form when a cold air mass is above a warm water or land mass. This causes violently convective (air-moving) conditions that lead to violent storms. A front or a consistent wind generally triggers the spinning effects, but the true nature of how these storms are formed is still somewhat of a mystery.

You can tell a lot about the weather by examining cloud formations. The following list explains the differences among the three types of cloud formations.

- **Cirriform:** *Cirrus* clouds are generally detached and wispy. They fly high and are generally non-convective, meaning they form when air movement due to temperature differences at different altitudes is minimal. Because of this, cirrus clouds are a sign of less turbulent weather conditions.

- **Cumuliform:** *Cumulus* clouds are mostly detached and fluffy. They are a product of local convective lift and indicate a more turbulent condition in the atmosphere.

- **Stratiform:** *Stratus* clouds are for the most part continuous and may have somewhat rippled form, sort of like a blanket. These clouds usually form on slow-moving fronts with high levels of convective lift and float a bit lower in the sky than their cumulus cousins. The convection is across a much larger area than the conditions that form cumulus clouds and indicates turbulent atmospheric conditions.

1. Which of the following presents the layers of Earth's atmosphere in the correct order from the ground up?

    (A) stratosphere, troposphere, mesosphere, thermosphere, exosphere

    (B) troposphere, stratosphere, mesosphere, thermosphere, exosphere

    (C) troposphere, thermosphere, mesosphere, stratosphere, exosphere

    (D) exosphere, troposphere, stratosphere, mesosphere, thermosphere

2. The ozone layer, which is located in the stratosphere, provides which of the following?

    (A) the oxygen you breathe

    (B) the nitrogen you breathe

    (C) protection against ultraviolet radiation

    (D) matter required for cloud formations

3. Which of the following conditions is most likely to cause a violent storm?

   (A) A colder, heavier air mass pushes under a warmer, lighter air mass.

   (B) A cold front meets a warm front.

   (C) An occluded front meets a warm front.

   (D) A mass of cold air moves in above a mass of warm, humid air.

4. Which atmospheric layer has the highest concentration of gases?

   (A) troposphere

   (B) stratosphere

   (C) mesosphere

   (D) thermosphere

Check your answers:

1. Choice (B): troposphere, stratosphere, mesosphere, thermosphere, exosphere.

2. The ozone layer protects against ultraviolet radiation, Choice (C).

3. Choice (D): When colder air is above warmer air, the warm air rises as the cold air sinks, often triggering violent storms.

4. The troposphere contains approximately 80 percent of the atmosphere's mass, so Choice (A) is the correct answer. It makes sense because gravity is stronger the nearer you get to the center of the Earth.

Swimming in Earth's hydrosphere

Earth's *hydrosphere* consists of all its water in every form — ice, snow, water, and water vapor. It includes surface water (oceans, lakes, rivers, streams, and puddles), water in and below the ground (groundwater, wells, and aquifers), and water in the air (clouds, rain, snow, and fog).

The movement of water is referred to as the *water cycle,* a continuous process in which water *evaporates* from the Earth's surface, *condenses* to form clouds, and falls back to Earth in some form of *precipitation* (see Figure 10-3). The water cycle also involves the movement of water in the form of rivers, streams, and ocean currents.

Note these important distinctions in water cycle lingo:

- **Condensation:** The process of changing from a vapor or gas into a liquid.

- **Evaporation:** The process of changing from a liquid into a vapor or gas.

- **Precipitation:** The product of condensation, which is released from clouds in the form of rain, snow, sleet, or hail.

- **Transpiration:** The transportation of water through plants from roots to small pores on leaves, where the water is converted to vapor.

Various natural forces power the water cycle, including the following:

- **Chemical properties of water:** Differences in water densities due to temperature and salinity contribute to the formation of ocean currents. For example, colder, saltier water is denser than warmer, fresh water, causing it to sink, producing currents.

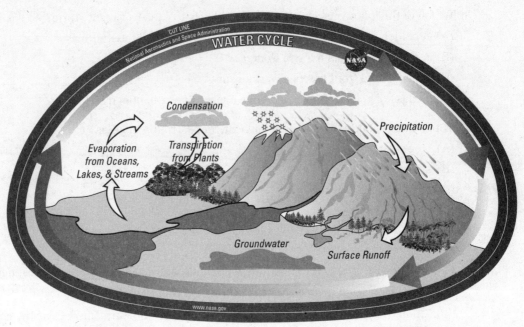

Figure 10-3:
The water
cycle.

✔ **Earth's rotation:** As the Earth spins on its axis, it deflects winds and currents, a phenomenon called the *Coriolis effect*. Earth's rotation combined with air and water movements cause a circular, spinning motion. North of the equator, storms tend to rotate clockwise. South of the equator, they tend to spin counterclockwise.

✔ **Earthquakes:** Earthquakes can displace vast amounts of water.

✔ **Gravity:** Gravitational fields surrounding the Earth and moon interact to cause currents to rise and fall, and the gravity on Earth causes water to flow in rivers and streams, which contributes to water movement in the bodies of water those rivers and streams empty into.

✔ **Sun:** Energy from the sun causes water to evaporate and provides fuel for plants to perform photosynthesis, which is responsible for transpiration.

✔ **Wind:** Wind moves the clouds that transport water through the sky, creates surface waves, contributes to the formation of ocean currents, and facilitates evaporation by moving drier air over water.

1. Which of the following is the best example of precipitation?

    (A) clouds

    (B) fog

    (C) dew

    (D) snow

2. Which of the following is the best example of condensation?

    (A) rain

    (B) fog

    (C) dew

    (D) sleet

3. Through which of the following processes does the water cycle remove salt from ocean water?

    (A) evaporation

    (B) condensation

    (C) transpiration

    (D) perspiration

4. Which of the following does *not* power the water cycle?

    (A) sun

    (B) moon

    (C) rocks

    (D) gravity

Check your answers:

1. Precipitation is water falling from the sky in liquid or solid form, so Choice (D) is the only correct answer.

2. Condensation is the product of vapor turning to water, which occurs when dew is formed, Choice (C).

3. When water evaporates, Choice (A), from the ocean's surface, the salt is left behind.

4. The sun, moon, and gravity power the water cycle. Rocks, Choice (C), do not.

Living it up as part of Earth's biosphere

Earth's *biosphere* is the total collection of all Earth's living and formerly living things organized into the following *biomes* (large communities of flora and fauna that occupy a major habitat):

- **Aquatic:** Covering approximately 71 percent of the Earth's surface, aquatic environments support a wide variety of plants, animals, and other living things. This biome is often broken down into freshwater and marine (saltwater):

    - **Freshwater:** Freshwater regions include ponds, lakes, rivers, streams, and wetlands (swamps).

    - **Marine:** Marine regions include oceans, coral reefs, and *estuaries* (where freshwater from rivers and streams mixes with ocean water).

- **Desert:** Covering about 10 percent of the Earth's surface or about 33 percent of the Earth's landmass, deserts support highly specialized plants and animals that require very little water to survive. Relatively few large animals call the desert home. Reptiles and small rodents adapt best to the typically hot/dry climate.

- **Forests:** Forests cover approximately 30 percent of the Earth's landmass and contain approximately 70 percent of the carbon present in living things. The forest biome is populated primarily by trees and other woody plants and a wide variety of animals and other living creatures. This biome can be divided into the following subcategories:

    - **Boreal forest:** Representing the largest land-based biome, boreal forests exist in a relatively broad band in the northern latitudes, extending through North America, Eurasia, Siberia, Scandinavia, Alaska, and Canada. Summers are typically warm, moist, and relatively short, and winters are long, cold, and dry.

- **Temperate deciduous forest:** These forests can be found in eastern North America, northeast Asia, and western and central Europe, where a moderate climate and a long growing season are common.

- **Tropical rain forest:** Tropical rain forests can be found around the equator, where the weather is warm year-round and seasons are distinguished as rainy or dry. The diversity of species, both plant and animal, is very high.

✔ **Grasslands:** Grasslands are open plains where various types of grasses, rather than shrubs and trees, dominate the landscape, and populations of large animals often graze. Alternating periods of rainfall and drought, grazing animals, and occasional fires are necessary to prevent the grassland from becoming a heavily wooded forest. The grassland biome is often categorized into the following two subtypes:

  - **Savanna:** Savannas are characterized by grassland with scattered trees and are typically located in areas with warm, hot climates and limited rainfall (over 50 centimeters but less than about 130 centimeters annually) concentrated in a six- to eight-month period.

  - **Temperate grassland:** Temperate grasslands have no trees or shrubs, a greater variation in temperature than do savannas, and less rainfall. Prairies are a type of temperate grassland characterized by tall grasses.

✔ **Tundra:** Tundra is flat, cold, dry, and treeless, with subsoil that's permanently frozen. Most of the nutrients are dead organic matter, and the growing season is very short, so biodiversity is low.

Ecology is a branch of biology that studies the relationships of organisms to one another and what's around them, including land and water. Ecology also has political relevance as a movement to preserve and protect the environment and the many biomes on the planet. Human activities have shrunk certain biomes, including rain forests, and turned fertile land to desert (a process called *desertification*), reducing the diversity of species on the planet. Ecology seeks to preserve and restore a more natural balance.

1. The thorny devil is a lizard that has horny scales on its back that collect dew and channel it down to the lizard's mouth. This adaptation is most likely due to the fact that the lizard resides in which of the following environments?

   (A) savanna

   (B) desert

   (C) tundra

   (D) forest

2. Bull sharks can adapt their osmoregulatory processes to survive in both freshwater and ocean water, which helps to explain which of the following?

   (A) Bull sharks are responsible for only a small number of shark attacks in the oceans.

   (B) White sharks are responsible for more attacks and human fatalities.

   (C) Bull sharks commonly attack other sharks.

   (D) Bull shark attacks are common in rivers.

3. Contrary to popular scientific opinion, a leading ecologist discovered that it was not over-grazing that turned grasslands into desert but lack of grazing. He has successfully restored desert lands to grasslands by bringing in large herds of animals to graze in ways that mimic the behaviors of large herds of animals that previously roamed the grasslands. Which of the following most likely explains why grazing is effective in restoring grasslands?

   (A) Grazing animals return nutrients to the soil.

   (B) Grazing animals compress the soil, so less water penetrates it.

(C) With less grass, more sun can reach the soil to promote seeds to germinate.

(D) Grazing animals reduce the population of weeds that compete with grasses for nutrients.

4. The biosphere consists of which of the following?

(A) all living creatures

(B) all living creatures and the environment in which they live

(C) all creatures living and formerly living and the environment in which they live

(D) large communities of flora and fauna

Check your answers:

1. The thorny devil is well adapted to living in the desert, Choice (B), where water is scarce.

2. If a bull shark can survive in both ocean water and freshwater, that would explain the bull shark attacks that occur in rivers (freshwater), Choice (D).

3. Grazing animals digest food and in the process break it down into waste products that can be further broken down into nutrients to help grow grasses, so Choice (A) is correct. Choice (D) would be a good second choice, but nothing supports the notion that grazing animals would choose to eat weeds instead of grasses.

4. The biosphere contains all creatures both living and dead and their environment, Choice (C). The other choices limit the biosphere to living creatures.

Seeing how Earth's systems interact

Earth's systems operate in concert, not as isolated entities. When a major event occurs in any of Earth's systems, other systems are often affected. In this section, we explore several ways that Earth's systems interact. These are only a few examples of the numerous interactions that can occur.

Chipping away at rocks

Earth has some awesome examples of how Earth systems interact. One example is the erosion of rock by wind or water. Holding a rock, you may consider it indestructible, but over a long period of time, wind, rain, and rivers can erode rocks into dust. For example, the Colorado River, which runs through the Grand Canyon, has been eroding the canyon for millions of years. It is now approximately 1,800 meters deep and 29 kilometers across, at its widest point.

The erosion of the Grand Canyon is an example of an interaction primarily between which two Earth systems?

(A) atmosphere and geosphere

(B) hydrosphere and atmosphere

(C) atmosphere and biosphere

(D) hydrosphere and geosphere

The Colorado River, part of the hydrosphere, has been eroding the canyon, part of the geosphere, for millions of years. Choice (D) is correct. Choice (A) would be a good second choice because wind probably contributes to the erosion. However, the question uses the word "primarily."

Looking at the fallout from a volcanic eruption

When a volcano erupts in the geosphere, all other systems are affected, including the geosphere itself:

- ✔ **Atmosphere:** Volcanic ash is blown miles high, blocking the sun and increasing cloud formation. The eruption also releases large amounts of carbon dioxide into the atmosphere.

- ✔ **Biosphere:** Ash falls from the sky, covering plants and often crushing or smothering them. Creatures on or below the ground may also be killed, harmed, or displaced. Molten lava flowing from the volcano may also burn and destroy plants and animals. Over time, the ash and lava enrich the soil and stimulate plant growth that supports other living creatures. The carbon dioxide released also helps to fuel plant growth.

- ✔ **Geosphere:** Falling ash and flowing lava add to the Earth's crust. Stimulated plant growth also adds to the planet's biomass, which, over a very long period of time and under the right conditions, can form future coal, oil, and natural gas supplies.

- ✔ **Hydrosphere:** Heat from the volcano may melt the snow and ice around the volcano, triggering floods and mud flows. Precipitation often increases after a volcanic eruption, as well.

Considering the ramifications of disappearing coral reefs

Coral reefs are formed by tiny animals called *polyps* that build large, complex living quarters out of calcium carbonate. Ecologists study and seek to preserve coral reefs for a number of reasons. The threat to coral reefs provides a good example of how Earth's systems interact.

> *Read the following excerpt from "Coral Reefs"* (`water.epa.gov/type/oceb/habitat/factsheet.cfm`) *and write a short response to the prompt that follows it, citing evidence in the passage to support your claims. Write your response on a separate sheet of paper. This item should take you approximately 10 minutes to complete. Remember, this is not timed separately; it is part of the 90 minutes you have to complete the test.*

What Is a Coral Reef?

Coral reefs are colonies of various types of reef-building stony hard corals. Each coral colony is composed of tiny animals, also known as polyps. Polyps stay fixed in one place to create a colony that provides a home to symbiotic algae.

Each polyp slowly secretes a hard calcium carbonate skeleton, which serves as the base or substrate for the colony. The living animal or polyp attaches itself to the skeletal base that it creates. The skeleton provides protection for the polyps and algae as predators approach.

Calcium carbonate is continuously deposited by the corals in the living colony, adding to the size and structure of the reef. It is these slow-growing hard skeletal structures that build up coral reefs over long periods of time.

Why Are Coral Reefs Important?

Coral reefs provide a source of food and shelter for a large variety of species including fish, shellfish, fungi, sponges, sea anemones, sea urchins, sea snakes, sea stars, worms, jellyfish, turtles, and snails.

Coral reefs protect coastlines from ocean storms and floods.

Coral reefs are environmental indicators of water quality because they can only tolerate narrow ranges of temperature, salinity, water clarity, and other water conditions.

Coral reefs make important contributions to local economies because they attract millions of tourists every year to enjoy beaches, water sports, and other activities.

Coral reefs are important sources of new medicines that can be used to treat diseases and other health problems.

What Is Affecting the Health of Coral Reefs?

Humans contribute to the deterioration of coral reefs through physical damage caused by boats and recreational contact, and through runoff of sediments, contaminants, and nutrients from agriculture, industry, sewage, and land clearing in the watershed.

Coral bleaching slows the growth and reproduction of corals. Bleaching occurs when environmental conditions no longer support the symbiotic relationship with photosynthetic algae, or zooxanthellae, found in coral polyps. When the colored algae leave the coral, the coral loses its color (bleaches) and its source of food.

Over the last three decades, several new coral diseases have caused widespread mortalities. The responsible agents are known in only a few cases, and some diseases may be caused by multiple organisms. Poor water quality, increased pollution, and elevated water temperatures increase the likelihood of coral disease.

How does the issue of protecting and preserving coral reefs illustrate the interaction of Earth's systems?

Write a short response to the prompt citing at least four pieces of evidence in the passage to support your claims.

Considering human-Earth system interactions

Human beings are also impacted by Earth systems and can impact those systems in both positive and negative ways, as we explain in this section.

Preventing and mitigating the effects of natural hazards

Natural hazards are any dangers posed by Earth system events, including the following, grouped by Earth system:

Atmospheric

Hailstorms

Hurricanes

Lightning

Tornadoes

Tropical storms

Biospheric

Crop failure

Wildfires

Plagues

Geospheric

Avalanches

Earthquakes

Landslides

Lava flows

Tsunamis

Volcanic eruptions

Hydrologic

Desertification

Drought

Erosion

Floods

Landslides

People have developed various scales to measure the intensity or magnitude of certain Earth system events, including the following:

- ✔ **The Fujita scale** classifies tornadoes on a scale of F0 to F5 based on wind speed and expected damage, as in this table:

Damage (f scale)	Little Damage	Minor Damage	Roof Gone	Walls Collapse	Blown Down	Blown Away
	f0	f1	f2	f3	f4	f5
Wind Speed (F scale)	40–73 mph	74–113 mph	114–158 mph	159–207 mph	208–261 mph	262–319 mph
	F0	F1	F2	F3	F4	F5

- ✔ **The Modified Mercalli scale** measures the intensity of an earthquake on a scale from I to XII.

- ✔ **The Richter scale** measures the magnitude or amount of energy released by an earthquake on a scale of 1 to 10. To date, the highest level recorded has been 9.

- ✔ **The Saffir-Simpson scale** classifies hurricanes by wind speed: Category 1 (119–153 km/h), Category 2 (154–177 km/h), Category 3 (178–209 km/h), Category 4 (210–249 km/h), Category 5 (250 km/h or higher).

Although Earth usually wins most head-to-head battles with humans, humans may be able to protect themselves from some potentially hazardous Earth system events. Here are a few examples of how human behavior has evolved or can evolve to avoid and mitigate potential threats.

- ✔ Restricting building on coastlines in certain areas to prevent damage and casualties from hurricanes and coastal flooding.

- ✔ Building and using storm shelters to prevent human casualties in the event of storms, tornadoes, and hurricanes.

- ✔ Designing and erecting buildings that are less susceptible to earthquake damage.

- ✔ Prohibiting the building of homes and businesses in flood zones.

✔ Building dikes in low-lying coastal areas to prevent coastal flooding.

✔ Reducing emissions from carbon-based fuels to lessen the severity and frequency of violent weather events.

✔ Performing controlled burns to prevent massive forest fires.

✔ Improving sanitation to prevent infection from bacteria, viruses, and parasites.

1. Deforestation is likely to increase the risk of which one of the following Earth system events?

   (A) hurricanes

   (B) tornadoes

   (C) earthquakes

   (D) landslides

2. A city is building a system to drain water from streets into a nearby stream. Upon completing the project, the city planners will have succeeded in raising the risk of ⬚.

3. To more accurately estimate the amount of damage from tornadoes, the modified Fujita scale accounts for building strength and looks like this. What F rating would you expect a strong frame house to withstand damage from a tornado? Use information from this and the previous table to reach an answer.

Building Type	Add to Convert f to F Scale	Rating	Rating	Rating	Rating	Rating	Rating
Weak outbuilding	−3	f3	f4	f5	f5	f5	f5
Strong outbuilding	−2	f2	f3	f4	f5	f5	f5
Weak frame house	−1	f1	f2	f3	f4	f5	f5
Strong frame house	0	F0	F1	F2	F3	F4	F5
Brick structure	+1	–	f0	f1	f2	f3	f4
Concrete building	+2	–	–	f0	f1	f2	f3

4. What sort of damage would you expect from a category F2 tornado striking a weak frame house?

   (A) roof gone and other minor damage

   (B) roof gone and walls collapsed

   (C) blown down

   (D) blown away

Check your answers:

1. Removing trees increases the likelihood of a landslide, Choice (D), because trees stabilize the ground they are grown in.

2. By directing water into a nearby stream, the city planners have increased the risk of flooding. (If you entered "flood(s)" or "flooding," count your answer correct.)

3. On the original Fujita scale, a damage rating of f5 is assigned to "blown away." Find "strong outbuilding" on the modified Fujita scale to see that you must add: −2 to the "f" rating to convert it to the "F" rating, which represents wind speed, so $f5 - 2 = F3$. Correct answer: F3.

4. At the top of the second column of the modified Fujita scale, you're instructed to add the number in that column that corresponds to the building type to the "f" rating to convert it to the "F" rating. For a weak frame house, $f3 - 1 = F2$, meaning an F2 tornado would cause an f3 level of damage to a weak frame house. According to the original Fujita scale, f3 damage is roof gone and walls collapsed, Choice (B).

Using natural resources wisely

Seven billion and growing, the human population places a significant strain on Earth's resources — not only oil and gas, which make the headlines, but each and every Earth system. Pollution threatens the atmosphere, hydrosphere, geosphere, and biosphere. Poor farming practices deplete nutrients from the soil and promote soil erosion and compaction. Increased use of fossil fuels depletes supplies for future generations while polluting the atmosphere and contributing to global warming. Overfishing, overhunting, and poaching reduce populations of certain creatures, disrupt food chains, and often lead to extinction, reducing biodiversity.

Humans have begun to realize that their survival hinges on the health of all Earth's systems and they must take steps toward *sustainability* — using natural resources in a way that promotes diversity and production in all Earth's systems. In a practical sense, sustainability can be achieved in a wide variety of areas, including the following:

- ✔ *Sustainable agriculture* means growing food using farming techniques that promote healthy soil and protect the environment, public health, human communities, and animal welfare.

- ✔ *Green building* is the practice of creating and using healthier and more resource-efficient construction, renovation, operation, maintenance, and demolition.

- ✔ *Recycling* supports the reuse of materials, which helps reduce pollution while conserving resources.

- ✔ *Opting for renewable energy sources*, such as solar energy, wind energy, and hydroelectric power, helps conserve nonrenewable energy sources, reduce pollution, and limit emissions of greenhouse gases.

   Renewable resources are those that are virtually unlimited (such as solar and wind energy) or can be replaced, such as biodiesel or forests. *Nonrenewable resources* are those that can be used up (such as certain minerals) or can be replaced only over a vast period of time (such as coal, oil, and natural gas).

- ✔ *Telecommuting* instead of driving to work conserves energy and other resources and reduces pollution, as does carpooling and taking public transportation, but not to the same extent.

- ✔ *Conserving water* promotes the natural functioning of the hydrosphere and helps reduce pollution.

1. Which of the following most fully describes what humans must do to ensure their future survival on Earth?

   (A) conserve oil and gas

   (B) protect and preserve the environment

   (C) recycle

   (D) use renewable energy sources

2. Which of the following is *not* a way the government can help promote sustainability?

   (A) charge a tax on carbon emissions

   (B) penalize companies for dumping toxins

(C) subsidize research into renewable energy research

(D) charge residents extra to provide curbside recycling

Check your answers:

1. Although all the choices are partially correct, only Choice (B) covers everything.

2. Charging residents for curbside recycling, Choice (D), could discourage people from recycling.

Wrapping Your Brain around the Structures and Organization of the Cosmos

The universe is a big place, and it's still growing. Astronomers continue to unlock mysteries and discover new mysteries of the universe, so the folks who developed the test don't expect you to be an expert. Having a general understanding of the universe and the galaxy and solar system in which you live, however, provides the contextual framework required to understand relevant reading passages and questions on the test. In this section we provide that framework, along with practice questions to help you retain your newly acquired knowledge and sharpen your skills.

Thinking big: Touring the universe

Start your journey by looking at the big picture — what the universe is and how it was created, the galaxies it contains, and some of the components of those galaxies. This provides you with some idea of where Earth fits in the big picture.

Getting started with the Big Bang theory

The *universe* is all existing matter and space — every star, planet, and other heavenly body, everything in and on those heavenly bodies, and everything in between — and it's getting bigger all the time. Scientists have good reasons to believe that the universe started with a Big Bang approximately 14 billion years ago. Prior to that time, it was a *singularity,* an infinitesimally small, infinitely hot and dense "something" that scientists don't quite understand. Some scientists think that the singularity from which the universe was born was actually nothing. What scientists do agree on, however, is that the universe has been expanding out from its point of origin for approximately 14 billion years and shows no signs of slowing.

Taking a look at galaxies

The universe contains more than 100 billion galaxies, each of which is a vast collection of stars, along with all matter and energy related to those stars, held together by their mutual gravitational forces and other unseen forces. Earth is in the Milky Way galaxy, which is nearly 100,000 light years across and believed to contain 200 to 400 billion stars. (A *light year* is the distance a ray of light travels in a year's time, approximately 6 trillion miles!)

In addition to the stars, planets, and other objects that astronomers can see through their telescopes, galaxies contain an estimated ten times as much *dark matter* that scientists can't see. Scientists postulate the existence of dark matter based on its gravitational effects on visible matter, measurements of radiation in space, and the fact that expansion of the universe seems to be speeding up instead of slowing down.

Scientists also believe that at the center of the Milky Way is a massive *black hole,* a region where the gravitational pull is so strong that no matter, light, or radiation can escape it. They base their belief on the fact that the stars are arranged in a spiral shape around the center and that vivid flares can be observed.

Following the life cycle of a star

Stars are constantly being born and dying across the galaxies. The process goes something like this for a relatively small star (up to about 1.5 times the mass of the sun):

1. Turbulence within a *nebula* (a cloud of gas and dust in space) creates a knot, a concentrated area of gas and dust.

2. If the knot is of sufficient density, it begins to collapse under the power of its own gravity.

3. As the knot collapses, its center begins to heat up, and the knot becomes a glowing *protostar,* a hot ball of spinning gases.

4. When the temperature and pressure are high enough, nuclear fusion reactions occur, generating massive amounts of energy. As the star releases energy, its contraction slows and it shines brighter. At this point, it's called a *main sequence star.*

5. The star burns bright until all its nuclear fuel is consumed. This process occurs much more quickly in larger stars than it does in smaller stars — millions of years compared to billions of years for smaller stars.

6. The remaining matter contracts and heats up, and the outer layers of the star expand and cool. The star begins to dim, becoming a *red giant.*

7. The outer layers form a gaseous shell that drifts away from the core, forming a *planetary nebula.*

8. When the star has lost all its core nuclear fuel and its gaseous shell has drifted away, it becomes a *white dwarf,* a very dense, dim body that continues to glow because of its remaining thermal energy.

9. The star eventually cools and stops glowing, becoming a *black dwarf.*

The life cycle of a large star follows a similar pattern until the end of Step 6. When a large star starts to dim, it becomes a *super red giant.* Then, a series of nuclear reactions occur around the dying star, forming an iron core surrounded by shells made of various elements. At some point, the star suddenly collapses and explodes, blowing away the outer layers and creating a *supernova* that shines very bright for a short time. If the core survives and is large (1.5 to 3 times the mass of the sun), it contracts to form a very dense *neutron star.* If the core is greater than 3 times the mass of the sun, it contracts to form a *black hole,* densely packed matter with extreme gravity.

Flying around with comets, asteroids, and other objects

Other objects fly around the universe, including the following:

- **Asteroid:** Also known as *planetoids* or *minor planets,* these are small celestial bodies that orbit the sun. Asteroids are similar to comets but don't have a visible coma (fuzzy outline and tail) like comets do. Made of rock and metal, they can also contain organic compounds. Some scientists think that asteroids could have delivered the chemicals necessary to start life on Earth, and certain businesses are looking into the possibility of mining asteroids for rare metals that are in short supply on Earth.

- **Asteroid belt:** One lies roughly between the orbits of Mars and Jupiter in the solar system. It is home to a large amount of irregular-shaped asteroids that range in size from dust through to the dwarf planet Ceres.

✔ **Comet:** A relatively small celestial body that orbits the sun. When close enough to the sun, comets display a visible *coma* (a fuzzy outline or atmosphere from solar radiation) and sometimes a tail. The coma is created as the comet gets closer to the sun, causing water, carbon dioxide, and other compounds to *sublime* (quickly change from solid to gas). Comets are made of ice, dust, and small rocky particles. `Aristotle`, a famous philosopher from ancient Greece, described comets as "stars with hair." Short-term comets (also known as *periodic comets*), such as Halley's Comet, have orbital periods of less than 200 years, while long-term comets have orbital periods of over 200 years.

✔ **Meteor:** A meteoroid that burns up as it passes through the Earth's atmosphere is known as a `meteor` or a *shooting star.* The Earth's atmosphere experiences millions of meteors every day. When many meteors occur in a short period of time in the same part of the sky, they form a *meteor shower.*

✔ **Meteorite:** A meteoroid (see the next bullet) that survives falling through the Earth's atmosphere and colliding with the Earth's surface is known as a `meteorite`.

✔ **Meteoroid:** This is a small rock or particle of debris in the solar system. Meteoroids range in size from dust to around 10 meters in diameter. The fastest meteoroids travel through the solar system at a speed of around 42 kilometers per second (26 miles per second).

1. In 1929, Edwin Hubble discovered that the farther a galaxy is from Earth, the faster it appears to move away, which gave rise to which of the following?

   (A) the explanation of how stars are formed

   (B) estimates of the size of the Milky Way

   (C) the Big Bang theory

   (D) a clearer understanding of black holes

2. When astronomers used the Hubble telescope to look at the Orion nebula, they discovered more about which of the following?

   (A) flight patterns of asteroids

   (B) how stars and planets are formed

   (C) the number of galaxies in the universe

   (D) the Big Bang theory

3. Which of the following objects is most likely to be confused with a planet?

   (A) asteroid

   (B) comet

   (C) meteor

   (D) star

4. The sun produces most of its energy through which of the following?

   (A) burning gases

   (B) nuclear fission

   (C) expanding and contracting

   (D) nuclear fusion

Check your answers:

   1. Movements of galaxies away from Earth suggests an expanding universe, which supports the Big Bang theory, Choice (C).

2. If the Hubble telescope is focused on a nebula, it's most probably being used to study the formation of stars and planets, Choice (B).

3. Asteroids, Choice (A), are most like planets and are even referred to as planetoids.

4. Stars, including the sun, produce most of their energy through nuclear fusion, Choice (D), merging two atoms of an element to form a new element.

Touring the solar system

Regardless of whether you're an amateur astronomer, you need to know a bit about the solar system to answer related questions. Most of what you need to know is about Earth's relationship to the sun and moon, but you may also encounter questions about other planets and heavenly bodies.

The first thing you need to know is what the solar system is. Figure 10-4 answers that question. The solar system consists of the sun and the heavenly bodies that orbit it. Eight planets revolve around the sun — four *inner* and four *outer* planets.

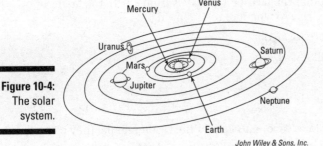

Figure 10-4:
The solar
system.

John Wiley & Sons, Inc.

Mercury, Venus, Earth, and Mars are the inner planets, often called *terrestrial* planets, because they have a rocky surface with similar features, including rifts, valleys, mountains, impact craters, and volcanoes. They all have refractory metals and minerals, such as silicates, that make up the majority of their crusts and mantles, and they all have cores that are composed of metals such as iron and nickel. (The term *refractory* means stable at high temperatures.) Three of the four planets (Venus, Earth, and Mars) have substantial enough atmospheres to generate winds and weather. The term *inner planet* or *terrestrial planet* should not be confused with the term *inferior planet*, which means any planet that is closer to the sun than Earth — Mercury and Venus. Following are some key facts about the inner planets.

✔ **Mercury:** Close proximity to the sun makes Mercury the hottest. It's also the smallest — slightly larger than Earth's moon. Speaking of moons, Mercury has none.

✔ **Venus:** Commonly considered Earth's sister planet, Venus is only slightly smaller than Earth, but it's a whole lot hotter. In fact, its claim to fame is that it has the hottest average temperature of all the planets at 855°F. It is also moon-less.

✔ **Earth:** The largest of the inner planets, this is the only planet in the solar system that supports life . . . although the jury is still out on that. Earth has one moon.

✔ **Mars:** Commonly known as the red planet, Mars is most like Earth. Because it's farther from the sun, it's much colder and requires about twice the time to travel around the sun. Mars has two moons.

Jupiter, Saturn, Uranus, and Neptune are the *outer planets,* also known as *gas giants* — gas because they're composed primarily of the gases hydrogen and helium, and giants because they're all much larger than the inner planets. The outer two gas giants, Uranus and Neptune, have more hydrocarbons and ices than Jupiter and Saturn and hence are often also referred to as the *ice giants.* Following are some additional important details about each of the outer planets:

- **Jupiter:** Jupiter is huge — 318 times the mass of the Earth and 2.5 times the mass of all the other planets combined. Jupiter's high internal heat is responsible for creating its characteristic cloud bands, and it has 63 known moons.

- **Saturn:** Saturn is a little over half the size of Jupiter in volume but less than a third of its size in mass, making it the least dense of the planets. Its characteristic rings are formed by ice and rock particles that circle the planet. Saturn has 62 confirmed moons, one of which (Titan) is larger than the planet Mercury.

- **Uranus:** This planet's claim to fame is that it's the coldest in the solar system with a temperature of about –322°F. It also spins on its side like a yo-yo, unlike most planets, which spin upright like tops. Because of this, a day or night on Uranus may last over 40 years. Uranus has 27 known moons.

- **Neptune:** Neptune is the farthest from the sun — 30 times as far as the Earth is from the sun — and it orbits the sun once every 165 Earth years. Its deep blue color is due to the blue light reflecting off of the methane gas in its atmosphere. Neptune is slightly warmer than Uranus, even though it's farther from the Sun, because it generates more internal heat. It has eight known moons.

Farther out past the outer planets is the zone known as the *trans-Neptune region* or the *outer solar system.* In this region reside a few *dwarf planets,* including Pluto, which had been considered a planet until 2006. This region also is believed to hold many other smaller asteroids and comets that periodically venture into the inner solar system, such as Halley's Comet.

Basking in sun facts and figures

The sun is classified as a G2V yellow dwarf star. G2 classifies the surface temperature of the sun to be approximately 5,500°C, or almost 10,000°F based on its yellow appearance. The sun is by far the chief component of the solar system, containing 99.9 percent of all mass in the solar system. The sun is 332,900 Earth masses, its diameter is 100 times that of Earth's, and its surface area is almost 12,000 times that of Earth's.

The sun is a huge ball of gas composed primarily of hydrogen (approximately 73 percent) and helium (approximately 25 percent), with smaller amounts of oxygen, iron, sulfur, neon, nitrogen, silicone, and magnesium. Even though these other elements are in smaller amounts relative to the mass of the sun, the amount of oxygen in the sun is more than 2,500 times the mass of Earth.

From inside out, the sun is composed of a *core, radiative zone, convective zone, photosphere, chromosphere,* and *corona.* The core is the hottest area of the sun and is where 99 percent of the fusion reaction takes place, generating heat and energy. The core is estimated to be about 15,000,000°C.

Zooming in on the Earth

Earth is close to home and may be nearer and dearer to the test developers, so pay particular attention to facts about the Earth. The most basic thing you need to know is that the Earth *rotates* on its axis and *revolves* around the sun. One rotation takes a little less than 24 hours, while a trip around the sun takes a little less than a year.

The Earth's axis is tilted at an angle of about $23\frac{1}{2}°$ and wobbles during the trip around the sun. As the North Pole tilts toward the sun during part of the Earth's orbit, the Northern Hemisphere experiences summer, while the Southern Hemisphere experiences winter. During the second half of Earth's orbit, the Southern Hemisphere is closer to the sun. This tilt also explains why night and day are not equal throughout the year. The vernal (spring) and autumnal equinoxes are the only two days of the year when day and night are of equal duration.

The Earth's relative position to the sun and moon explain two key phenomena — tides and eclipses:

✔ **Tides:** The sun and moon team up to create tides, with the moon playing a larger role. As the sun sets and the moon rises, the gravitational pull of the moon causes the ocean nearest the moon to bulge out toward the moon, causing the tide to rise locally and fall everywhere else around the globe.

✔ **Solar eclipse:** A solar eclipse occurs when the moon passes between the Earth and the sun, partially or totally blocking the rays of the sun.

✔ **Lunar eclipse:** A lunar eclipse occurs when the Earth passes between the sun and the moon, partially or totally preventing the rays of the sun from striking and reflecting off of the moon.

One of the most important stars in the sky is the North Star, or *Polaris*. The North Star is virtually stationary in the night sky in the Northern Hemisphere and points north because it's almost exactly in line with the North Pole. Due to its stationary appearance, it has been used as an aid to navigation throughout history.

1. Mercury, Venus, Earth, and Mars are called the *terrestrial* planets because

   (A) they are close to the sun.

   (B) they have solid, rocky surfaces.

   (C) they are capable of supporting rudimentary life forms.

   (D) they are in the terrestrial part of the solar system.

2. Which of the following planets are known as *ice giants?*

   (A) Uranus and Neptune

   (B) Mercury and Saturn

   (C) Jupiter and Saturn

   (D) Venus and Uranus

3. Looking for good sites to land a spaceship on Mars, scientists discovered signs of erosion on the planet's surface, which would suggest which of the following?

   (A) Life exists on Mars.

   (B) Mars probably has or has had water on its surface.

   (C) Asteroids have probably collided with Mars.

   (D) It frequently rains on Mars.

4. Why would NASA be unable to land a spaceship on Saturn's surface?

   (A) It is too rocky.

   (B) It is too icy.

   (C) It is too far.

   (D) It is too gassy.

Check your answers:

1. Mercury, Venus, Earth, and Mars all have solid, rocky surfaces, Choice (B).

2. Uranus and Neptune, Choice (A), are considered to be ice giants.

3. Erosion would suggest that Mars has or has had water on its surface, Choice (B). There are other sources of erosion, but these are not listed as choices; you need to select the best answer from those offered.

4. Saturn is composed primarily of gas, so ships can't land on its surface, Choice (D). Below the gas is a layer of liquid hydrogen, and below that is a layer of liquid helium, so if a spaceship were able to get down that far without being crushed by the atmospheric pressure, it probably wouldn't last very long.

Part III
Testing Your Science Skills and Knowledge

Five Ways to Simulate the GED Science Test Environment

- ✔ Find a quiet place to work, where you won't be distracted or interrupted.
- ✔ Put away cellphones, music players, and all other electronic devices. They won't be permitted on test day.
- ✔ Use a separate pad of paper to take notes, draw pictures, reason out science problems, and perform calculations.
- ✔ Set a timer to count down from the 90 minutes allocated for the Science section of the test.
- ✔ Don't take a break during the test.

 Check out www.dummies.com/extras/gedsciencetest for a free article that provides strategies for boosting your score on test day.

In this part . . .

✔ See how your stamina measures up by taking a full-length practice GED Science test.

✔ Score your test quickly with the answer key.

✔ Discover how to improve your performance by reading through the answer explanations for all practice test questions.

Chapter 11

Taking a GED Science Practice Test

The GED Science test consists of multiple-choice, fill-in-the-blank, drag-and-drop, hot-spot, and short-answer items intended to measure general concepts in science. The questions are based on short passages that may include a graph, chart, or figure. Study the information given and then answer the question(s) following it. Refer to the passage information as often as necessary in answering the questions, but remember that you have a time limit, and you should try to spend as little time on any item as you can and still get the correct answer.

You have 90 minutes to complete the GED Science test, including answering two short-answer items, which should take about 10 minutes each. (Note that the short-answer questions are not timed separately, so you have to manage your time and aim to spend about 10 minutes on each one, so that you have about 70 minutes to complete all the other questions.) The answers and explanations to this test's questions are in Chapter 12. Go through the explanations to *all* the questions, even for the ones you answered correctly. The explanations are a good review of the techniques we discuss throughout the book.

Unless you require accommodations, you'll be taking the GED test on a computer. Instead of marking your answers on a separate answer sheet, as you do for the practice tests in this book, you'll see clickable ovals and fill-in-the-blank text boxes, and you'll be able to click with your mouse and drag and drop items where indicated. We formatted the questions and answer choices in this book to make them appear as similar as possible to what you'll see on the computer-based test, but we had to retain some A, B, C, and D choices for marking your answers, and we provide an answer sheet for you to do so.

Answer Sheet for Practice Test, Science

1.		26.	Ⓐ Ⓑ Ⓒ Ⓓ
2. Ⓐ Ⓑ Ⓒ Ⓓ		27.	Ⓐ Ⓑ Ⓒ Ⓓ
3. Ⓐ Ⓑ Ⓒ Ⓓ		28.	Ⓐ Ⓑ Ⓒ Ⓓ
4. Ⓐ Ⓑ Ⓒ Ⓓ		29.	
5. Ⓐ Ⓑ Ⓒ Ⓓ		30.	Ⓐ Ⓑ Ⓒ Ⓓ
6. Ⓐ Ⓑ Ⓒ Ⓓ		31.	
7. Ⓐ Ⓑ Ⓒ Ⓓ		32.	Ⓐ Ⓑ Ⓒ Ⓓ
8.		33.	
		34.	
9. Ⓐ Ⓑ Ⓒ Ⓓ		35.	Ⓐ Ⓑ Ⓒ Ⓓ
10. Ⓐ Ⓑ Ⓒ Ⓓ		36.	
11. Ⓐ Ⓑ Ⓒ Ⓓ		37.	Ⓐ Ⓑ Ⓒ Ⓓ
12. Ⓐ Ⓑ Ⓒ Ⓓ		38.	
13. Ⓐ Ⓑ Ⓒ Ⓓ		39.	Ⓐ Ⓑ Ⓒ Ⓓ
14. Ⓐ Ⓑ Ⓒ Ⓓ		40.	Ⓐ Ⓑ Ⓒ Ⓓ
15. Ⓐ Ⓑ Ⓒ Ⓓ		41.	Ⓐ Ⓑ Ⓒ Ⓓ
16. Ⓐ Ⓑ Ⓒ Ⓓ		42.	Ⓐ Ⓑ Ⓒ Ⓓ
17. Ⓐ Ⓑ Ⓒ Ⓓ		43.	Ⓐ Ⓑ Ⓒ Ⓓ
18. Ⓐ Ⓑ Ⓒ Ⓓ		44.	Ⓐ Ⓑ Ⓒ Ⓓ
19. Ⓐ Ⓑ Ⓒ Ⓓ		45.	Ⓐ Ⓑ Ⓒ Ⓓ
20.		46.	Ⓐ Ⓑ Ⓒ Ⓓ
21. Ⓐ Ⓑ Ⓒ Ⓓ		47.	Ⓐ Ⓑ Ⓒ Ⓓ
22.		48.	Ⓐ Ⓑ Ⓒ Ⓓ
23. Ⓐ Ⓑ Ⓒ Ⓓ		49.	Ⓐ Ⓑ Ⓒ Ⓓ
24. Ⓐ Ⓑ Ⓒ Ⓓ		50.	
25.			

Science Test

Time: 90 minutes

Directions: Read each item carefully and mark your answer on the answer sheet provided by filling in the corresponding oval or writing your answer in the blank box.

Questions 1–2 refer to the following excerpt from the U.S. Environmental Protection Agency's website on climate change (www.epa.gov/climatechange).

As temperatures increase, the habitat ranges of many North American species are moving northward in latitude and upward in elevation. While this means a range expansion for some species, for others it means a range reduction or a movement into less hospitable habitat or increased competition. Some species have nowhere to go because they are already at the northern or upper limit of their habitat.

For example, boreal forests are invading tundra, reducing habitat for the many unique species that depend on the tundra ecosystem, such as caribou, arctic fox, and snowy owl. Other observed changes in the United States include expanding oak-hickory forests, contracting maple-beech forests, and disappearing spruce-fir forests. As rivers and streams warm, warm water fish are expanding into areas previously inhabited by cold water species. Cold water fish, including many highly valued trout species, are losing their habitats. As waters warm, the area of feasible, cooler habitats to which species can migrate is reduced. Range shifts disturb the current state of the ecosystem and can limit opportunities for fishing and hunting.

1. As temperatures become warmer and ranges move, the new territory may prove to be less ☐ for specific species.

2. When cold water fish are replaced by warm water species, this creates problems for human beings because

   (A) humans depend on fish as a source of protein

   (B) fishing is a sport that aids local economies

   (C) many cold water fish are valued as food or prey

   (D) all of the above

3. Although people often talk about building a home on solid ground, the truth is that

   (A) Earth is capable of supporting huge buildings anywhere on its surface

   (B) the ground is solid and stable

   (C) the ground is capable of sudden dramatic movement

   (D) people should not live near an active volcano

Go on to next page ⟩

Question 4 refers to the following excerpt from NASA's website (www.nasa.gov).

It would be impractical, in terms of volume and cost, to completely stock the International Space Station (ISS) with oxygen or water for long periods of time. Without a grocery store in space, NASA scientists and engineers have developed innovative solutions to meet astronauts' basic requirements for life. The human body is two-thirds water. It has been estimated that nearly an octillion (10^{27}) water molecules flow through our bodies daily. It is therefore necessary for humans to consume a sufficient amount of water, as well as oxygen and food, on a daily basis in order to sustain life. Without water, the average person lives approximately three days. Without air, permanent brain damage can occur within three minutes. Scientists have determined how much water, air, and food a person needs per day per person for life on Earth. Similarly, space scientists know what is needed to sustain life in space.

4. Why is it necessary to recycle air and water on a spaceship?

(A) to keep the interior smelling clean

(B) astronauts can only survive for three days with limited oxygen

(C) astronauts require oxygen and water to survive

(D) so that astronauts don't get thirsty between meals

5. If you were sitting around with a group of friends complaining about how many baseball games had been rained out this season, you would be complaining about the

(A) precipitation

(B) condensation

(C) evaporation

(D) perspiration

Question 6 refers to the following diagram.

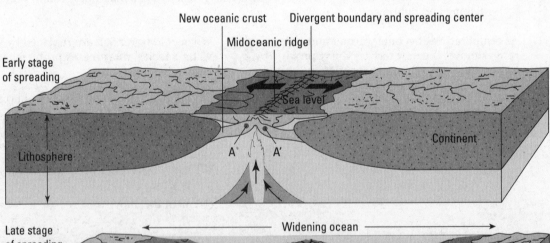
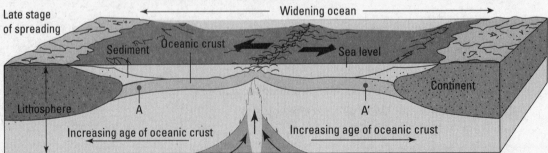

Illustration courtesy of U.S. Geological Survey and National Park Service

Go on to next page

6. This diagram shows an area where a "hot spot" in the lithosphere allows magma to work its way through Earth's crust to the surface. Because this is taking place beneath the ocean, it has resulted in a ridge that runs most of the way from Antarctica to the arctic down the middle of the North and South Atlantic. How does that explain the continent's moving farther apart as the arrows in the diagram indicate?

   (A) The magma creates gaps in the sea floor, which are filled by fresh magma.

   (B) The magma cools, forming ridges, which break open as new magma pushes its way up.

   (C) Repeated intrusions of magma widen the gaps, fill them in, and then create new gaps.

   (D) All the processes above occur, causing the continents to move.

Questions 7–8 refer to the following passage.

Rocket Propulsion

Have you ever wondered how a rocket ship moves? Perhaps you have seen science-fiction movies in which a captain uses a blast of the rocket engines to save the ship and its crew from crashing into the surface of a distant planet.

Usually, a fuel, such as the gasoline in a car, needs an oxidizer, such as the oxygen in the air, to create combustion, which powers the engine. In space, there is no air and, thus, no oxidizer. The rocket ship, being a clever design, carries its own oxidizer. The fuel used may be a liquid or a solid, but the rocket ship always has fuel and an oxidizer to mix together. When the two are mixed and combustion takes place, a rapid expansion is directed out the back of the engine. The force pushing backward moves the rocket ship forward. In space, with no air, the rocket ship experiences no resistance to the movement. The rocket ship moves forward, avoids the crash, or does whatever the crew wants it to do.

7. Why is the rocket engine the perfect propulsion method for space travel?

   (A) It is very powerful.

   (B) It carries its own oxidizer.

   (C) It carries a lot of fuel.

   (D) It produces a forward thrust.

8. Fuel on a rocket ship may be a ☐ or a ☐.

Questions 9–16 refer to the following passage.

Where Does All the Garbage Go?

When we finish using something, we throw it away, but where is "away"? In our modern cities, "away" is usually an unsightly landfill site, piled high with all those things that we no longer want. A modern American city generates solid waste or garbage at an alarming rate. Every day, New York City produces 17,000 tons of garbage and ships it to Staten Island, where it is added to yesterday's 17,000 tons in a landfill site. We each produce enough garbage every five years to equal the volume of the Statue of Liberty. In spite of all the efforts to increase recycling, we go on our merry way producing garbage without thinking about where it goes.

In any landfill, gone is not forgotten by nature. By compacting the garbage to reduce its volume, we slow the rate of decomposition, which makes our garbage last longer. In a

Go on to next page ⟶

modern landfill, the process produces a garbage lasagna. There's a layer of compacted garbage covered by a layer of dirt, covered by a layer of compacted garbage and so on. By saving space for more garbage, we cut off the air and water needed to decompose the garbage and, thus, preserve it for future generations. If you could dig far enough, you might still be able to read 40-year-old newspapers. The paper may be preserved, but the news is history.

One of the answers to this problem is recycling. Any object that can be reused in one form or another is an object that shouldn't be found in a landfill. Most of us gladly recycle our paper, which saves energy and resources. Recycled paper can be used again and even turned into other products. Recycling old newspapers is not as valuable as hidden treasure, but when the cost of landfills and the environmental impact of producing more and more newsprint is considered, it can be a bargain. If plastic shopping bags can be recycled into a cloth-like substance that can be used to make reusable shopping bags, maybe American ingenuity can find ways to reduce all that garbage being stored in landfills before the landfills overtake the space for cities.

9. Why are the disposal methods used in modern landfills as much a part of the problem as a part of the solution?

(A) They look very ugly.

(B) They take up a lot of valuable land.

(C) The process used is counterproductive.

(D) Newspapers are readable after 50 years.

10. Why is recycling paper important?

(A) It saves money.

(B) It reduces the need for new landfill sites.

(C) Newspaper is not biodegradable.

(D) None of the above.

11. Why is solid waste compacted in a modern landfill?

(A) to reduce the odor

(B) to help the bacteria decompose the waste

(C) to make the landfill look better

(D) to reduce the amount of space it occupies

12. What is the modern landfill compared to?

(A) an efficient way of ridding cities of solid waste

(B) a garbage cannelloni

(C) a place for bacteria to decompose solid waste

(D) none of the above

13. Why is it important for cities to establish recycling programs?

(A) It makes people feel good about their garbage.

(B) It reduces the volume of waste to store.

(C) Recycling lets someone else look after your problem.

(D) It makes garbage collection faster.

14. What can individual Americans do to reduce the amount of waste that is going into the landfills?

(A) eat less

(B) reuse and recycle as much as possible

(C) stop using paper

(D) import more nitrogen

15. Bacteria provide what helpful purpose in composting?

(A) They help get rid of rodents.

(B) They take part in chemical reactions.

(C) They are part of the inorganic cycle.

(D) They help decompose composting waste.

16. If municipalities lose money recycling paper, why do they continue?

(A) The cost is less than acquiring more landfill sites.

(B) Municipalities don't have to make money.

(C) The public likes to recycle paper.

(D) The politicians don't care they are losing money.

Go on to next page

Questions 17–18 refer to the following passage.

The Surface of the Moon

The surface of the moon is a hostile, barren landscape. Astronauts have found boulders as large as houses in huge fields of dust and rock. They've had no maps to guide them but have survived, thanks to their training for the mission.

17. The aspect of the lunar landscape that may make landing there dangerous is that

(A) astronauts have to consider the possibility of hostile aliens

(B) the moon has very rough terrain

(C) the moon has unlit landing fields with uncertain footings

(D) there are no maps of the moon

18. What aspect of the moon makes the height of a boulder unimportant for the astronauts moving about?

(A) Low gravity makes climbing easier, if it's necessary.

(B) There are special tools for flying over boulders.

(C) Astronauts can drive around an obstruction.

(D) Astronauts have training in flying.

Questions 19–21 refer to the following passage.

Pushing Aside the Water

The Titanic struck an iceberg presumably because the captain of the ship did not see it, which is reasonable. Approximately $\frac{7}{8}$ of an iceberg is below the surface of the water. You can observe this same phenomenon when you place an ice cube in a glass of water. Most of the ice cube is below the surface of the water, but a small portion remains above the surface. This is because the ice cube displaces an amount of water that weighs slightly less than the weight of the ice cube. Another way to look at it is that water is denser than ice; that is, the same volume of water, say 1 cubic foot, weighs more than an equivalent volume of ice.

When you enter a swimming pool, the water rises because your body displaces a certain amount of the water equal to the volume of your body that's below the surface. You may notice that some people tend to float in a pool while others sink. People with a lower percentage of body fat (more muscle) tend to sink, whereas those with a higher percentage of body fat tend to float because water is denser than fat. When someone with a greater percentage of body fat is in a pool, the weight of the water the person displaces is greater than the weight of the person, so the person floats. On the other hand, a person with low body fat sinks (unless he takes a big breath of air) because the weight of the water he displaces is less than the weight of his body.

19. If you sink to the bottom of a pool, you displace

(A) an amount of water equal to your weight

(B) an amount of water more than your weight

(C) an amount of water less than your weight

(D) more water than the volume of your body

20. A freight liner carrying 3,000 tons of cargo travels across the Atlantic Ocean (a large body of saltwater) and enters the St. Lawrence Seaway (a body of freshwater). Given that saltwater is denser than freshwater, does the boat float higher or lower in the St. Lawrence Seaway than it does in the Atlantic Ocean? [   ]

Go on to next page ⟶

21. If you wanted to find the volume of an irregularly shaped object, how could you do it?

(A) Immerse the object in a premeasured volume of water and measure the amount of water displaced.

(B) Measure the object and calculate the volume.

(C) Weigh the object.

(D) Float it on the surface of the water and see how much water it displaced.

Questions 22–23 refer to the following passage.

Air Bags

Most new cars are equipped with air bags. In a crash, the air bags quickly deploy, protecting the driver and front-seat passenger by inflating to absorb the initial force of the crash. Air bags deploy so quickly and with such force that they can injure a short adult sitting too close to the dashboard or a child in a car seat. This safety device has to be treated with respect. With the proper precautions, air bags save lives. In fact, a person in the front seat of a modern car equipped with air bags who also wears a seat belt stands a much better chance of surviving a crash than an unbelted person. The two safety devices work together to save lives but must be used properly.

22. In a front-end collision, the [   ] absorbs the initial force of the crash.

23. Where is the safest place for an infant in a car seat in a car equipped with air bags?

(A) in the rear seat

(B) in the front seat

(C) on the right side of the car

(D) on the left side of the car

Question 24 refers to the following passage.

Newton's Second Law of Motion

Newton's second law of motion states that when a body changes its velocity because an external force is applied to it, that change in velocity is directly proportional to the force and inversely proportional to the mass of the body. That is, the faster you want to stop your car, the harder you must brake. The brakes apply an external force that reduces the velocity of the car. The faster you want to accelerate the car, the more force you must apply. Increasing the horsepower of an engine allows it to apply greater force in accelerating. That is why drag racer cars seem to be all engine.

24. If you want a car that accelerates quickly, which attributes give you the best acceleration?

(A) light weight and two doors

(B) automatic transmission

(C) automatic transmission and two doors

(D) light weight and high horsepower

Go on to next page

Questions 25–26 refer to the following passage from the National Institute of Justice (`www.nij.gov/topics/forensics/evidence/dna/basics/pages/analyzing.aspx`).

Overview of Steps in Analyzing DNA Evidence

Several basic steps are performed during DNA testing regardless of the type of test being done. The general procedure includes: 1) the isolation of the DNA from an evidence sample containing DNA of unknown origin, and generally at a later time, the isolation of DNA from a sample (blood, for example) from a known individual; 2) the processing of the DNA so that test results may be obtained; 3) the determination of the DNA test results (or types), from specific regions of the DNA; and 4) the comparison and interpretation of the test results from the unknown and known samples to determine whether the known individual is not the source of the DNA or is included as a possible source of the DNA.

The Federal Bureau of Investigation (FBI) has chosen 13 specific STR loci to serve as the standard for the Combined DNA Index System (CODIS) (DNA databases and software used to match DNA evidence against DNA samples collected from convicted offenders). The purpose of establishing a core set of STR loci is to ensure that all forensic laboratories can establish uniform DNA databases and, more importantly, share valuable forensic information. If the forensic or convicted offender CODIS index is to be used in the investigative stages of unsolved cases, DNA profiles must be generated by using STR technology and the specific 13 core STR loci selected by the FBI.

25. DNA testing compares the DNA from an ☐ sample with the DNA of a known individual.

26. CODIS enables law enforcement agencies to
    (A) compare DNA evidence to that of convicts
    (B) compare DNA evidence to that of known suspects
    (C) compare DNA from convicts to that of known suspects
    (D) compare DNA evidence to that of everyone in the country

Questions 27–28 refer to the following passage.

Work

When we think of work, we think of people sitting at desks operating computers or building homes or making some other effort to earn money. When a physicist thinks of work, she probably thinks of a formula — force exerted over a distance. If you don't expend any energy — resulting in a force of zero — or if your force produces no movement, no work has been done. If you pick up your gigantic super-ordinary 2-pound hamburger and lift it to your mouth to take a bite, you do work. If you want to resist temptation and just stare at your hamburger, you do no work. If your friend gets tired of you playing around and lifts your hamburger to feed you, you still do no work, but your friend does. In scientific terms, two elements are necessary for work to be done: A force must be exerted and the object to which the force has been exerted must move.

Go on to next page

27. If the formula for work is
Work = Force × Distance, how much more work would you do in lifting a 10-pound barbell 3 feet instead of 2 feet?

    (A) half as much

    (B) three times as much

    (C) one-third as much

    (D) one and a half times as much

28. Though you may see that you do work in climbing a flight of stairs, why do you also do work when you descend a flight of stairs?

    (A) It is hard to climb down stairs.

    (B) You have exerted a force over a distance.

    (C) You feel tired after descending stairs.

    (D) It is easier to climb down stairs.

Question 29 refers to the following excerpt from Womenshealth.gov.

Stimulus:

"Mirror, mirror on the wall . . . who's the thinnest one of all?" According to the National Eating Disorders Association, the average American woman is 5 feet 4 inches tall and weighs 140 pounds. The average American model is 5 feet 11 inches tall and weighs 117 pounds. All too often, society associates being "thin" with "hardworking, beautiful, strong, and self-disciplined." On the other hand, being "fat" is associated with being "lazy, ugly, weak, and lacking willpower." Because of these harsh critiques, rarely are women completely satisfied with their image. As a result, they often feel great anxiety and pressure to achieve and/or maintain an imaginary appearance.

Eating disorders are serious medical problems. Anorexia nervosa, bulimia nervosa, and binge-eating disorder are all types of eating disorders. Eating disorders frequently develop during adolescence or early adulthood but can occur during childhood or later in adulthood. Females are more likely than males to develop an eating disorder.

29. Prompt:

On a separate sheet of paper, write a short response explaining how the depictions of females on television and in print media gives a false impression of body image to young women, and how that can lead to serious problems in later life.

This item should take about 10 minutes to complete.

Question 30 refers to the following excerpt from NASA's Earth Observatory website (www.earthobservatory.nasa.gov).

If Kepler's laws define the motion of the planets, Newton's laws define motion. Thinking on Kepler's laws, Newton realized that all motion, whether it was the orbit of the moon around the Earth or an apple falling from a tree, followed the same basic principles. "To the same natural effects," he wrote, "we must, as far as possible, assign the same causes." Previous Aristotelian thinking, physicist Stephen Hawking has written, assigned different causes to different types of motion. By unifying all motion, Newton shifted the scientific perspective to a search for large, unifying patterns in nature. Newton outlined his laws in *Philosophiae Naturalis Principia Mathematica (Mathematical Principles of Natural Philosophy),* published in 1687.

30. Newton was inspired by

    (A) Hawking

    (B) Aristotle

    (C) Kepler

    (D) Einstein

Go on to next page

> *Question 31 refers to the following excerpt from the U.S. Environmental Protection Agency's website on climate change (www.epa.gov/climatechange).*

Climate change, along with habitat destruction and pollution, is one of the important stressors that can contribute to species extinction. The IPCC estimates that 20–30% of the plant and animal species evaluated so far in climate change studies are at risk of extinction if temperatures reach levels projected to occur by the end of this century. Projected rates of species extinctions are 10 times greater than recently observed global average rates and 10,000 times greater than rates observed in the distant past (as recorded in fossils).

31. One of the great dangers to Earth as a result of climate change is the ⬚ of species.

> *Question 32 refers to the following excerpt from the National Science Foundation website (www.nsf.gov).*

By observing galaxies formed billions of years ago, astronomers have been able to paint an increasingly detailed picture of how the universe evolved. According to the widely accepted Big Bang theory, our universe was born in an explosive moment approximately 15 billion years ago. All the universe's matter and energy — even the fabric of space itself — was compressed into an infinitesimally small volume and then began expanding at an incredible rate. Within minutes, the universe had grown to the size of the solar system and cooled enough so that equal numbers of protons, neutrons, and the simplest atomic nuclei had formed.

32. According to astronomers, how did the universe form?

    (A) The sun attracted all the particles orbiting around it.

    (B) All matter and energy became compressed.

    (C) In a monumental explosion.

    (D) None of the above.

> *Question 33 refers to the following definition from the U.S. Environmental Protection Agency's climate change glossary (www.epa.gov/climatechange).*

Carbon cycle is all parts (reservoirs) and fluxes of carbon. The cycle is usually thought of as four main reservoirs of carbon interconnected by pathways of exchange. The reservoirs are the atmosphere, terrestrial biosphere (usually includes freshwater systems), oceans, and sediments (includes fossil fuels). The annual movements of carbon, the carbon exchanges between reservoirs, occur because of various chemical, physical, geological, and biological processes. The ocean contains the largest pool of carbon near the surface of the Earth, but most of that pool is not involved with rapid exchange with the atmosphere.

33. The largest pool of carbon in close proximity to the surface of the Earth is the ⬚.

Go on to next page ⟶

Questions 34–35 refer to the following passage.

Hibernating Plants

We have many perennial plants in our gardens. Plants such as roses and irises grow and flower year after year. They hibernate through the winter and then come back to life at various times throughout the spring and early summer. Tulips are beautiful flowers that are among the earliest to come up every spring. They are fragile in appearance but manage to survive the uncertain weather of spring, blooming for a while and then sleeping for the rest of the year. The next year, they are ready to peek out of the earth and brighten your spring again.

Tulips survive because they grow from bulbs. Each bulb stores moisture and food during good weather. When the weather turns, the plant hibernates: The roots and leaves dry out and fall off, but the bulb develops a tough outer skin to protect itself. The bulb becomes dormant until the following spring, when the whole cycle begins again.

34. The ⬚ of the tulip allows it to survive a rough winter.

35. The word "perennial" means

    (A) blossoms continuously

    (B) dies in the winter

    (C) continues to live from one year to the next

    (D) grows from bulbs

Questions 36–37 refer to the following passage.

Gunpowder

Have you ever wondered how the bullet is propelled out of a gun when the trigger is pulled? A cartridge (also referred to as a round or a shell) is made of two parts — the case and the bullet. The case is filled with gunpowder and an ignition device, and when the ignition device is hit, the gunpowder explodes, hurling the bullet out of the barrel of the gun.

Early bullets were primarily made of lead, but when fired at high velocities, the lead would tend to melt from the hot gas behind it and the friction inside the barrel. To prevent this melting, Major Eduard Rubin invented the copper-jacketed bullet with a lead core wrapped in a layer of copper. Copper is harder than lead and has a higher melting point, so these bullets could be shot at greater velocities.

36. In the movies, guns with blank cartridges are used to produce the shooting sound without endangering the actors, in which case the ⬚ is missing.

37. If you wanted to reduce the force with which a bullet is hurled out of the barrel, you would

    (A) use a jacketed bullet

    (B) use a larger cartridge

    (C) use an unjacketed bullet

    (D) use less gunpowder in the cartridge

Go on to next page

Questions 38–40 refer to the following passage.

Why Don't Polar Bears Freeze?

Watching a polar bear lumber through the frigid Arctic wilderness, you may wonder why it doesn't freeze. If you were there, you would likely freeze. In fact, you may feel cold just looking at photographs of polar bears.

Professor Stephan Steinlechner of Hanover Veterinary University in Germany set out to answer the question of why polar bears don't freeze. Polar bears have black skin. This means that, in effect, polar bears have a huge solar heat collector covering their bodies. Covering this black skin are white hollow hairs. These hairs act as insulation, keeping the heat inside the fur covering. This is like an insulated house. The heat stays in for a long period of time.

This is an interesting theory and does answer the question, except you may still wonder how they keep warm at night, when the sun isn't out!

38. The most important element in retaining the polar bear's body heat is its ☐.

39. What part of the polar bear absorbs heat?

(A) caves

(B) ice

(C) its furry coat

(D) its skin

40. If you had to live in the Arctic, what sort of clothing would be least appropriate?

(A) insulated coats

(B) silk underwear

(C) black clothing with fur covering

(D) white clothing with fur covering

Questions 41–46 refer to the following passage.

Space Stuff

Each space flight carries items authorized by NASA, but the quirky little items carried in astronauts' pockets are what catch the interest of collectors. Auction sales have been brisk for material carried aboard various space flights.

On the second manned Mercury flight, Gus Grissom carried two rolls of dimes. He was planning to give these to the children of his friends after he returned to Earth. If you carried two rolls of dimes worth ten dollars around the world, they would still add up to ten dollars. When Gus Grissom returned to Earth after a space flight, however, these dimes became space mementos, each worth many times its face value.

Although NASA does not permit the sale of items carried aboard space missions, many items have found their way to market. Eleven Apollo 16 stamps, autographed by the astronauts, sold for $27,000 at auction, but the corned beef sandwich that John Young offered to Gus Grissom never returned to Earth.

Go on to next page

41. Why did Gus Grissom carry rolls of dimes on a space mission?

    (A) he forgot they were in his pocket

    (B) to give to the children of friends

    (C) to sell at auction

    (D) he was a coin collector

42. What happened to John Young's corned beef sandwich?

    (A) It was sold.

    (B) It was left on the moon.

    (C) It was eaten.

    (D) Not enough information is given.

43. What is so special about souvenirs carried in an astronaut's pocket?

    (A) Weightlessness changes their composition.

    (B) They are very rare.

    (C) Lunar radiation affects them.

    (D) The pockets are made of a special material.

44. What would NASA not authorize astronauts to carry into space?

    (A) potential valuable souvenirs

    (B) extra oxygen

    (C) tools for experiments

    (D) not stated in the passage

45. Why would a stamp collector be especially interested in stamps that had been carried by an astronaut into space?

    (A) Collectors like to collect items that are rare.

    (B) Because most people will never travel in outer space, this would be one of the possible items from space flight available to them.

    (C) Collectors prefer items associated with famous people.

    (D) All of the above.

46. What makes stamps a safer choice for an unauthorized space souvenir than coins?

    (A) There are more stamp collectors than coin collectors.

    (B) Stamps made of paper are more easily autographed than other small items such as coins.

    (C) They weigh less.

    (D) All of the above.

Question 47 refers to the following definition from the U.S. Environmental Protection Agency's climate change glossary (www.epa.gov/climatechange).

The most abundant greenhouse gas, water vapor is the water present in the atmosphere in gaseous form. Water vapor is an important part of the natural greenhouse effect. While humans are not significantly increasing its concentration through direct emissions, it contributes to the enhanced greenhouse effect because the warming influence of greenhouse gases leads to a positive water vapor feedback. In addition to its role as a natural greenhouse gas, water vapor also affects the temperature of the planet because clouds form when excess water vapor in the atmosphere condenses to form ice and water droplets and precipitation.

47. Water vapor is a positive influence on the Earth because

    (A) it is the most abundant greenhouse gas

    (B) it counteracts carbon emissions

    (C) it has a neutral effect on the temperature of Earth

    (D) it moisturizes your skin

Go on to next page

> *Questions 48–49 refers to the following excerpt from NASA's website (www.nasa.gov).*

Saving lives does not have to be as complex as robotic surgery, but can be as simple as providing the life-giving source of clean water. This specifically is of utmost importance to a community in rural Mexico, showing the far-reaching benefits of the water purification component of NASA's Environmental and Life Control Support System (ECLSS). ECLSS provides clean water for drinking, cooking, and hygiene aboard the space station. This technology has been adapted on Earth to aid remote locations or places devastated by natural disaster that do not have access to clean drinking water.

In Chiapas, Mexico, many people are at risk of illness from drinking contaminated water from wells, rivers, or springs not treated by municipal water systems. Children in Chiapas, previously sickened by parasites and stomach bugs, now have access during school to clean, safe drinking water. This is due to the installation of the ECLSS-derived water purification plant. Renewable solar energy powers the water treatment technology for the community in Chiapas. Results include improved overall health and cost savings from not having to buy purified water or medication to treat waterborne illnesses.

48. How do innovations by NASA help a little town in Mexico?

   (A) by setting up space industries

   (B) by providing for food

   (C) by supplying potable water

   (D) by ridding the area of parasites

49. Why would NASA choose solar energy to power the filtration plant?

   (A) There was a factory manufacturing solar panels nearby.

   (B) It is safer than hydro-electric electricity.

   (C) It costs less per kwh in this area.

   (D) It is renewable energy.

Directions: *Read the stimulus from the Environmental Protection Agency website (www.epa.gov/heatisland) and write a short response to the following prompt on separate sheets of paper.*

---

50. Prompt

   Explain how heat islands alter the temperature in the area surrounding a big city. This item should take about 10 minutes.

Heat Island Impacts

On a hot, sunny summer day, roof and pavement surface temperatures can be 50–90°F (27–50°C) hotter than the air, while shaded or moist surfaces — often in more rural surroundings — remain close to air temperatures.[1] These surface urban heat islands, particularly during the summer, have multiple impacts and contribute to atmospheric urban heat islands. Air temperatures in cities, particularly after sunset, can be as much as 22°F (12°C) warmer than the air in neighboring, less developed regions.[2]

Elevated temperatures from urban heat islands, particularly during the summer, can affect a community's environment and quality of life. While some impacts may be beneficial, such as lengthening the plant-growing season, the majority of them are negative. These impacts include

Go on to next page

- Increased energy consumption
- Elevated emissions of air pollutants and greenhouse gases
- Compromised human health and comfort
- Impaired water quality

Increased Energy Consumption

Elevated summertime temperatures in cities increase energy demand for cooling. Research shows that electricity demand for cooling increases 1.5–2.0% for every 1°F (0.6°C) increase in air temperatures, starting from 68 to 77°F (20 to 25°C), suggesting that 5–10% of community-wide demand for electricity is used to compensate for the heat island effect.[2]

Urban heat islands increase overall electricity demand, as well as peak demand, which generally occurs on hot summer weekday afternoons, when offices and homes are running cooling systems, lights, and appliances. During extreme heat events, which are exacerbated by urban heat islands, the resulting demand for cooling can overload systems and require a utility to institute controlled, rolling brownouts or blackouts to avoid power outages.

Elevated Emissions of Air Pollutants and Greenhouse Gases

As described above, urban heat islands raise demand for electrical energy in summer. Companies that supply electricity typically rely on fossil fuel power plants to meet much of this demand, which in turn leads to an increase in air pollutant and greenhouse gas emissions. The primary pollutants from power plants include sulfur dioxide (SO_2), nitrogen oxides (NOx), particulate matter (PM), carbon monoxide (CO), and mercury (Hg). These pollutants are harmful to human health and also contribute to complex air quality problems such as the formation of ground-level ozone (smog), fine particulate matter, and acid rain. Increased use of fossil-fuel-powered plants also increases emissions of greenhouse gases, such as carbon dioxide (CO_2), which contribute to global climate change.

In addition to their impact on energy-related emissions, elevated temperatures can directly increase the rate of ground-level ozone formation. Ground-level ozone is formed when NOx and volatile organic compounds (VOCs) react in the presence of sunlight and hot weather. If all other variables are equal, such as the level of precursor emissions in the air and wind speed and direction, more ground-level ozone will form as the environment becomes sunnier and hotter.

Compromised Human Health and Comfort

Increased daytime temperatures, reduced nighttime cooling, and higher air pollution levels associated with urban heat islands can affect human health by contributing to general discomfort, respiratory difficulties, heat cramps and exhaustion, non-fatal heat stroke, and heat-related mortality.

Heat islands can also exacerbate the impact of heat waves, which are periods of abnormally hot, and often humid, weather. Sensitive populations, such as children, older adults, and those with existing health conditions, are at particular risk from these events.

Excessive heat events, or abrupt and dramatic temperature increases, are particularly dangerous and can result in above-average rates of mortality. The Centers for Disease Control and Prevention estimates that from 1979–2003, excessive heat exposure contributed to more than 8,000 premature deaths in the United States.[3] This figure exceeds the number of mortalities resulting from hurricanes, lightning, tornadoes, floods, and earthquakes combined.

Go on to next page →

Impaired Water Quality

High pavement and rooftop surface temperatures can heat storm water runoff. Tests have shown that pavements that are 100°F (38°C) can elevate initial rainwater temperature from roughly 70°F (21°C) to over 95°F (35°C).[4] This heated storm water generally becomes runoff, which drains into storm sewers and raises water temperatures as it is released into streams, rivers, ponds, and lakes.

Water temperature affects all aspects of aquatic life, especially the metabolism and reproduction of many aquatic species. Rapid temperature changes in aquatic ecosystems resulting from warm storm water runoff can be particularly stressful, even fatal to aquatic life.

References

1. Berdahl, P., and Bretz, S. 1997. Preliminary Survey of the Solar Reflectance of Cool Roofing Materials. *Energy and Buildings,* 25:149–158.

2. Akbari, H. 2005. Energy Saving Potentials and Air Quality Benefits of Urban Heat Island Mitigation. Lawrence Berkeley National Laboratory.

3. Centers for Disease Control and Prevention. 2006. Extreme Heat: A Prevention Guide to Promote Your Personal Health and Safety.

4. James, W. 2002. Green Roads: Research into Permeable Pavers. *Stormwater,* 3(2):48–40.

Go on to next page

Go on to next page

DO NOT TURN THE PAGE UNTIL TOLD TO DO SO.
DO NOT RETURN TO A PREVIOUS TEST.

Chapter 12

Answers and Explanations for GED Science Practice Test

• •

*I*n this chapter, we provide the answers and explanations to every question on the Science practice test in Chapter 11. If you just want a quick look at the answers, check out the abbreviated answer key at the end of this chapter. However, if you have the time, it's more useful for study purposes to read all the answer explanations carefully. Doing so will help you understand why some answers were correct and others not, especially when the choices were really close. It will also point you to areas where you may need to do more review. Remember, you learn as much from your errors as from the correct answers.

Go through the explanations to all the questions, even for the ones you answered correctly. The explanations are a good review of the techniques we discuss throughout the book.

Answers and Explanations

1. **hospitable.** As the passage states, the new territory may be less *hospitable* because of the natural conditions of the territory.

2. **(D) all of the above.** All the choices are possible answers to the question. It is assumed that you would be aware that both Choices (A) and (B) answer the question. Choice (C) is so general that it would be correct because the answer begins with "many," which is very general and makes it unlikely that the answer would be wrong.

3. **(C) the ground is capable of sudden dramatic movement.** You've probably heard of volcanic eruptions, earthquakes, and landslides, all of which are examples of sudden dramatic movement of the Earth. Choices (A) and (B) don't match general knowledge or experience, and Choice (D) is probably a good idea but not the answer.

4. **(C) astronauts require oxygen and water to survive.** Without a constant supply of air and water, the astronauts couldn't survive in space, and because carrying a sufficient supply of air and water would be impossible given weight restrictions, they must be recycled. Choice (A) is a pleasant thought but not a priority for space travel. Choice (B) is incorrect based on the information given in the passage, and Choice (D) is irrelevant compared to the other issues involved in space travel.

5. **(A) precipitation.** *Precipitation* is rain that falls from the sky. *Condensation* is water that forms on the outside of a cold object when warm, humid air comes in contact with it. *Evaporation* is water that vaporizes into the air. *Perspiration* is the process of sweating to remain cool.

6. **(D) All the processes above occur, causing the continents to move.** Sea floor spreading is caused when magma forces its way into faults or thinner or softer areas of the Earth's crust. The thinnest areas are typically located under an ocean. As the magma forces its way up through the sea floor filling cracks in the crust, it forces the crust apart slightly and

creates ridges. It cools, solidifies, and then is subjected to pressure from underneath yet again. More cracks are filled with magma, and in the process, ridges are created, the sea floor is forced farther and farther apart, and the gap is filled with magma.

7. **(B) It carries its own oxidizer.** This question is about space travel, and Choices (A) and (C) would be irrelevant in space. Choice (D) would cause the ship to go backward. Because there's no oxygen in space and rockets require oxygen to operate, carrying its own oxidizer would solve this problem. Therefore, Choice (B) is correct.

8. **liquid** or **solid.** The passage states that the fuel used is either a liquid or a solid.

9. **(C) The process used is counterproductive.** Although dump sites aren't attractive, looking good isn't part of the problem, so Choice (A) is incorrect. By their nature, dump sites are large and take up a lot of space. Using a lot of valuable land makes no economic sense, and Choice (B) is irrelevant. The ability to read a newspaper after a period of time is interesting but is neither part of the problem nor the solution, so Choice (D) is wrong. Creating a garbage "lasagna" creates problems of its own, and Choice (C) would be the best answer.

10. **(B) It reduces the need for new landfill sites.** The less garbage dumped, the less there is to decompose and the less need there is for new landfill sites, so Choice (B) is the best answer. Choice (A) is a common municipal goal but not the best answer. Choice (C) is incorrect.

11. **(D) to reduce the amount of space it occupies.** Compacting reduces the space needed for the refuse, so Choice (D) is correct. Choices (A), (B), and (C) are incorrect.

12. **(D) none of the above.** Choices (A), (B), and (C) are incorrect according to the passage, so Choice (D) must be correct. Don't assume that "none of the above" is correct. For it to be the answer, all the other choices must be incorrect. Read carefully to make sure.

13. **(B) It reduces the volume of waste to store.** Landfills are really storage facilities for garbage. A good recycling program diverts some or all of the recyclable materials out of the landfill to places that can reuse, manufacture something else out of, or alter the composition of the components or materials. It makes little difference how people feel about their garbage if they're drowning in a sea of waste, so Choice (A) is not a valid answer. Unfortunately, there is no someone else to look after the amount of garbage generated but us, so Choice (C) is not an appropriate answer. The speed of garbage collection is not the issue, so Choice (D) is wrong.

14. **(B) reuse and recycle as much as possible.** Reusing and recycling is not only a clever catch-phrase, it's a way of life that will reduce the flow of materials to the landfill. Choices (A) and (C) are cutesy answers but will do nothing to reduce the amount of waste produced by the population and are incorrect. Choice (D) sounds very scientific when skimming but is completely incorrect.

15. **(D) They help decompose composting waste.** Bacteria interact with decomposable materials to break them down and turn them into compost, so Choice (D) is correct. Choice (A) may be a wish of every landfill, but garbage attracts rodents, who find it a source of food, so Choice (A) is wrong. The reaction is not chemical, nor does the cycle involve inorganic materials, so Choices (B) and (C) are wrong.

16. **(A) The cost is less than acquiring more landfill sites.** Landfills occupy urban land, and urban land is expensive. The money lost in recycling paper is still less than the cost of acquiring new sites for ever-expanding landfills, so Choice (A) is correct. Choice (B) is a dream. If municipalities lose money, people are the source of that shortfall, and Choice (B) must be wrong. The public by and large are tired at the end of the day or in a hurry at the beginning. Recycling paper is one more chore and is not valued as an activity by most of the population, making Choice (C) incorrect. Politicians like to balance the budget, especially around election time, and losing votes is connected to losing money and makes them care, so Choice (D) is very wrong.

17. **(B) the moon has very rough terrain.** The moon has boulders as big as houses, and landing on one the wrong way or at the wrong speed could cause a serious collision. The other choices have no basis in the passage.

18. **(A) Low gravity makes climbing easier, if it's necessary.** The low gravity on the moon would make it very easy to climb steep terrain. D is wrong. B and C might be right if they had been mentioned in the passage.

19. **(C) an amount of water less than your weight.** The weight of water you displace is equal to your weight. Think about it this way: If you drop a bowling ball in a tub of water, it sinks because it's denser than the water; the weight of the water displaced is less than the weight of the bowling ball.

20. **lower.** The boat would float lower in the St. Lawrence Seaway. Because freshwater isn't as dense as saltwater, the relative density of the ship would be greater in freshwater than in saltwater and would make it float lower in the water.

21. **(A) Immerse the object in a premeasured volume of water and measure the amount of water displaced.** You can't really calculate the volume of the object with measurements if it's irregularly shaped, so Choice (B) is wrong. Weighing the object gives its weight, not its volume, so eliminate Choice (C). And unless the object sinks, it doesn't displace its total volume of water, so Choice (D) is wrong.

22. **airbag** According to the passage, the airbag absorbs the initial force of the crash.

23. **(A) in the rear seat.** The passage states that an airbag can be dangerous to a short person sitting too close to the dashboard or a child in a car seat. Choice (A) is the closest answer because Choice (D) would imply that if the infant were sitting on the left side in the front, she would be driving, and Choice (C) would indicate that if the child were in the front seat, she would be in danger from the air bag. If Choices (C) and/or (D) had indicated that the infant would be in the rear seat, those answers may have been acceptable, but without this, Choice (A) is still the best answer.

24. **(D) light weight and high horsepower.** According to Newton's Law, acceleration (change in velocity) would be greatest with increased force and decreased mass, which is Choice (D). The type of transmission or the number of doors is irrelevant, so Choices (A), (B), and (C) are wrong.

25. **evidence.** DNA from samples collected at the crime scene is compared to DNA of known individuals (suspects) to include or exclude them as suspects in the investigation.

26. **(A) compare DNA evidence to that of convicts.** CODIS consists of DNA databases and software used to match DNA evidence against DNA samples collected from convicted offenders. Choice (B) is wrong because CODIS isn't needed to compare DNA evidence to that of known suspects; investigators merely obtain a sample from the suspect and compare the DNA from that sample to the DNA collected at the crime scene. Choice (C) doesn't make sense, because there would be no reason to compare the DNA from convicts to that of known suspects. You can also rule out Choice (D) because only the DNA of convicted offenders is placed in CODIS.

27. **(D) one and a half times as much.** The formula indicates a direct relationship between force and distance. $\frac{3}{2} = 1\frac{1}{2}$, so the answer is Choice (D). Choices (A), (B), and (C) are mathematically incorrect if you use the equation.

28. **(B) You have exerted a force over a distance.** Choice (B) is the definition of work and is correct. Choices (A) and (D) contradict each other, and both are wrong. Choice (C) could be correct in the real world, but it has nothing to do with the passage, so it's irrelevant.

29. The short-answer item has no correct answer except that it should be written in response to the prompt and the stimulus and written in standard English, with an introduction and a conclusion.

Check out the GED Science Test Short Answer Resource Guide for Adult Educators (www.gedtestingservice.com/uploads/files/89097368525e28544f77607f31391c4f.pdf) to see how short-answer items are scored, and try to apply the same criteria to your work. Better yet, have a friend score your short answer response using the material from the resource guide and discuss it with them. Although this material is meant for teachers, because you're working independently, you're your own teacher. Now you have to become your own objective marker. Doing this will help you immeasurably on the test as you write the response.

30. **(C) Kepler.** The passage states that Kepler was one of the inspirations for Newton's train of thought on gravity. Common knowledge is that Einstein lived during recent times, long after Newton, so Choice (D) must be wrong. Aristotle was a Greek philosopher who lived long before Newton and didn't inspire him, except perhaps with his curiosity about the world. Still, it's not the best answer.

31. **extinction.** This is stated in the passage.

32. **(C) In a monumental explosion.** The only choice mentioned in the passage is Choice (C), which means that Choice (D) cannot be correct. Choice (B) sounds plausible, but it is not mentioned in the passage, and Choice (A) is wrong.

33. **ocean.** The passage outlines the four main reservoirs of carbon, one of which is the ocean. It then goes on to state explicitly that the ocean is the largest pool of carbon near the surface of the Earth.

34. **bulb.** The passage states that the bulb enables the tulip to survive the winter.

35. **(C) continues to live from one year to the next.** The word "perennial" indicates that the plant continues to live from one year to the next, even though it may go dormant for a time.

36. **bullet.** If a gun is firing blanks and making a shooting sound but not endangering anyone's life, the bullet must be missing.

37. **(D) use less gunpowder in the cartridge.** Because the gunpowder provided the explosive energy to expel the bullet from the barrel, less gunpowder produces less force. Choices (A) and (C) are both wrong because whether the bullet is jacketed or not has no direct effect on the velocity of the bullet. Choice (B) could be correct if you used a larger cartridge with the same amount or less of gunpowder, but without more information, that choice isn't the best.

38. **fur.** Reading the passage carefully and ignoring the poor joke at the end, the black skin warms the polar bear, but the fur helps retain the heat.

39. **(D) its skin.** The black skin of the polar bear absorbs heat and acts like a huge heat collector.

40. **(B) silk underwear.** This is a question that's worded with the negative "least." Always be careful with any question worded with a negative because when you're in a rush, you may tend to skim questions and answers. From the passage, which is about polar bears living in a frigid environment, the choice "silk underwear" seems silly, but when you read the question carefully, it's the best choice. Read everything carefully. The questions aren't there to trick you or be mean but to make sure that you read and understand what's written.

41. **(B) to give to the children of friends.** The passage clearly states that Grissom wanted to give them to the children of his friends as a memento of the trip into space. Neither Choice (A) nor Choice (D) is mentioned anywhere in the passage. The passage also states that NASA doesn't permit the sale of such items, and Choice (C) states that he wanted to sell them at auction, which is incorrect.

42. **(D) Not enough information is given.** The passage states that the sandwich never returned to Earth but doesn't indicate what may have happened to it. They may have left it on the moon, Grissom may have eaten it, or the astronauts may have shared it. Nowhere in the passage are you told, so Choice (D) is the best answer.

43. **(B) They are very rare.** Until such time as space travel is a regular commute, anything or anyone who has traveled in space is very rare. Choices (A) and (C) are incorrect, and Choice (D) may or may be correct, but nothing is mentioned about it in the passage, so it must be ignored as a "best" answer.

44. **(D) not stated in the passage.** The passage doesn't state what astronauts are allowed or prohibited from taking on space missions, but it does state that NASA doesn't permit the sale of items carried aboard space missions.

45. **(D) All of the above.** Choices (A), (B), and (C) are all possibly correct, which makes Choice (D) the correct answer.

46. **(D) All of the above.** The first three answers are all part of common knowledge, so Choice (D) is the best answer.

47. **(A) it is the most abundant greenhouse gas.** Water vapor is the most abundant greenhouse gas according to the passage. The passage doesn't mention Choices (B) or (C), and Choice (D) may be right but is not mentioned in the paragraph.

48. **(C) by supplying potable water.** The passage mentions the provision of clean drinking (potable) water to the village. Choice (A) may be a worthy result but is not mentioned in the passage. Neither Choice (B) nor Choice (D) is mentioned, so they're incorrect, as well.

49. **(D) It is renewable energy.** Solar energy is renewable and would be best for an area without a sophisticated infrastructure. The other choices are interesting but wrong.

50. The short answer item has no correct answer except that it should be written in response to the prompt and the stimulus and written in standard English, with an introduction and a conclusion. The Science short-answer questions receive a score between 0 and 3 points. To earn 3 points, you need to provide a clear and detailed answer, along with supporting evidence from the passage. You must ensure you actually answer the question and use facts and data from the passage to support your answer. The answer can be one or two paragraphs, ranging from 50 to 300 words. The answer must be clear and to the point, and your statements justified by the content and your interpretation of that content. Writing style, grammar, and spelling are not part of the evaluation. If you did that, give yourself a 3. (For some samples, with evaluation, go to www.gedtestingservice.com/uploads/files/89097368525e28544f77607f31391c4f.pdf.)

Answer Key

1. **hospitable**	2. **D**
3. **C**	4. **C**
5. **A**	6. **D**
7. **B**	8. **liquid** or **solid**
9. **C**	10. **B**
11. **D**	12. **D**
13. **B**	14. **B**
15. **D**	16. **A**
17. **B**	18. **A**
19. **C**	20. **lower**
21. **A**	22. **airbag**
23. **A**	24. **D**
25. **evidence**	26. **A**
27. **D**	28. **B**
29. **Short-answer response**	30. **C**
31. **extinction**	32. **Big Bang**
33. **ocean**	34. **bulb**
35. **C**	36. **bullet**
37. **D**	38. **fur**
39. **D**	40. **B**
41. **B**	42. **D**
43. **B**	44. **D**
45. **A**	46. **D**
47. **A**	48. **C**
49. **D**	50. **Short-answer response**

Part IV
The Part of Tens

In this part . . .

- ✔ Boost your score with ten performance-enhancing tips, including how to improve reading speed and comprehension, interpret visual presentations of data, hone the skills evaluated on the test, get up to speed on key science concepts, and nurture your curious self.

- ✔ Discover ten fun and very useful science facts and concepts, including the fact that matter exists in three different states, heat flows in one direction, bigger objects have more gravitational attraction to each other than do smaller objects, photosynthesis and respiration are flip sides of the same chemical coin, and more!

Chapter 13

Ten Performance-Enhancing Tips

In This Chapter

▶ Ramping up reading speed and comprehension

▶ Sharpening key skills, including math skills

▶ Getting up to speed on key science concepts

▶ Practicing with sample science tests

According to the GED Testing Service, all you need is a general knowledge of science to do well on the test, but that's kind of vague. In this chapter, we provide additional details in the form of ten skills to focus on leading up to test day.

Improving Reading Comprehension and Speed

By far, the most important skill you need to perform well on the GED Science test is reading comprehension and speed. You need to read carefully enough to understand the reading passages, questions, and answer choices and quickly enough to complete the test in the allotted time. To improve both reading speed and comprehension, here's what you do:

✔ Practice reading challenging science passages. Read textbooks and science magazines on a wide range of topics.

✔ Build your science vocabulary. Understanding basic concepts and terms enables you to understand what you're reading while spending less time trying to figure out what something means.

See Chapter 5 for more suggestions.

Writing a Short Answer Response

The Science test contains questions that prompt you to write a short essay in 10 minutes or less. That's not much time. To save time and write a more coherent essay, take the following steps:

1. **Read the stimulus (one or more reading passages) and the prompt (instructions for what to write).**

2. **Write one sentence that clearly states your point or approach in response to the prompt.**

3. **Write down three to four points that support your claim based on evidence in the passage, and arrange the points from most to least important.**

4. **Write a one or more paragraph answer, starting with your thesis statement, introducing each point in order. Add supporting evidence for each point from the stimulus.**

5. **Write a conclusion summing up your assertions and referring back to the prompt.**

Your essay doesn't have to be perfect. Because of the length or the answer and time allocated, the evaluation concentrates on the facts you present, not your writing style. The scorers expect a competent answer to the stimulus with first draft writing quality.

Interpreting Visual Presentations of Data

Many of the questions on the GED Science test include visuals — graphs, maps, illustrations, and tables. These visual presentations of data actually make it easier to understand the data than if it were presented only in the form of text, so when you see these items, don't panic. Be thankful that you don't need to wade through a paragraph to pick out bits of information.

The key to reading graphs and other visual presentations of data is to look at everything, especially any text at the top, bottom, left, or right of the image. This text often provides important information for answering the question.

Practice reading visuals. Flip through science textbooks and magazines in search of graphs, tables, illustrations, and other representations of data and look them over carefully, until you're comfortable extracting data from visuals. Most visuals present relative data. Don't spend forever trying to find data to an impossible degree of accuracy.

Reading Broadly

You don't need to be a biologist, physicist, chemist, or geologist to perform well on the Science test. In fact, a broad understanding of all fields of science serves you best. Questions on the test are divvied up among the following science content areas:

Content Area	Percentage of Questions
Physical science (physics and chemistry)	40%
Life science	40%
Earth and space science	20%

You may be drawn more to one science field than another, so strive to broaden your reading in areas that you don't know as well or that you find less interesting. You may just be surprised.

Honing the Required Skills

Although all questions on the test are relevant to the world of science, you really don't need a huge body of scientific knowledge to do well on the test. The test is designed to evaluate your skills — your ability to understand information presented in different formats and use your power of reason to arrive at the correct answer. More specifically, the test evaluates the following skills:

- ✔ Identify textual evidence that supports a conclusion.
- ✔ Extract details from information presented visually in graphs, tables, illustrations, and so on.
- ✔ Determine the meaning of symbols, terms, and phrases used in a scientific context.
- ✔ Reason from data or evidence presented to a conclusion.
- ✔ Make a reasonable prediction based on data or evidence presented.
- ✔ Identify and refine a hypothesis for a scientific investigation.
- ✔ Find possible sources of error in an experimental design.
- ✔ Understand and apply scientific models, theories, and laws and related formulas.
- ✔ Summarize a data set in statistical terms.
- ✔ Express scientific information numerically, symbolically, and visually.
- ✔ Determine the probability of an event occurring.
- ✔ Use counting and permutations to gauge possibilities.

Sharpening Your Math Skills

Expect to encounter basic math on the Science test. You don't need to memorize formulas, but you may need to calculate an average or percentage or use a formula included with a question to calculate a specific answer.

Note: There will be an onscreen calculator, a model TI-30XS. You are allowed to bring your own TI-30XS calculator, but check with the GED Testing Service on the specific model allowed because that has changed in the past.

If you haven't taken the GED Mathematical Reasoning test yet, you may want to prepare for and take that test first, so your mathematical brain cells are warmed up for any math you need to do on the Science test. Check out our other book *GED Mathematical Reasoning Test For Dummies* (Wiley) for additional guidance.

Wrapping Your Brain around Key Science Concepts

Having a conceptual framework in place provides you with a general understanding that improves your ability to read and understand science information, regardless of the format used to present it. Here are some key concepts to focus on as you prepare for the science test:

- ✔ **Atomic theory:** The theory that all matter is made of tiny, invisible particles. (See Chapter 9.)
- ✔ **Cell theory:** The theory that the cell is the building block for all forms of life. (See Chapter 8.)

- **Classification of living things:** The system used to classify everything from single-cell bacteria up to human beings. (See Chapter 8.)

- **Conservation of energy:** The fact that in a closed system, energy is neither created nor destroyed, and the applications of that fact. (See Chapter 9.)

- **Earth systems:** Earth's atmosphere (air), hydrosphere (water), geosphere (land), and biosphere (living creatures) and how the systems interact. (See Chapter 10.)

- **Energy transfer in ecosystems:** How energy from the sun is converted and used to power the production of all life on Earth. (See Chapter 8.)

- **Evolution through natural selection:** The theory that all creatures on Earth evolve through a process of genetic mutation and selection of traits that enable creatures to thrive in certain conditions. (See Chapter 8.)

- **Genetics/heredity:** The molecular basis of inherited traits. (See Chapter 8.)

- **Newton's laws of motion:** Several laws that describe the relationships among forces, objects, and movement. (See Chapter 9.)

- **Scientific method:** The process scientists use to formulate and test a hypothesis in order to develop explanations for natural phenomena. (See Chapter 6.)

Sharpening Your Thinking Skills

You can look at some questions on the test and know the answer before you even glance at the answer choices because you have some previous knowledge that's relevant. In other cases, even if you don't have that knowledge, you can often reason your way to the correct answer. Here are the skills you need to focus on:

- **Comprehension:** Understanding the meaning or intended meaning of what you read (text) or see (visual presentation of data).

- **Application:** Using information from a passage or visual in a concrete situation.

- **Analysis:** Exploring the relationships among ideas and being able to recognize when certain information doesn't logically fit.

- **Evaluation:** Assessing the soundness or accuracy of information and the methods used to produce, collect, and report data.

To sharpen your thinking skills, ask questions as you read, especially questions about how reliable or trustworthy certain information being presented really is.

Nurturing Your Curious Self

Curiosity may have killed the cat, but it can do you a great deal of good as you prepare for the Science test. As you read through this book, you're likely to feel curious about some of the science topics you're reading about. Who wouldn't be? Science is fascinating. Instead of squelching that curiosity, nurture it by poking around on the Web for more information. Let your curiosity lead you on a journey through the natural world of science, where you can discover more about yourself and the universe you live in than you could ever imagine. Along the way, you'll be preparing for the test and having so much fun doing it that it won't even feel like work.

Taking More Practice Tests

The Web is packed with sample science tests, some of which are aligned with the GED Science test and others that aren't but can still provide valuable practice for taking the GED version. Start with the GED Testing Service's practice tests at www.gedtestingservice. com/educators/freepracticetest and then expand your search. You search for general science tests using search phrases such as "sample science test questions," or look for questions that apply to a specific area of science, such as "newton laws of motion sample test questions." Use your imagination to think up other search terms to find the science questions you're looking for. And finally, a shameless plug: In the latest version *GED Test For Dummies,* we offer several additional tests, as well as access to some online tests.

Chapter 14

Ten Essential Science Facts and Concepts

A general understanding of science and a properly functioning brain are all you need to pass the GED Science test, but it doesn't hurt to have a basic knowledge of some key science facts and concepts under your belt. Knowing that molecules in gas form are farther apart than the same molecules in liquid or solid form, for example, may enable you to answer a particular question in the blink of an eye, so you have more time to reason out other questions.

In this chapter, we present ten essential and interesting science facts and concepts that may come in handy on the test.

Recognizing Matter in Different States

Matter (stuff) comes in three different states (see Figure 14-1):

✔ **Solid:** As a solid, the atoms or molecules are close together and arranged in a pattern.

✔ **Liquid:** As a liquid, the atoms or molecules are close together but not arranged in any pattern.

✔ **Gas:** As a gas, the atoms or molecules are far apart and flying wildly around.

Figure 14-1:
Matter comes in three different states.

Solid   Liquid   Gas

John Wiley & Sons, Inc.

Atoms and molecules move faster and farther apart when energy is added, which explains how matter changes state from a solid to a liquid to a gas. If you remove energy from matter, the atoms or molecules get closer and closer together until they crystallize, at which point the atoms or molecules are locked in place.

Following Heat Flow

The first statement of the second law of thermodynamics is that heat flows spontaneously from a hot to a cold body.

Looking at Figure 14-2, which is hotter, the ball or the air around the ball?

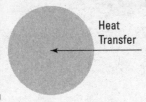

Figure 14-2:
Heat flows spontaneously from hot to cold.

Heat Transfer

John Wiley & Sons, Inc.

The air around the ball would need to be hotter than the ball for the heat to flow into the ball. You may notice this if you leave your beach ball out in the hot sun and the air inside it expands.

Also note that heat transfer occurs in three ways:

- ✔ **Conduction:** Heat travels from one molecule to another when the two touch.

- ✔ **Convection:** Heat rises because it's less dense than cooler air, causing air currents that mix the colder and warmer air.

- ✔ **Radiation:** Heat travels by waves. Solar energy is radiant energy, traveling through space in the form of waves.

Noting the Difference between Reflection and Refraction

If you encounter a question involving the reflection or refraction of light, note these differences (see Figure 14-3):

- ✔ **Reflection:** Light rays bounce off a surface.
- ✔ **Refraction:** Light rays bend as they pass through a substance, such as water.

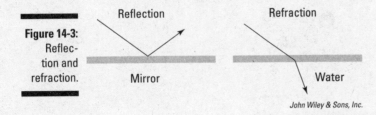

Figure 14-3:
Reflection and refraction.

Reflection   Refraction

Mirror   Water

John Wiley & Sons, Inc.

Ballparking Gravitational Attraction

According to Newton's universal law of gravitation, the gravitational force attracting two objects to each other is directly proportional to their mass and inversely proportional to the distance between them. In other words, two large, dense objects close together are going to be more attracted to each other (gravitationally speaking) than two smaller (in terms of mass) objects that are far apart.

Brushing Up on Energy Transfer in Ecosystems

In an ecosystem, all energy comes from the sun. Through the process of *photosynthesis,* plants use radiant energy from the sun to convert water and carbon dioxide into carbohydrates (chemical energy) that other organisms in the ecosystem can consume and digest to extract the energy. Members of an ecosystem are divided into producers, consumers, and decomposers (see Figure 14-4):

✔ **Producers:** The plants that convert the sun's radiant energy into chemical energy.

✔ **Consumers:** Organisms that eat the plants or other consumers.

✔ **Decomposers:** Organisms that break down waste products, including dead producers and consumers.

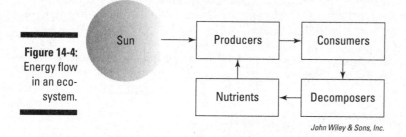

Figure 14-4: Energy flow in an ecosystem.

John Wiley & Sons, Inc.

Differentiating between Photosynthesis and Respiration

In an ecosystem, two crucial chemical reactions take place:

✔ **Photosynthesis:** Plants use sunlight to convert carbon dioxide and water into carbohydrates, and they release oxygen as a byproduct:

$$CO_2 + H_2O \rightarrow Carbohydrates + O_2$$

✔ **Respiration:** Animals eat and digest the plants and breathe oxygen, converting the carbohydrates back into carbon dioxide and water.

$$Carbohydrates + O_2 \rightarrow CO_2 + H_2O$$

Defining Earth's Systems

Earth has four systems that constantly interact to determine conditions on the planet:

- ✓ **Atmosphere:** Air that envelops the Earth in five layers: troposphere (closest to the surface), stratosphere, mesosphere, thermosphere, and exosphere (farthest out). The troposphere is where most cloud and weather formations occur.

- ✓ **Biosphere:** All living things, plants and animals.

- ✓ **Geosphere:** Land, including all layers below the ground you walk on. The geosphere is divided into several layers: the core (center), mantle, and crust (thin outer layer). The *lithosphere* is the rocky area that comprises a portion of the crust and mantle and is where geological activity takes place, such as earthquakes and volcanoes.

- ✓ **Hydrosphere:** Water in all its many states — liquid (water), solid (ice and snow), and gas (vapor). For more, skip to the next section about the water cycle.

Tracing the Water Cycle

The water cycle describes the movement of water around the Earth, as shown in Figure 14-5. The sun and gravity are the biggest drivers of the water cycle. The sun provides the energy to fuel evaporation from oceans, lakes, and streams and from plants that release water as part of the *transpiration process* (the movement of water from the roots to the leaves). Changes in temperature cause the water vapor to condense and fall as precipitation, and then gravity takes over to move the water from higher to lower areas through the ground or through water channels, such as rivers and streams.

Other factors influence water movement as well, such as wind and the chemical properties of water, including temperature and salinity.

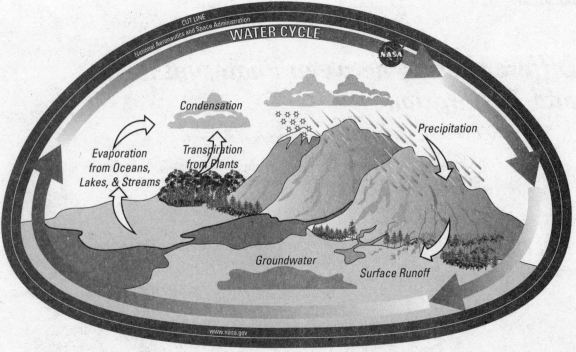

Illustration courtesy of NASA

Figure 14-5: Earth's water cycle.

Telling the Difference between Kinetic and Potential Energy

Energy comes in many forms, but it can be broken down into two categories (see Figure 14-6):

✔ **Potential energy:** Stored energy that an object has due to its position or configuration. In Figure 14-6, the ball at position A has the greatest potential energy.

✔ **Kinetic energy:** Energy that an object has due to its motion. In Figure 14-6, the ball at position B has the greatest kinetic energy.

At position C in the figure, the ball has a combination of potential and kinetic energy.

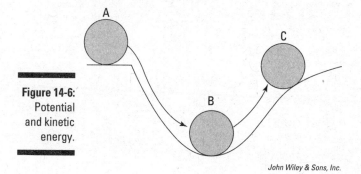

Figure 14-6:
Potential and kinetic energy.

John Wiley & Sons, Inc.

Saving Work with Machines

Machines are generally constructed to enable people to perform work without having to exert as much force as would otherwise be required. Machines are based on a law in physics that can best be described in the formula Work = Force × Distance. Most machines increase the distance over which a force is applied. Using a simple pulley, for example, you would need to pull 4 feet of rope to lift an object 2 feet off the ground, but you would find that you needed only half the strength to lift it. The same is true with any simple machine. For example, pushing a cart 50 yards up a gently sloping hill is easier than pushing the same cart a shorter distance up a steeper hill.

When you see a question with a pulley, ramp, lever, wheel, or other simple machine, put the Work = Force × Distance formula to work for you.

Index

• D •

About the Authors

Achim K. Krull, BA, MAT, is a graduate of the University of Toronto, with specialist qualifications in history and geography. He has taught at both the high school and adult education level. Achim worked for many years in the academic alternative schools of the Toronto District School Board, as administrator/curriculum leader of Subway Academy One, and as cofounder of SOLE. He has written textbooks, teachers' guides, and a large variety of other learning materials with Murray Shukyn, including scripts for educational videos, as well as newspaper and magazine articles. Achim designed and currently teaches an academic upgrading program for young adults preparing to enter apprenticeships.

Murray Shukyn, BA, is a graduate of the University of Toronto, with professional qualifications as a teacher at the elementary and secondary levels, including special education. He has taught at the elementary, secondary, and university levels and developed training programs for adult learners in the coffee and food-service industries. During his extensive career, spanning more than 50 years, Murray has taught professional development programs for educators and is acknowledged as a Canadian leader in the field of alternative education. He was instrumental in the creation of such innovative programs for the Toronto Board of Education as SEED, Learnxs, Subway Academy One, SOLE, and ACE. In 1995, Murray became Associate Director of the Training Renewal Foundation, which introduced the GED in the province of Ontario. As a consultant to government, media, and public relations companies, he has coauthored numerous textbooks and magazine and periodical articles with Achim Krull and coauthored several books to prepare adults to take the GED test with both Achim Krull and Dale Shuttleworth.

Dedication

From Murray: To Bev, Deb, and Ron, who have always provided ongoing support and encouragement for all the projects I find myself involved in.

Authors' Acknowledgments

We wish to say a special word of thanks to Grace Freedson of Grace Freedson's Publishing Network for all her efforts in negotiating for these books and guiding us through the often murky waters of negotiations.

Thanks to John Wiley & Sons acquisitions editor Lindsay Lefevere for choosing us to write this book and for pulling together a talented team of professionals to help us produce a top-quality product.

We thank Chrissy Guthrie of Guthrie Writing & Editorial, LLC, for shepherding our manuscript through the editorial process and to production and providing the guidance we needed to make a good manuscript great. Thanks also to our copy editor, Todd Lothery, for weeding out any errors in spelling, grammar, and punctuation and, more important, ensuring the clarity of our prose.

Special thanks to our technical editor, Sonia Chaumette, for detecting and eliminating any substantive errors and omissions that would otherwise undermine the accuracy and utility of this book.

Publisher's Acknowledgments

Executive Editor: Lindsay Sandman Lefevere

Editorial Project Manager and Development Editor: Christina Guthrie

Copy Editor: Todd Lothery

Technical Editor: Sonia Chaumette

Art Coordinator: Alicia B. South

Project Coordinator: Siddique Shaik

Cover Image: ©Getty Images/BlackJack3D

Apple & Mac

iPad For Dummies, 6th Edition
978-1-118-72306-7

iPhone For Dummies, 7th Edition
978-1-118-69083-3

Macs All-in-One For Dummies,
4th Edition
978-1-118-82210-4

OS X Mavericks For Dummies
978-1-118-69188-5

Blogging & Social Media

Facebook For Dummies, 5th Edition
978-1-118-63312-0

Social Media Engagement For Dummies
978-1-118-53019-1

WordPress For Dummies, 6th Edition
978-1-118-79161-5

Business

Stock Investing For Dummies,
4th Edition
978-1-118-37678-2

Investing For Dummies, 6th Edition
978-0-470-90545-6

Personal Finance For Dummies,
7th Edition
978-1-118-11785-9

QuickBooks 2014 For Dummies
978-1-118-72005-9

Small Business Marketing Kit
For Dummies, 3rd Edition
978-1-118-31183-7

Careers

Job Interviews For Dummies, 4th Edition
978-1-118-11290-8

Job Searching with Social Media
For Dummies, 2nd Edition
978-1-118-67856-5

Personal Branding For Dummies
978-1-118-11792-7

Resumes For Dummies, 6th Edition
978-0-470-87361-8

Starting an Etsy Business For Dummies,
2nd Edition
978-1-118-59024-9

Diet & Nutrition

Belly Fat Diet For Dummies
978-1-118-34585-6

Mediterranean Diet For Dummies
978-1-118-71525-3

Nutrition For Dummies, 5th Edition
978-0-470-93231-5

Digital Photography

Digital SLR Photography All-in-One
For Dummies, 2nd Edition
978-1-118-59082-9

Digital SLR Video & Filmmaking
For Dummies
978-1-118-36598-4

Photoshop Elements 12 For Dummies
978-1-118-72714-0

Gardening

Herb Gardening For Dummies,
2nd Edition
978-0-470-61778-6

Gardening with Free-Range Chickens
For Dummies
978-1-118-54754-0

Health

Boosting Your Immunity For Dummies
978-1-118-40200-9

Diabetes For Dummies, 4th Edition
978-1-118-29447-5

Living Paleo For Dummies
978-1-118-29405-5

Big Data

Big Data For Dummies
978-1-118-50422-2

Data Visualization For Dummies
978-1-118-50289-1

Hadoop For Dummies
978-1-118-60755-8

Language & Foreign Language

500 Spanish Verbs For Dummies
978-1-118-02382-2

English Grammar For Dummies,
2nd Edition
978-0-470-54664-2

French All-in-One For Dummies
978-1-118-22815-9

German Essentials For Dummies
978-1-118-18422-6

Italian For Dummies, 2nd Edition
978-1-118-00465-4

Math & Science

Algebra I For Dummies, 2nd Edition
978-0-470-55964-2

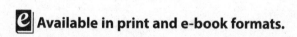 **Available in print and e-book formats.**

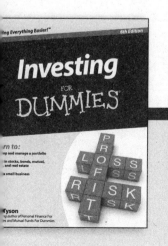

Available wherever books are sold. **For more information or to order direct visit www.dummies.com**

Anatomy and Physiology For Dummies, 2nd Edition
978-0-470-92326-9

Astronomy For Dummies, 3rd Edition
978-1-118-37697-3

Biology For Dummies, 2nd Edition
978-0-470-59875-7

Chemistry For Dummies, 2nd Edition
978-1-118-00730-3

1001 Algebra II Practice Problems
For Dummies
978-1-118-44662-1

Microsoft Office

Excel 2013 For Dummies
978-1-118-51012-4

Office 2013 All-in-One For Dummies
978-1-118-51636-2

PowerPoint 2013 For Dummies
978-1-118-50253-2

Word 2013 For Dummies
978-1-118-49123-2

Music

Blues Harmonica For Dummies
978-1-118-25269-7

Guitar For Dummies, 3rd Edition
978-1-118-11554-1

iPod & iTunes For Dummies, 10th Edition
978-1-118-50864-0

Programming

Beginning Programming with C
For Dummies
978-1-118-73763-7

Excel VBA Programming For Dummies,
3rd Edition
978-1-118-49037-2

Java For Dummies, 6th Edition
978-1-118-40780-6

Religion & Inspiration

The Bible For Dummies
978-0-7645-5296-0

Buddhism For Dummies, 2nd Edition
978-1-118-02379-2

Catholicism For Dummies, 2nd Edition
978-1-118-07778-8

Self-Help & Relationships

Beating Sugar Addiction For Dummies
978-1-118-54645-1

Meditation For Dummies, 3rd Edition
978-1-118-29144-3

Seniors

Laptops For Seniors For Dummies,
3rd Edition
978-1-118-71105-7

Computers For Seniors For Dummies,
3rd Edition
978-1-118-11553-4

iPad For Seniors For Dummies,
6th Edition
978-1-118-72826-0

Social Security For Dummies
978-1-118-20573-0

Smartphones & Tablets

Android Phones For Dummies,
2nd Edition
978-1-118-72030-1

Nexus Tablets For Dummies
978-1-118-77243-0

Samsung Galaxy S 4 For Dummies
978-1-118-64222-1

Samsung Galaxy Tabs For Dummies
978-1-118-77294-2

Test Prep

ACT For Dummies, 5th Edition
978-1-118-01259-8

ASVAB For Dummies, 3rd Edition
978-0-470-63760-9

GRE For Dummies, 7th Edition
978-0-470-88921-3

Officer Candidate Tests For Dummies
978-0-470-59876-4

Physician's Assistant Exam For Dummies
978-1-118-11556-5

Series 7 Exam For Dummies
978-0-470-09932-2

Windows 8

Windows 8.1 All-in-One For Dummies
978-1-118-82087-2

Windows 8.1 For Dummies
978-1-118-82121-3

Windows 8.1 For Dummies, Book + DVD
Bundle
978-1-118-82107-7

Take Dummies with you everywhere you go!

Whether you are excited about e-books, want more from the web, must have your mobile apps, or are swept up in social media, Dummies makes everything easier.

Leverage the Power

For Dummies is the global leader in the reference category and one of the most trusted and highly regarded brands in the world. No longer just focused on books, customers now have access to the For Dummies content they need in the format they want. Let us help you develop a solution that will fit your brand and help you connect with your customers.

Advertising & Sponsorships

Connect with an engaged audience on a powerful multimedia site, and position your message alongside expert how-to content.

Targeted ads • Video • Email marketing • Microsites • Sweepstakes sponsorship

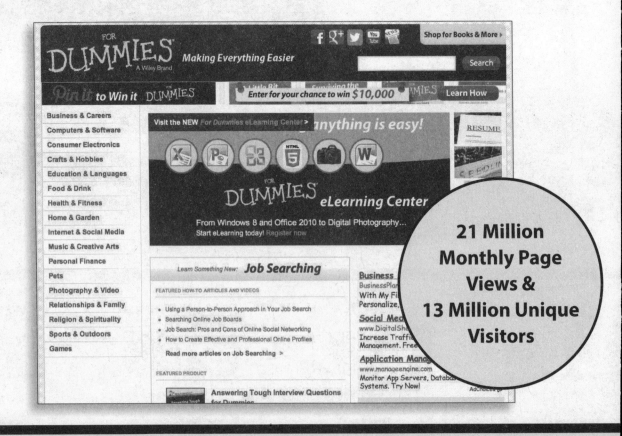

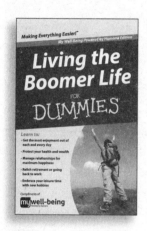

Dummies products make life easier!

- DIY
- Consumer Electronics
- Crafts

- Software
- Cookware
- Hobbies

- Videos
- Music
- Games
- and More!

Dummies.com